Advances in MATHEMATICAL ECONOMICS

Aims and Scope. The project is to publish *Advances in Mathematical Economics* once a year under the auspices of the Research Center for Mathematical Economics. It is designed to bring together those mathematicians who are seriously interested in obtaining new challenging stimuli from economic theories and those economists who are seeking effective mathematical tools for their research.

The scope of *Advances in Mathematical Economics* includes, but is not limited to, the following fields:

- Economic theories in various fields based on rigorous mathematical reasoning.
- Mathematical methods (e.g., analysis, algebra, geometry, probability) motivated by economic theories.
- Mathematical results of potential relevance to economic theory.
- Historical study of mathematical economics.

Authors are asked to develop their original results as fully as possible and also to give a clear-cut expository overview of the problem under discussion. Consequently, we will also invite articles which might be considered too long for publication in journals.

S. Kusuoka, A. Yamazaki (Eds.)

Advances in Mathematical Economics

Volume 11

Springer

Shigeo Kusuoka
Professor
Graduate School of Mathematical Sciences
University of Tokyo
3-8-1 Komaba, Meguro-ku
Tokyo, 153-0041 Japan

Akira Yamazaki
Professor
Department of Economics
Meisei University
Hino
Tokyo, 191-8506 Japan

ISBN 978-4-431-99845-7 e-ISBN 978-4-431-77784-7

Printed on acid-free paper
Springer is a part of Springer Science+Business Media
springer.com

Printed in Japan

Camera-ready copy prepared from the authors' LaTeX files.

Table of Contents

Research Articles

Adv. Math. Econ. 11, 1–10 (2008)

Advances in
MATHEMATICAL
ECONOMICS

Optimal hedging strategies on asymmetric functions

Takuji Arai*

Department of Economics, Keio University, 2-15-45 Mita, Minato-ku, Tokyo 108-8345, Japan
(e-mail: arai@econ.keio.ac.jp)

Received: June 26, 2007
Revised: November 7, 2007

JEL classification: G10

Mathematics Subject Classification (2000): 91B28, 52A41, 60H05

Abstract. We treat in this paper optimal hedging problems for contingent claims in an incomplete financial market, which problems are based on asymmetric functions. In summary, we consider the problem

$$\min_{\vartheta \in \Theta} E[f(H - G_T(\vartheta))],$$

where H is a contingent claim, Θ, which is a suitable set of predictable processes, represents the collection of all admissible strategies, $G_T(\vartheta)$ is a portfolio value at the maturity T induced by an admissible strategy ϑ, and $f : \mathbf{R} \to \mathbf{R}_+$ is a differentiable strictly convex function with $f(0) = 0$. In particular, under the assumption that there exist two positive constants c_0 and C_1 such that, for any $x \in \mathbf{R}$ being far away from 0 sufficiently, $c_0|x|^p \leq f(x)$, and $|f'(x)| \leq C_1|x|^{p-1}$, where $1 < p < \infty$, we shall prove the unique existence of a solution and shall discuss its mathematical property.

Key words: mathematical finance, incomplete market, convex function, semimartingale, stochastic integral

* The author would like to thank Jan Kallsen and Shigeo Kusuoka for their valuable comments and discussion, and is very grateful to an anonymous referee for helpful comments, which has greatly improved the paper. The financial support of the author has been partially granted by Grant-in-Aid for Young Scientists (B) No.16740062 and Scientific Research (C) No.19540144 from the Ministry of Education, Culture, Sports, Science and Technology of Japan.

1. Introduction

Let $(\Omega, \mathcal{F}, P)$ be a complete probability space. We fix $T > 0$, and suppose that $\mathbf{F} = \{\mathcal{F}_t\}_{t\in[0,T]}$ is a filtration satisfying the so-called usual condition, that is, $\mathbf{F}$ is right-continuous and $\mathcal{F}_0$ contains all null sets of $\mathcal{F}$. In addition, we assume that $\mathcal{F}_0$ is trivial and $\mathcal{F}_T = \mathcal{F}$. Let X be an $\mathbf{F}$-adapted $\mathbf{R}^d$-valued RCLL semimartingale on $(\Omega, \mathcal{F}, P)$. X is not assumed to be continuous. Moreover, Θ denotes some subspace of $\mathbf{R}^d$-valued X-integrable predictable processes. We define $G_t(\vartheta) := \int_0^t \vartheta_s dX_s$ for any $t \in [0, T]$ and any $\vartheta \in \Theta$, and $G_T := \{G_T(\vartheta)|\vartheta \in \Theta\}$. Note that Θ and G_T is assumed to be linear spaces.

Consider an incomplete financial market which consists of one riskless asset and d risky assets whose fluctuation is described by the semimartingale X. We regard the fixed $T > 0$ as the maturity of our market. Suppose that the interest rate of our market is given by 0, namely, the price of the riskless asset is 1 at all times. Furthermore, we consider the set Θ of predictable processes as the collection of all admissible strategies. Thus, we call each element of Θ an admissible strategy. Let H be a contingent claim which is a kind of pay-off at T. Mathematically, H is an $\mathcal{F}_T$-measurable random variable. We assume an investor who intends to hedge the contingent claim H with a suitable strategy which belongs to Θ. Suppose that the initial endowment of the investor is 0, and the investor attempts to construct her portfolio to approach, in some rational sense, the contingent claim as much as possible at the maturity. The mean-variance hedging is well-known as one of strong candidates for such optimal hedging strategies. However, it depends only on the size of the hedging error, which is the difference between the value of the contingent claim and the portfolio value at the maturity. In general, investors are interested whether their hedging error is positive or negative. Hence, it is important to widen the width of problems which we can treat.

Throughout this paper, we shall make, in the light of the above matters, a new attack on the following minimization problem:

$$\inf_{\vartheta\in\Theta} E[f(H - G_T(\vartheta))], \tag{1}$$

where $f : \mathbf{R} \to \mathbf{R}_+$ is a differentiable strictly convex function with $f(0) = 0$, $\mathbf{R}_+ = [0, \infty)$, and Θ is defined so that $f(H - G_T(\vartheta))$ may be integrable for any $\vartheta \in \Theta$. The case of $f(x) = x^2$ and $= |x|^p$ for $1 < p < \infty$ are corresponding to the mean-variance hedging and the p-optimal hedging undertaken by Arai [1], respectively. Indeed, optimal hedging strategies depending only on the size of the hedging error are corresponding to the case where f is symmetric, in which problem (1) become a norm minimization problem which is in an easy to handle mathematically. On the other hand, in order to reflect the sign of the hedging error, we have to treat asymmetric functions. Hence, our aim in this paper is to extend the mean-variance hedging or the p-optimal hedging to the asymmetric case.

Remark 1. We can rewrite (1) as follows:

$$\inf_{x \in G_T} E[f(H - x)], \tag{2}$$

since the operator $G_T(\cdot) : \Theta \to G_T$ is an injection under the no-arbitrage condition. Throughout this paper, we regard (2) as the primal problem.

Let us sketch out the problem (2). Let $x^H \in G_T$ be fixed. We assume that $E[f'(H - x^H)x] = 0$ for any $x \in G_T$. The convexity of f implies that, for any $x \in G_T$,

$$\begin{aligned} E[f(H - x)] &\geq E[f(H - x^H) + f'(H - x^H)(H - x - (H - x^H))] \\ &= E[f(H - x^H)] + E[f'(H - x^H)(x^H - x)] \\ &= E[f(H - x^H)]. \end{aligned}$$

The following theorem is based on the above fact.

Theorem 1. *Suppose that there exists an $x^H \in G_T$ satisfying $E[f'(H - x^H)x] = 0$ for any $x \in G_T$. Then, x^H is the unique solution to (2).*

Proof. We have only to prove the uniqueness. Suppose that there exist two solutions x_0 and x_1. Remark that $E[f(H - x_0)] = E[f(H - x_1)]$. Denoting $x_\alpha := \alpha x_1 + (1-\alpha)x_0$ for any $\alpha \in (0, 1)$, $H - x_\alpha = \alpha(H - x_1) + (1-\alpha)(H - x_0)$. Since f is convex, we have

$$f(H - x_\alpha) \leq \alpha f(H - x_1) + (1 - \alpha) f(H - x_0).$$

Now, we set $A_\alpha := \{f(H - x_\alpha) < \alpha f(H - x_1) + (1 - \alpha) f(H - x_0)\}$, which satisfies $P(A_\alpha) > 0$, since $x_0 \neq x_1$ and the strict convexity of f. Then, we obtain that

$$\begin{aligned} E[f(H - x_\alpha)] &= E[f(H - x_\alpha)1_{A_\alpha} + f(H - x_\alpha)1_{A_\alpha^c}] \\ &< E[\alpha f(H - x_1) + (1 - \alpha) f(H - x_0)] \\ &= E[f(H - x_1)], \end{aligned}$$

which is contradiction. As a result, the solution exists uniquely.

Next, we consider a dual problem under the assumption of Theorem 1. We define the convex dual $\widetilde{f}$ of f as $\widetilde{f}(y) := \sup_{x \in \mathbf{R}}[xy - f(x)]$, and the orthogonal complement of G_T as

$$G^\perp := \{y | (H - x^H)y - \widetilde{f}(y) \text{ is integrable and } E[xy] = 0 \text{ for any } x \in G_T\},$$

where x^H is the unique solution to (2). Then, we have the following:

Theorem 2. *Under the same assumption as the previous theorem, we have*

$$\inf_{x \in G_T} E[f(H-x)] = \sup_{y \in G^{\perp}} E[Hy - \widetilde{f}(y)]. \tag{3}$$

Proof. Letting $I(y) := (f')^{-1}(y)$, we have $\widetilde{f}(y) = yI(y) - f(I(y))$ for any $y \in \mathbf{R}$. Since $\widetilde{f}(y) \geq xy - f(x)$ for any $x, y \in \mathbf{R}$, $\inf_{x \in G_T} E[f(H-x)] = E[f(H-x^H)] \geq E[(H-x^H)y - \widetilde{f}(y)]$, where we take a random variable y so that the right hand side should be integrable. Thus, for any $y \in G^{\perp}$, $\inf_{x \in G_T} E[f(H-x)] \geq \sup_{y \in G^{\perp}} E[(H-x^H)y - \widetilde{f}(y)] = \sup_{y \in G^{\perp}} E[Hy - \widetilde{f}(y)]$.

We prove the reverse inequality. The assumption in Theorem 1 guarantees that $f'(H-x^H) \in G^{\perp}$. Thus, we have

$$\begin{aligned}
\inf_{x \in G_T} E[f(H-x)] &= E[f(H-x^H)] \\
&= E[(H-x^H)f'(H-x^H) - \widetilde{f}(f'(H-x^H))] \\
&\leq \sup_{y \in G^{\perp}} E[(H-x^H)y - \widetilde{f}(y)] = \sup_{y \in G^{\perp}} E[Hy - \widetilde{f}(y)].
\end{aligned}$$

Consequently, Theorem 2 follows.

Note that these results are obtained under the assumption in Theorem 1. In general, it is very difficult to check whether a concrete model given satisfies the assumption or not. Thus, we shall focus on a sufficient condition for the assumption. In order to achieve this goal, it might be important how we set the underlying market and define the set Θ. The closedness of G_T might be a significant keyword.

In Sect. 2, we define admissible strategies and confirm that the space of all their stochastic integrals is closed. Moreover, under the setting introduced in Sect. 2, we prove in Sect. 3 the unique existence of a solution x^H to the problem (2) under the condition which there are two positive constants c_0 and C_1 such that, for any $x \in \mathbf{R}$ whose absolute value is sufficient large,

$$c_0|x|^p \leq f(x), \quad \text{and} \quad |f'(x)| \leq C_1|x|^{p-1}.$$

In addition, we mention that $E[f'(H-x^H)x] = 0$ for any $x \in G_T$. For all unexplained notation, we refer to Dellacherie and Meyer [4] and Černý and Kallsen [3].

2. Setup

In this section, we address our standing assumptions and define admissible strategies. Throughout this section, let $1 < p < \infty$ be fixed arbitrarily.

The asset price process X is an $\mathbf{R}^d$-valued RCLL semimartingale. Moreover, suppose that X is locally bounded. Firstly, we define simple strategies and admissible strategies.

Definition 1. (1) *An $\mathbf{R}^d$-valued process ϑ is called simple if it is a linear combination of processes of the form $Y1_{(\tau_1,\tau_2]}$, where $\tau_1 \le \tau_2$ denote stopping times and Y a bounded $\mathcal{F}_{\tau_1}$-measurable random variable.*

(2) *We define $K^{simple} := \{G_T(\vartheta) | \vartheta$ is a simple strategy$\}$, and $K_p := \overline{K^{simple}}$, where the bar means the $\mathcal{L}^p(P)$-closure.*

(3) *We call an X-integrable predictable process ϑ admissible, if there exists a sequence $(\vartheta^n)_{n\ge1}$ of simple strategies such that $G_t(\vartheta^n) \to G_t(\vartheta)$ in probability for any $t \in [0,T]$, and $G_T(\vartheta^n) \to G_T(\vartheta)$ in $\mathcal{L}^p(P)$.*

(4) *Denote by $\overline{\Theta}$ the space of all admissible strategies.*

The financial interpretation of a simple strategy $Y1_{(\tau_1,\tau_2]}$ is explicit, since this means that the investor buys, for $i = 1, \dots, d$, Y^i shares of the i-th asset at τ_1 and sells them at τ_2. Thus, $\overline{\Theta}$, which is, as it were, a space of limitations of simple strategies, is reasonable as the set of all admissible strategies. Now, we should look into the closedness of $\overline{\Theta}$. To do it, we state our standing assumptions after the introduction of σ-martingales and signed σ-martingale measures (SσMM).

Definition 2. (1) *A semimartingale S is called a σ-martingale, if there exists an increasing sequence $(D_n)_{n\ge1}$ of predictable sets such that $D_n \uparrow \Omega \times \mathbf{R}_+$ up to an evanescent set and $\int 1_{D_n} dS$ is a uniformly integrable martingale for any $n \in \mathbf{N}$.*

(2) *A signed measure Q is said to be an absolutely continuous signed σ-martingale measure (SσMM), if $Q \ll P$ with $Q(\Omega) = 1$, and XZ^Q is a P-σ-martingale, where Z^Q is the density process of Q defined as*

$$Z_t^Q := E\left[\frac{dQ}{dP} | \mathcal{F}_t\right].$$

We describe our standing assumptions as follows:

Assumption 1. (1) $\sup\{E[|X_\tau^i|^p] | \tau$ *is a stopping time* $, i = 1, \dots, d\} < \infty$.

(2) *There exists a probability measure $Q \sim P$ satisfying $E[(dQ/dP)^q] < \infty$ and being an SσMM, where q is the conjugate index of p, that is, $\frac{1}{p} + \frac{1}{q} = 1$.*

Under the above standing assumptions, we have one proposition and two corollaries, which are extensions of Černý and Kallsen [3] to the $\mathcal{L}^p$-setting. Since these extensions are straightforward, we omit their proofs.

Proposition 1 **([3, Lemma 2.4]).** *For $A \in \mathcal{L}^p(P)$, the following are equivalent:*

(1) $A \in K_p$.
(2) $E_Q[A] = 0$ *for any SσMM Q with* $\frac{dQ}{dP} \in \mathcal{L}^q(P)$.
(3) *There exists a* $\vartheta \in \overline{\Theta}$ *such that* $A = G_T(\vartheta)$.
(4) *There exists an X-integrable predictable process* ϑ *such that* $A = G_T(\vartheta)$ *and* $G(\vartheta)Z^Q$ *is a uniformly integrable martingale for any SσMM Q with* $\frac{dQ}{dP} \in \mathcal{L}^q(P)$, *where* Z^Q *is the density process of Q.*

Corollary 1 **([3, Corollary 2.5]).** *The following are equivalent:*

(1) $\vartheta \in \overline{\Theta}$.
(2) ϑ *is an X-integrable predictable process,* $G_T(\vartheta) \in \mathcal{L}^p(P)$, *and* $G(\vartheta)Z^Q$ *is a uniformly integrable martingale for any SσMM Q with* $\frac{dQ}{dP} \in \mathcal{L}^q(P)$, *where* Z^Q *is the density process of Q.*

Corollary 2 **([3, Corollary 2.9]).** *Denoting* $\widetilde{\Theta} := \{\vartheta | \vartheta$ *is an X-integrable predictable process, and* $G(\vartheta) \in \mathcal{S}^p\}$, *we have the following:*

(1) $\widetilde{\Theta} \subset \overline{\Theta}$.
(2) $\overline{\{G_T(\vartheta) | \vartheta \in \widetilde{\Theta}\}} = K_p = \{G_T(\vartheta) | \vartheta \in \overline{\Theta}\}$, *where the bar means the* $\mathcal{L}^p(P)$*-closure.*

The last corollary asserts that the space $\overline{\Theta}$ is appropriate as the collection of all admissible strategies, because we have $K_p = \{G_T(\vartheta) | \vartheta \in \overline{\Theta}\}$, which is closed in $\mathcal{L}^p(P)$. Although there are some papers which treat $\widetilde{\Theta}$ as the collection of all admissible strategies, we have to add some standing assumptions to ensure the closedness of $\{G_T(\vartheta) | \vartheta \in \widetilde{\Theta}\}$. Thus, we adopt $\overline{\Theta}$ in this paper.

3. The unique existence of the solution

Throughout this section, we assume Assumption 1, and fix $1 < p < \infty$ and $H \in \mathcal{L}^p(P)$ arbitrarily. We denote $G_T := \{G_T(\vartheta) | \vartheta \in \overline{\Theta}\} (= K_p)$, which is a non-empty closed convex subspace of $\mathcal{L}^p(P)$. Note that $\mathcal{L}^p(P)$ is a reflexive Banach space. We assume furthermore that $f : \mathbf{R} \to \mathbf{R}_+$ is differentiable, strictly convex function with $f(0) = 0$. In addition to this, suppose hereafter that there are two positive constants c_0 and C_1 such that, for any $x \in \mathbf{R}$ whose absolute value is sufficient large,

$$c_0|x|^p \le f(x), \quad \text{and} \quad |f'(x)| \le C_1|x|^{p-1}.$$

More precisely, the following two conditions are assumed:

(i) there exist two positive constants c_0 and M such that, for any $x \in \mathbf{R}$,

$$c_0|x|^p 1_{\{|x|>M\}} \le f(x), \tag{4}$$

(ii) there exist two positive constants C_1 and C_2 such that, for any $x \in \mathbf{R}$,

$$|f'(x)| \le C_1|x|^{p-1} + C_2. \tag{5}$$

Example 1. The following is one of typical functions satisfying all the above conditions:

$$f(x) = \begin{cases} x^p, & x \ge 0, \\ \delta|x|^p, & x < 0, \end{cases}$$

where $\delta > 0$.

When we define $\Phi : G_T \to \mathbf{R}_+$ as $\Phi(x) := E[f(H - x)]$, we shall show the unique existence of a solution to the problem

$$\inf_{x \in G_T} \Phi(x),$$

which is equivalent to (2), and shall introduce a mathematical property which the solution satisfies.

The Gâteaux derivative of Φ is defined as

$$D\Phi(x, y) := \lim_{t \to 0} \frac{1}{t}[\Phi(x + ty) - \Phi(x)], \quad \text{for any } x, y \in G_T.$$

Note that the above definition is slightly different from one of the Gâteaux-differential in [5]. Firstly, we calculate the Gâteaux derivative of Φ.

Proposition 2. *For any $x, y \in G_T$, we have*

$$D\Phi(x, y) = -E[f'(H - x)y].$$

Proof. We begin with one preparation which is a well-known result in the measure theory.

Lemma 1 ([2, Theorem 16.8]). *Let I be an open interval. A measurable function $h(\omega, t)$ on $\Omega \times I$ is assumed to be partial differentiable on t P-a.s., and integrable on ω for each $t \in I$. Moreover, we suppose that there exists an integrable function $g(\omega)$ such that*

$$\left| \frac{\partial h}{\partial t}(\omega, t) \right| \le g(\omega) \; P\text{-a.s.} \quad \textit{for any } t \in I.$$

Then, we have $\dfrac{\partial}{\partial t}\displaystyle\int_\Omega h(\omega, t)dP = \int_\Omega \frac{\partial h}{\partial t}(\omega, t)dP$ *for each $t \in I$.*

Fix $x, y \in G_T$ arbitrarily, and set $I := (-1, 1)$. We define a function h on $\Omega \times I$ as $h(\omega, t) := f(H - x - ty)$. The integrability of h on ω and the partial differentiability of h on t are obvious. We have

$$\frac{\partial h}{\partial t}(\omega, t) = -f'(H - x - ty)y.$$

The assumption (5) implies that $|f'(H - x - ty)| \leq C_1|H - x - ty|^{p-1} + C_2$. Thus, we have and define

$$\begin{aligned}\left|\frac{\partial h}{\partial t}(\omega, t)\right| &\leq C_1|H - x - ty|^{p-1}|y| + C_2|y| \\ &\leq C_1 \max_{t \in I} |H - x - ty|^{p-1}|y| + C_2|y| =: g(\omega).\end{aligned}$$

Now, we show the integrability of g. Firstly, we have

$$\begin{aligned}|H - x - ty|^{p-1} &\leq (|H - x| + |ty|)^{p-1} \\ &\leq 2^{p-2}|H - x|^{p-1} + 2^{p-2}|t|^{p-1}|y|^{p-1} \\ &\leq 2^{p-2}|H - x|^{p-1} + 2^{p-2}|y|^{p-1}.\end{aligned}$$

Thus, Hölder's inequality yields that

$$\begin{aligned}E[|g|] &\leq C_1 2^{p-2} E\left[|H - x|^{p-1}|y| + |y|^p\right] + C_2 E[|y|] \\ &\leq C_1 2^{p-2}\left\{E^{\frac{1}{q}}\left[|H - x|^p\right]\|y\|_p + \|y\|_p^p\right\} + C_2 E[|y|] < \infty,\end{aligned}$$

where $\|\cdot\|_p$ represents the $\mathcal{L}^p(P)$-norm. Hence, we can apply the above lemma. We have then

$$\begin{aligned}D\Phi(x, y) &= \lim_{t \to 0} \frac{1}{t}[\Phi(x + ty) - \Phi(x)] = \lim_{t \to 0} \frac{1}{t} E[h(t) - h(0)] \\ &= \frac{\partial}{\partial t} E[h(t)]\Big|_{t=0} = E\left[\frac{\partial}{\partial t} h(t)\Big|_{t=0}\right] = -E[f'(H - x)y],\end{aligned}$$

from which Proposition 2 follows.

Before stating our main results, we have to prepare some terminology. $\Phi : G_T \to \mathbf{R}$ is lower semi-continuous (l.s.c.), if, for any $a \in \mathbf{R}$, $\{x \in G_T | \Phi(x) \leq a\}$ is closed. Moreover, Φ is proper, if it nowhere takes the value $-\infty$ and is not identically equal to $+\infty$. Thus, any Φ in our setting is convex proper. Below is an important result to prove the unique existence of a solution to the problem (2).

Lemma 2 ([5, Proposition II.1.2]). *Assume that Φ is strictly convex, l.s.c. and proper. In addition to this, we assume that Φ is coercive, i.e., for any sequence $x_n \in G_T$ such that $\|x_n\|_p \to \infty$, $\Phi(x_n)$ converges to ∞. Then, there exists a solution to (2) uniquely.*

We have to verify that our model satisfies the conditions of the above lemma. Firstly, we prove that Φ is l.s.c.. Denoting $\Phi'(x) := -f'(H-x)$, we have $\Phi'(x) \in \mathcal{L}^q(P)$ for any $x \in G_T$, and $D\Phi(x, y) = E[\Phi'(x)y]$ for any $x, y \in G_T$. Proposition I.5.4 of [5] yields that

$$\Phi(x) - \Phi(y) > E[\Phi'(y)(x-y)], \tag{6}$$

for any $x, y \in G_T, x \neq y$. Now, we fix an $x \in G_T$ and a sufficient small number $\delta > 0$. If $\|x-y\|_p < \delta$, then we have

$$|\Phi(x) - \Phi(y)| < C_1\delta\{\|H-x\|_p + \delta\}^{p-1} + C_2\delta. \tag{7}$$

Let us prove (7). When $\Phi(x)-\Phi(y) \geq 0$, the inequality (6), Hölder's inequality, Minkowski's inequality and the condition (5) imply that

$$\begin{aligned}\Phi(x) - \Phi(y) &< -E[\Phi'(x)(y-x)] \leq E^{1/q}[|f'(H-x)|^q]\|y-x\|_p \\ &\leq E^{1/q}[C_1^q|H-x|^p]\|y-x\|_p + C_2\|y-x\|_p \\ &< C_1\delta\|H-x\|_p^{p-1} + C_2\delta.\end{aligned}$$

On the other hand, when $\Phi(x) - \Phi(y) \leq 0$, we have $\Phi(x) - \Phi(y) > E[\Phi'(y)(x-y)]$. Thus,

$$\begin{aligned}|\Phi(x) - \Phi(y)| &< |E[f'(H-y)(x-y)]| \leq E^{1/q}[|f'(H-y)|^q]\|x-y\|_p \\ &< C_1\delta\|H-y\|_p^{p-1} + C_2\delta.\end{aligned}$$

Moreover, for any $y \in G_T$ such that $\|x-y\|_p < \delta$, we have

$$\|H-y\|_p \leq \|H-x\|_p + \|x-y\|_p < \|H-x\|_p + \delta.$$

Consequently, (7) holds, that is, Φ is continuous, not only l.s.c..

Next, we confirm that Φ is coercive. Let $\{x_n\}_{n\geq 1}$ be a sequence on G_T such that $\|x_n\|_p \to \infty$. The condition (4) implies that

$$\begin{aligned}\Phi(x_n) &= E[f(H-x_n)] \geq c_0E[|H-x_n|^p 1_{\{|H-x_n|>M\}}] \\ &\geq c_0E[|H-x_n|^p 1_{\{|H-x_n|>M\}}] + c_0E[|H-x_n|^p 1_{\{|H-x_n|\leq M\}}] - c_0M^p \\ &= c_0E[|H-x_n|^p] - c_0M^p \geq c_0\{E[|x_n|^p] - E[|H|^p] - M^p\} \\ &\to \infty,\end{aligned}$$

as n tends to ∞, from which Φ is coercive.

Remark 2. Let us confirm that, if Φ satisfies all conditions of Lemma 2 and $D\Phi(x^H, y) = 0$ for any $y \in G_T$, then Theorems 1 and 2 hold.

As in the inequality (6), Proposition I.5.4 of [5] asserts that $D\Phi(x, y-x) < \Phi(y) - \Phi(x)$ for any $x \neq y \in G_T$. We have then $\Phi(x^H) < \Phi(y)$ for any $y \in G_T$. Hence, this fact results in Theorem 1.

Moreover, we define a convex function $F : \mathcal{L}^p \to \mathbf{R} \cup \{+\infty\}$ as

$$F(x) := \begin{cases} \Phi(H-x), & \text{if } H-x \in G_T, \\ +\infty, & \text{otherwise.} \end{cases}$$

The assertion of Theorem 2 then is rewritten as $(\Phi(x^H) =) F(H-x^H) = F^{**}(H-x^H)$, which is the bipolar function of F, and whose definition is introduced in Sect. I.4.2.of [5]. The characterization (5.2) of Chap. I in [5] implies $0 \in \partial F(H-x^H)$. As regards the definition of the subdifferential ∂F, see Definition I.5.1 of [5]. Consequently, (5.3) of Chap. I in [5] asserts that $F(H-x^H) = F^{**}(H-x^H)$, which completes the proof of Theorem 2.

In conclusion, we obtain the following theorem:

Theorem 3. *The problem (2) has a unique solution* $x^H \in G_T$.

Moreover, we have the following mathematical property with respect to the unique solution x^H.

Theorem 4. *The solution* $x^H \in G_T$ *to the problem (2) satisfies*

$$E[f'(H-x^H)x] = 0 \quad \text{for any } x \in G_T. \tag{8}$$

Proof. By Proposition 2, we rewrite (8) as $D\Phi(x^H, y) = 0$ for any $y \in G_T$. We have $D\Phi(x, ay) = aD\Phi(x, y)$ for any $x, y \in G_T$ and any $a \in \mathbf{R}$ as a general property of the Gâteaux derivatives. Now, we assume that (8) does not hold. There exists then some $y \in G_T$ such that $D\Phi(x, y) \neq 0$. Thus, even if $D\Phi(x^H, y) > 0$, we have $D\Phi(x^H, -y) < 0$, which is contradiction. Hence (8) holds.

Remark 3. Theorems 3 and 4 mean that, when we regard $\overline{\Theta}$ as the set of all admissible strategies and impose the conditions (4) and (5) on f, Assumption 1 is a sufficient condition for the condition in Theorems 1 and 2.

References

1. Arai, T.: $\mathcal{L}^p$-projections of random variables and its application to finance. Preprint (2007)
2. Billingsley, P.: Probability and Measure, 3rd edn. Wiley, New York 1995
3. Černý, A., Kallsen, J.: On the structure of general mean-variance hedging strategies. Ann. Prob. **35**, 1479–1531 (2007)
4. Dellacherie, C., Meyer, P.A.: Probabilities and Potential B. North-Holland, Amsterdam 1982
5. Ekeland, I., Témam, R.: Convex Analysis and Variational Problems. Society for Industrial & Applied, Philadelphia 1999

Adv. Math. Econ. 11, 11–44 (2008)

Advances in
MATHEMATICAL
ECONOMICS

Tightness conditions and integrability of the sequential weak upper limit of a sequence of multifunctions

Charles Castaing[1], **Christian Hess**[2] **and Mohamed Saadoune**[3]

[1] Département de Mathématiques, Université Montpellier II, Place E. Bataillon, 34095 Montpellier cedex, France
(e-mail: castaing@math.univ-montp2.fr)

[2] Centre de Recherche Stratégies et Dynamiques Financières, Université Paris Dauphine, 75775 Paris cedex 16, France
(e-mail: christian.hess@dauphine.fr)

[3] Département de Mathématiques, Université Ibn Zohr, Lot. Addakhla, B.P. 8106, Agadir, Maroc
(e-mail: msaadoune@hotmail.com)

Received: September 11, 2006
Revised: May 30, 2007

Abstract. Various notions of tightness for measurable multifunctions are introduced and compared. They are used to derive results on the existence of integrable selections for the sequential weak upper limit of a sequence of multifunctions. Similar questions are examined for multifunctions with values in a dual space. Some results are particularized in the single-valued case, and applications to the multidimensional Fatou Lemma, both in the primal and in the dual space, are derived. This is achieved under conditions weaker than or noncomparable to L^1-boundedness.

Key words: Tightness conditions, Upper limit of a sequence of multifunctions, Measurable selection, Integrable selection, Fatou's Lemma in several dimensions.

1. Introduction

Given a sequence of points in a Banach space, it is often useful to consider the set of its cluster points and to get information about the properties of this set. Especially, when the points depend on a parameter that models randomness, one needs tractable results on the measurable dependance of the set of cluster points with respect to the parameter. Further, measurable and integrable selections are of importance. The same type of question also arises for a sequence of subsets.

In this more general setting, a pertinent concept is that of sequential upper limit. On the other hand, in the infinite dimensional setting, the sequential upper limit with respect to the weak topology, namely the sequential weak upper limit has shown to be of interest in many existence problems.

More precisely, let $(\Omega, \mathcal{F}, \mu)$ be a complete probability space, E a separable Banach space and 2^E the collection of all subsets of E. The sequential-weak upper limit of a sequence (X_n) of measurable multifunctions (alias set-valued functions) $X_n : \Omega \to 2^E$ is a multifunction denoted by $w - ls\, X_n$. The study of its measurability and integrability properties was initiated by the second author in [11,12]. But, older references concerning similar problems in finite dimensional spaces or in special topological spaces can be found in [11]. The main result of [11] (Theorem 5.5), that we shall often referred to, reads as follows: if the real-valued function

$$\omega \to \liminf_{n \to +\infty} d(0, X_n(\omega))$$

is integrable and if there exists a $\mathcal{R}(E_w)$-valued multifunction Γ such that for all $n \geq 1$ and all $\omega \in \Omega$

$$X_n(\omega) \subseteq \Gamma(\omega)$$

then the multifunction w-ls X_n admits at least one measurable and integrable selection. Here $\mathcal{R}(E_w)$ denotes the collection of all nonempty weakly closed and weakly ball-compact subsets of E (see Sect. 2).

Motivated by the study of Fatou type lemmas in Mathematical Economics, we present several variants of Hess' result via new conditions of tightness for measurable multifunctions. It is well known that the multidimensional Fatou Lemma allows one to prove the existence of equilibrium for an economy including infinitely many agents. The reader is referred to the book by Hildenbrand [14] for an extensive study of this topic. For the case of a dual space one can look at the contributions of Benabdellah and Castaing [5], Cornet and Martins da Rocha [9] and Balder and Sambucini [4]. In the present paper, we provide versions the Fatou Lemma in several dimensions for functions with values in E or in E^*. In these results the integrability conditions have been relaxed, namely the L^1-boundedness assumption is no longer required.

The paper is organised as follows. In Sect. 2 we set our notation and definitions, and summarize needed results. In Sect. 3, we present several tightness conditions for sequences of measurable multifunctions and we study their relations. In Sect. 4, combining the tightness conditions given in Sect. 3 with various integrability conditions, we establish several theorems on the existence of integrable selections for the sequential weak upper limit of a sequence of measurable multifunctions. In Sect. 5, we present results similar to those given in Sect. 4 for sequences of E-scalarly integrable multifunctions taking on convex weakly-star compact values in E^*, the topological dual space of E. Specific applications to the Fatou Lemma in several dimensions are provided at the end of Sects. 4 and 5.

2. Notation and preliminaries

In the sequel, E stands for a separable Banach space, whose norm is denoted by $|.|$, and E^* for the topological dual of E. The closed unit ball of E is denoted by B and the closed ball of radius r centered at 0 is denoted by rB. By s (resp. w), we denote the norm topology (resp. the weak topology) of E. The space E endowed with topology s (resp. w) will be denoted by E_s (resp. E_w). On E^*, the weak-star topology is denoted by w^*. It is known that the separability of E implies the existence of a countable w^*-dense subset D^* of E^*.

The collection of all subsets of E is denoted by 2^E. Several subcollections of 2^E will be considered, for example, the space $bd(E)$ of bounded subsets of E and the space $\mathcal{K}(E_w)$ of weakly compact subsets of E. Further, recall that a subset C of E is said to be *w-ball-compact* if the intersection of C with every closed ball is weakly compact. By the notation $\mathcal{R}(E_w)$ we mean the space of all weakly closed and weakly ball-compact subsets of E. In addition, it is convenient to indicate that the sets are convex by the subscript 'c'. For example $\mathcal{K}_c(E_w)$ stands for the set of convex weakly compact subsets of E and $\mathcal{R}_c(E_w)$ for the space of closed, convex, weakly ball-compact subsets of E. As to the set of Borel sets, we note that, due to the separability assumption, the Borel σ-fields $\mathcal{B}(E_s)$ and $\mathcal{B}(E_w)$ coincide. Thus we shall simply use the notation $\mathcal{B}(E)$.

The *distance function* of a subset C in E is defined by

$$d(x, C) = \inf_{y \in C} |x - y| \qquad x \in E.$$

We also set

$$|C| = \sup\{|x| : x \in C\}.$$

When C is empty, we apply the usual convention $d(0, C) = +\infty$ and $|C| = 0$. For any nonempty subset C, one has $d(0, C) \leq |C|$.

Let $(C_n)_{n\geq 1}$ be a sequence in 2^E, the collection of all subsets of E. The *sequential weak upper limit* $w - ls\, C_n$ of (C_n) is defined by

$$w - ls\, C_n = \left\{ x \in E : x = w - \lim_{j \to +\infty} x_{n_j}\,,\ x_{n_j} \in C_{n_j} \right\}$$

where $(C_{n_j})_{j\geq 1}$ denotes any subsequence of (C_n). In particular, the sequence $(n_j)_{j\geq 1}$ is increasing, whence tends to infinity. The *topological weak upper limit* $w - LS\, C_n$ of (C_n) is denoted by $w - LS\, C_n$ and is defined by

$$w - LS\, C_n = \bigcap_{n \geq 1} w - \text{cl} \bigcup_{k \geq n} C_n$$

where $w - \text{cl}$ denotes the closed hull operation in the weak topology. Recall that the topological weak upper limit is the set of those $x \in E$ such that every weak neighborhood of x meets infinitely many subsets C_n. The following inclusion is easy to check

$$w - ls\, C_n \subseteq w - LS\, C_n.$$

Conversely, if the C_n are contained in a fixed weakly compact subset K, then both sides coincide. The equality also holds if K is only assumed to be bounded, provided E^* be strongly separable (see e.g. Proposition 3.5 of [11]). In both cases, this follows from the metrizability of the restriction of the weak topology to K. On the other hand, since any weakly convergent sequence is bounded the following equality holds

$$w - ls\, C_n = \bigcup_{k \geq 1} w - ls\, (C_n \cap kB)\,. \tag{2.1}$$

Let $(\Omega, \mathcal{F}, \mu)$ be a complete[1] probability space. We denote by $L^0(\mu)$ (resp. by $L^1(\mu)$) the space of all (classes of) μ-measurable functions (resp. of μ-measurable and μ-integrable) functions. An E-valued function f is said to be *measurable* if $f^{-1}(B) \in \mathcal{F}$ for all $B \in \mathcal{B}(E)$. If the integral

$$\int_\Omega |f| d\mu$$

is finite, it is possible to define the integral $\int_\Omega f d\mu$ by the usual Bochner construction (see e.g. [1] or [10]).

A multifunction X with values in E, i.e. a map $X : \Omega \to 2^E$, is said to be *$\mathcal{F}$-measurable* (shortly *measurable*) if its graph $Gr(X)$, defined by

$$Gr(X) = \{(\omega, x) \in \Omega \times X : x \in X(\omega)\}$$

belongs to $\mathcal{F} \otimes \mathcal{B}(E)$. Given a measurable multifunction X and a Borel set $G \in \mathcal{B}(E)$, the set

$$X^- G = \{\omega \in \Omega : X(\omega) \cap G \neq \emptyset\}$$

is measurable, that is $X^- G \in \mathcal{F}$. In view of the completeness hypothesis on the probability space, this is a consequence of the Projection Theorem (see e.g. Theorem III.23 of [8] or Theorem 17.24 of [1]) and of the equality

[1] The completion hypothesis is not indispensable, but it simplifies the presentation and the statements of results.

$$X^{-}G = \mathrm{proj}_{\Omega}\{Gr(X) \cap (\Omega \times G)\}.$$

Conversely, if X is closed valued and satisfies $X^{-}U \in \mathcal{F}$ for each open set U, then $Gr(X) \in \mathcal{F} \otimes \mathcal{B}(E)$. In particular, if X is measurable, the *domain* of X, defined by

$$\mathrm{dom}\, X = \{\omega \in \Omega : X(\omega) \neq \emptyset\}$$

is measurable, because $\mathrm{dom}\, X = X^{-}E$. Another useful measurability criterion can be mentioned: the separability of E implies that a closed valued multifunction X is measurable if and only if the map $\omega \to d(x, X(\omega))$ is measurable for all $x \in E$.

The measurability of multifunctions is preserved under several operations. For example, given a sequence $(X_n)_{n\geq 1}$ of measurable multifunctions, the intersection $\bigcap_{n\geq 1} X_n$ and the union $\bigcup_{n\geq 1} X_n$ are measurable multifunctions too.

A *selection* of a multifunction X is a map $f : \Omega \to E$ such that $f(\omega) \in X(\omega)$ for all $\omega \in \mathrm{dom}\, X$. It is known that a measurable multifunction with nonempty domain admits at least one measurable selection (see e.g. [1] or [8]). The above measurability issues remain valid if E is replaced with a complete separable metric space, because the linear structure of E is not involved in the definitions and results just recalled.

Let $L^1_E(\Omega, \mathcal{F}, \mu)$ (shortly $L^1_E(\mu)$) be the space (of classes) of Bochner integrable E valued functions. For any multifunction $X : \Omega \to 2^E$, we denote by $\mathcal{S}^1_X(\mathcal{F}, \mu)$, or $\mathcal{S}^1_X$ for short, the set of all $\mathcal{F}$-measurable, Bochner μ-integrable selections of X, namely

$$\mathcal{S}^1_X = \{u \in L^1_E(\mu) : u(\omega) \in X(\omega) \quad \mu - \text{a.e.}\}.$$

X is said to be *μ-integrable* if the set $\mathcal{S}^1_X$ is nonempty. A simple measurable selection argument shows that a measurable multifunction X is integrable if and only if the distance function $\omega \to d(0, X(\omega))$ is integrable (see e.g. Lemma 5.1 of [11]). The multifunction X is said to be *integrably bounded* if the function

$$\omega \to |X(\omega)|$$

is integrable. A nonempty valued, integrably bounded multifunction is integrable, but the converse implication is false as simple examples show.

Given a subcollection $\mathcal{C}$ of 2^E we denote by $\mathcal{M}(\mathcal{C})$ the space of all $\mathcal{C}$ valued measurable multifunctions. Further, the space of all μ-integrably bounded multifunctions X in $\mathcal{M}(\mathcal{C})$ is denoted by $\mathcal{L}^1_{\mathcal{C}}(\mu)$ or, sometimes, $\mathcal{L}^1(\mathcal{C}, \mu)$. A sequence (X_n) in $\mathcal{L}^1_{bd(E)}(\mu)$ is said to be *bounded* if the sequence $(|X_n|)$ is bounded in $L^1(\mu)$.

3. Tightness conditions for sequences of multifunctions

In the present section several tightness properties are examined for sequences of multifunctions with values in a separable Banach space E. Let $\mathcal{C}$ be a subcollection of 2^E and $(X_n)_{n\geq 1}$ be a sequence of multifunctions taking on values in 2^E. It will be convenient to say that a property (P) relative to (X_n) is satisfied *infinitely often* (i.o.) if (P) holds for infinitely many indices n. Consider the following four conditions.

$\mathcal{I}(\mathcal{C})$: there exists $\Gamma \in \mathcal{M}(\mathcal{C})$ such that for μ-almost all $\omega \in \Omega$ one has

$$X_n(\omega) \bigcap \Gamma(\omega) \neq \emptyset \qquad i.o.$$

$\mathcal{S}(\mathcal{C})$: there exists $\Gamma \in \mathcal{M}(\mathcal{C})$ such that for μ-almost all $\omega \in \Omega$ one has

$$X_n(\omega) \subseteq \Gamma(\omega) \qquad i.o.$$

$\mathcal{D}(\mathcal{C})$: there exists $\Gamma \in \mathcal{M}(\mathcal{C})$ such that for μ-almost all $\omega \in \Omega$ one has

$$\liminf_{n\to+\infty} d(0, X_n(\omega) \bigcap \Gamma(\omega)) < +\infty$$

$\mathcal{D}'(\mathcal{C})$: there exists $\Gamma \in \mathcal{M}(\mathcal{C})$ such that for μ-almost all $\omega \in \Omega$ one has

$$\limsup_{n\to+\infty} d(0, X_n(\omega) \bigcap \Gamma(\omega)) < +\infty$$

A sequence (X_n) of multifunctions satisfying condition $\mathcal{I}(\mathcal{C})$ will be said to be $\mathcal{I}(\mathcal{C})$-tight. Similarly, we shall speak of $\mathcal{S}(\mathcal{C})$, $\mathcal{D}(\mathcal{C})$ or $\mathcal{D}'(\mathcal{C})$-tightness. In order to avoid trivialities, we assume that multifunction Γ is nonempty valued.

Remark 3.1. (i) The measurability hypotheses imply that the multifunctions $X_n \cap \Gamma$ are measurable.

(ii) The following implications hold: $\mathcal{D}'(\mathcal{C}) \Rightarrow \mathcal{D}(\mathcal{C}) \Rightarrow \mathcal{I}(\mathcal{C})$. Further, consider the condition

$$\text{for } \mu\text{-almost all } \omega \in \Omega,\ X_n(\omega) \neq \emptyset \quad \forall n \geq 1. \tag{*}$$

Obviously condition $(*)$ and $\mathcal{S}(\mathcal{C})$ together imply $\mathcal{I}(\mathcal{C})$. On the other hand, if $(X_n)_{n\geq 1}$ is $\mathcal{I}(\mathcal{C})$-tight, the sequence (Y_n) defined by $Y_n = X_n \cap \Gamma$ is $\mathcal{S}(\mathcal{C})$-tight.

In particular, if the X_n's are single-valued, i.e. $X_n = f_n$ where $f_n : \Omega \to E$ are measurable, $\mathcal{I}(\mathcal{C})$-tightness and $\mathcal{S}(\mathcal{C})$-tightness are equivalent.

Let us introduce now four new concepts of tightness that can be seen as approximate versions of the above conditions. The connections with the previous ones will be examined soon. These notions are denoted by $\mathcal{I}(\mathcal{C})_\varepsilon$, $\mathcal{S}(\mathcal{C})_\varepsilon$, $\mathcal{D}(\mathcal{C})_\varepsilon$ and $\mathcal{D}'(\mathcal{C})_\varepsilon$. The definitions go as follows.

$\mathcal{I}(\mathcal{C})_\varepsilon$: for every $\varepsilon > 0$, there exists a multifunction $\Gamma_\varepsilon \in \mathcal{M}(\mathcal{C})$ such that if the subsets $A_{n\varepsilon}$ are defined by $A_{n\varepsilon} = \{X_n \bigcap \Gamma_\varepsilon \neq \emptyset\}$, we have

$$\mu(\limsup_{n\to+\infty} A_{n\varepsilon}) \geq 1 - \varepsilon$$

$\mathcal{S}(\mathcal{C})_\varepsilon$: for every $\varepsilon > 0$, there exists a multifunction $\Gamma_\varepsilon \in \mathcal{M}(\mathcal{C})$ such that if we set $A_{n\varepsilon} = \{X_n \subseteq \Gamma_\varepsilon\}$, we have

$$\mu(\limsup_{n\to+\infty} A_{n\varepsilon}) \geq 1 - \varepsilon$$

$\mathcal{D}(\mathcal{C})_\varepsilon$: for every $\varepsilon > 0$ there exists a multifunction $\Gamma_\varepsilon \in \mathcal{M}(\mathcal{C})$ such that

$$\Omega_\varepsilon = \{\omega \in \Omega : \liminf_{n\to+\infty} d(0, X_n(\omega) \bigcap \Gamma_\varepsilon(\omega)) < +\infty\}$$

satisfies $\mu(\Omega_\varepsilon) \geq 1 - \varepsilon$.

$\mathcal{D}'(\mathcal{C})_\varepsilon$: for every $\varepsilon > 0$ there exists a multifunction $\Gamma_\varepsilon \in \mathcal{M}(\mathcal{C})$ such that

$$\Omega_\varepsilon = \{\omega \in \Omega : \limsup_{n\to+\infty} d(0, X_n(\omega) \bigcap \Gamma_\varepsilon(\omega)) < +\infty\}$$

satisfies $\mu(\Omega_\varepsilon) \geq 1 - \varepsilon$.

The following result connects conditions of exact tightness and approximate tightness.

Proposition 3.1. *The following equivalences are valid.*

$$\mathcal{I}(\mathcal{C}) \Leftrightarrow \mathcal{I}(\mathcal{C})_\varepsilon \qquad \mathcal{S}(\mathcal{C}) \Leftrightarrow \mathcal{S}(\mathcal{C})_\varepsilon \qquad \mathcal{D}(\mathcal{C}) \Leftrightarrow \mathcal{D}(\mathcal{C})_\varepsilon \qquad \mathcal{D}'(\mathcal{C}) \Leftrightarrow \mathcal{D}'(\mathcal{C})_\varepsilon.$$

Proof. The implications

$$\mathcal{I}(\mathcal{C}) \Rightarrow \mathcal{I}(\mathcal{C})_\varepsilon \qquad \mathcal{S}(\mathcal{C}) \Rightarrow \mathcal{S}(\mathcal{C})_\varepsilon \qquad \mathcal{D}(\mathcal{C}) \Rightarrow \mathcal{D}(\mathcal{C})_\varepsilon \qquad \mathcal{D}'(\mathcal{C}) \Rightarrow \mathcal{D}'(\mathcal{C})_\varepsilon$$

are easy. Indeed, for proving the implication $\mathcal{I}(\mathcal{C}) \Rightarrow \mathcal{I}(\mathcal{C})_\varepsilon$, it is enough to set for each $\varepsilon > 0$ and $n \geq 1$

$$\Gamma_\varepsilon = \Gamma \qquad \text{and} \qquad A_{n\varepsilon} = \{X_n \cap \Gamma \neq \emptyset\}.$$

which gives $\mu(\limsup_{n\to+\infty} A_{n\varepsilon}) = 1$.

The proof of implication $\mathcal{S}(\mathcal{C}) \Rightarrow \mathcal{S}(\mathcal{C})_\varepsilon$ is done similarly, but $A_{n\varepsilon}$ is defined by $A_{n\varepsilon} = \{X_n \subseteq \Gamma\}$ for all n, ε. As for implication $\mathcal{D}(\mathcal{C}) \Rightarrow \mathcal{D}(\mathcal{C})_\varepsilon$, we set this time for every $\varepsilon > 0$

$$\Omega_\varepsilon = \left\{ \liminf_{n\to+\infty} d(0, X_n \bigcap \Gamma) < +\infty \right\}$$

and we deduce $\mu(\Omega_\varepsilon) = 1$. Implication $\mathcal{D}'(\mathcal{C}) \Rightarrow \mathcal{D}'(\mathcal{C})_\varepsilon$ is proved in the same way. We turn now to the non trivial implications.

$\mathcal{I}(\mathcal{C})_\varepsilon \Rightarrow \mathcal{I}(\mathcal{C})$: We consider $\varepsilon = \varepsilon_q$ where $q \geq 0$ is an integer and we assume that the sequence (ε_q) is decreasing and tends to 0. We set as above $A_{n\varepsilon} = \{X_n \cap \Gamma_\varepsilon \neq \emptyset\}$ and, to simplify the notation, $A_{nq} = A_{n\varepsilon_q}$ and $\Gamma_q = \Gamma_{\varepsilon_q}$. Now, we define the sequence $(\Omega_q)_{q\geq 1}$ by

$$\Omega_q = \limsup_{n\to+\infty} A_{nq}.$$

Further, since for each $q \geq 1$,

$$\mu(\limsup_{n\to+\infty} A_{nq}) \geq 1 - \varepsilon_q,$$

we get $\lim_{q\to\infty} \mu(\Omega_q) = 1$. We also define the multifunction Γ on Ω by

$$\Gamma = 1_{\Omega'_1}\Gamma_1 + \sum_{q\geq 2} 1_{\Omega'_q}\Gamma_q$$

where $\Omega'_1 = \Omega_1$ and $\Omega'_q = \Omega_q \setminus \cup_{i<q}\Omega_i$ for all $q \geq 1$. For each $\omega \in \Omega_q$ one has

$$\omega \in A_{nq} = \{X_n \cap \Gamma \neq \emptyset\} \quad \text{i.o.},$$

which proves implication $\mathcal{I}(\mathcal{C})_\varepsilon \Rightarrow \mathcal{I}(\mathcal{C})$. Implications $\mathcal{S}(\mathcal{C})_\varepsilon \Rightarrow \mathcal{S}(\mathcal{C})$, $\mathcal{D}(\mathcal{C})_\varepsilon \Rightarrow \mathcal{D}(\mathcal{C})$ and $\mathcal{D}'(\mathcal{C})_\varepsilon \Rightarrow \mathcal{D}'(\mathcal{C})$ can be proved in the same way. □

The notion of $\mathcal{D}(\mathcal{C})$-tightness has an alternate formulation involving bounded sets or balls as the following proposition shows.

Proposition 3.2. *If $\mathcal{C}$ is a family of subsets and $(X_n)_{n\geq 1}$ a sequence of measurable multifunctions, the following two statements (a) and (b) are equivalent.*

(a) *(X_n) is $\mathcal{D}(\mathcal{C})$-tight*
(b) *there exists a positive measurable function r such that the sequence $(X_n \cap rB)_{n\geq 1}$ is $\mathcal{I}(\mathcal{C})$-tight.*

Proof. Let us first show that (a) $\Rightarrow$ (b). By assumption, there exists a measurable multifunction $\Gamma : \Omega \to \mathcal{C}$ such that $\liminf_n d(0, X_n \cap \Gamma) < +\infty$ holds μ-almost surely. Let r be a positive measurable function such that

$$\liminf_{n\to+\infty} d(0, X_n(\omega) \cap \Gamma(\omega)) < r(\omega) \qquad \mu - \text{a.s.} \tag{3.1}$$

It is readily seen that (3.1) implies

$$X_n(\omega) \cap \Gamma(\omega) \cap r(\omega)B \neq \emptyset \qquad \text{i.o.}$$

The converse implication goes similarly. □

In view of some results that we plan to prove (namely Theorems 4.4 and 4.7), it is also interesting to introduce stronger notions of tightness, namely $\mathcal{I}_+(\mathcal{C})_\varepsilon$-tightness and $\mathcal{S}_+(\mathcal{C})_\varepsilon$-tightness. Let $\mathcal{C}$ be a collection of subsets of E.

$\mathcal{I}_+(\mathcal{C})_\varepsilon$: A sequence (X_n) of $\mathcal{C}$-valued multifunctions is said to be $\mathcal{I}_+(\mathcal{C})_\varepsilon$-tight if, for every $\varepsilon > 0$, there is a measurable multifunction $\Gamma_\varepsilon \in \mathcal{M}(\mathcal{C})$ such that if we set

$$A_{n\varepsilon} = \{X_n \cap \Gamma_\varepsilon \neq \emptyset\},$$

we have

$$\inf_{n\geq 1} \mu(A_{n\varepsilon}) \geq 1 - \varepsilon$$

$\mathcal{S}_+(\mathcal{C})_\varepsilon$: A sequence (X_n) of $\mathcal{C}$-valued multifunctions is said to be $\mathcal{S}_+(\mathcal{C})_\varepsilon -$ *tight* if, for every $\varepsilon > 0$, there is a multifunction $\Gamma_\varepsilon \in \mathcal{M}(\mathcal{C})$ such that if we set $A_{n\varepsilon} = \{X_n \subseteq \Gamma_\varepsilon\}$, we have

$$\inf_{n\geq 1} \mu(A_{n\varepsilon}) \geq 1 - \varepsilon$$

Remark 3.2. Proposition 3.1 is useful, because conditions $\mathcal{I}(\mathcal{C})$, $\mathcal{S}(\mathcal{C})$, $\mathcal{D}(\mathcal{C})$ and $\mathcal{D}'(\mathcal{C})$ are simpler than the corresponding approximate tightness conditions $\mathcal{I}(\mathcal{C})_\varepsilon$, $\mathcal{S}(\mathcal{C})_\varepsilon$, $\mathcal{D}(\mathcal{C})_\varepsilon$ and $\mathcal{D}'(\mathcal{C})_\varepsilon$. However, condition $\mathcal{I}(\mathcal{C})_\varepsilon$ (resp. $\mathcal{S}(\mathcal{C})_\varepsilon$) is easier to compare with $\mathcal{I}_+(\mathcal{C})_\varepsilon$ (resp. $\mathcal{S}_+(\mathcal{C})_\varepsilon$)

Remark 3.3. (i) The tightness condition $\mathcal{I}_+(\mathcal{C})_\varepsilon$ resembles condition $\mathcal{I}(\mathcal{C})_\varepsilon$, but is stronger. This follows from the inequalities

$$\mu(\limsup_{n\to\infty} A_n) \geq \limsup_{n\to\infty} \mu(A_n) \geq \inf_{n\geq 1} \mu(A_n)$$

valid for any sequence (A_n) in $\mathcal{F}$. Easy examples show that these inequalities may be strict. Similarly, the implication $\mathcal{S}_+(\mathcal{C})_\varepsilon \Rightarrow \mathcal{S}(\mathcal{C})_\varepsilon$ also holds and it is strict.

(ii) In the definition of $\mathcal{S}_+(\mathcal{C})_\varepsilon$-tightness, the measurability of the multifunction Γ_ε is not essential, but in the definition of $\mathcal{I}_+(\mathcal{C})_\varepsilon$-tightness, the measurability of Γ_ε is necessary in order to get the measurability of multifunctions $X_n \cap \Gamma_\varepsilon$ (for $n \geq 1$ and $\varepsilon > 0$).

In the following proposition, two further properties of tight sequences are provided.

Proposition 3.3. (i) *Let (X_n) be an $\mathcal{I}_+(\mathcal{R}(E_w))_\varepsilon$-tight sequence. If it is bounded in $\mathcal{L}^1(bd(E), \mu)$, then it is also $\mathcal{I}_+(\mathcal{K}(E_w))_\varepsilon$-tight.*

(ii) *Let $\mathcal{C} = \mathcal{K}(E_w)$ (resp. $bd(E)$). If (X_n) is $\mathcal{I}_+(\mathcal{C})_\varepsilon$-tight, then it is $\mathcal{D}(\mathcal{C})_\varepsilon$-tight.*

Proof. (i) Let $\varepsilon > 0$. By hypothesis, there exists a multifunction $\Gamma_\varepsilon \in \mathcal{M}(\mathcal{R}(E_w))$ such that

$$\inf_{n\geq 1} \mu(A_{n\varepsilon}) \geq 1 - \varepsilon$$

where $A_{n\varepsilon} = \{X_n \cap \Gamma_\varepsilon \neq \emptyset\}$ for each $n \geq 1$. Since $(|X_n|)$ is $L^1(\mu)$-bounded, one can find $r_\varepsilon > 0$ such that

$$\inf_{n\geq 1} \mu(|X_n| \leq r_\varepsilon) \geq 1 - \varepsilon.$$

Define the multifunction Δ_ε by $\Delta_\varepsilon = \Gamma_\varepsilon \cap r_\varepsilon B$. Then, Δ_ε is measurable and $\mathcal{K}(E_w)$-valued. For each $n \geq 1$, one has

$$A_{n\varepsilon} \cap \{|X_n| \leq r_\varepsilon\} \subseteq \{X_n \cap \Delta_\varepsilon \neq \emptyset\},$$

whence

$$\inf_{n\geq 1} \mu(\{X_n \cap \Delta_\varepsilon \neq \emptyset\}) \geq 1 - 2\varepsilon.$$

(ii) We first look at the case $\mathcal{C} = \mathcal{K}(E_w)$. Let $\varepsilon > 0$ and $\Gamma_\varepsilon \in \mathcal{M}(\mathcal{K}(E_w))$ be the multifunction that appears in the $\mathcal{I}_+(\mathcal{K}(E_w))$-tightness condition. It satisfies

$$\inf_{n\geq 1} \mu(A_{n\varepsilon}) \geq 1 - \varepsilon \tag{3.2}$$

where for each $n \geq 1$, $A_{n\varepsilon}$ is defined as in the proof of part (i). Inequality (3.2) implies $\mu(\limsup A_{n\varepsilon}) \geq 1 - \varepsilon$. Now, for each $\omega \in \limsup A_{n\varepsilon}$, there exists an increasing sequence $(n_k)_{k\geq 1}$ of positive integers such that $\omega \in A_{n_k\varepsilon}$ for all $k \geq 1$. Thus, we have the following chain of inequalities

$$\liminf_{n\to+\infty} d(0, X_n(\omega) \cap \Gamma_\varepsilon(\omega)) \leq \liminf_{k\to+\infty} d(0, X_{n_k}(\omega) \cap \Gamma_\varepsilon(\omega)) \leq |\Gamma_\varepsilon(\omega)|$$

Consequently, it follows

$$\mu(\{\omega \in \Omega : \liminf_{n\to+\infty} d(0, X_n(\omega) \cap \Gamma_\varepsilon(\omega)) < +\infty\}) \geq \mu(\limsup_{n\to+\infty} A_{n\varepsilon}) \geq 1 - \varepsilon$$

which proves the $\mathcal{D}(\mathcal{K}(E_w))$-tightness. The proof of the $\mathcal{D}(bd(E))$-tightness only needs obvious modifications. □

Remark 3.4. For sake of comparison with the results in [11], it is interesting to say that a sequence (X_n) of multifunctions with values in E is $\mathcal{I}_{++}(\mathcal{C})$-tight if there exists a measurable multifunction $\Gamma : \Omega \to \mathcal{C}$ such that

$$X_n(\omega) \cap \Gamma(\omega) \neq \emptyset \qquad \omega \in \Omega$$

for all $n \geq 1$.

Similarly (X_n) is said to be $\mathcal{S}_{++}(\mathcal{C})$-tight if there exists a multifunction $\Gamma : \Omega \to \mathcal{C}$ (possibly non measurable) such that

$$X_n(\omega) \subseteq \Gamma(\omega) \qquad \omega \in \Omega$$

for all $n \geq 1$.

Consider the sequence (Y_n) defined by $Y_n = X_n \cap \Gamma$. If the condition

$$X_n(\omega) \neq \emptyset \qquad \text{i.o.} \qquad \omega \in \Omega$$

is satisfied, then the following implication holds:

$$(X_n) \text{ is } \mathcal{I}_{++}(\mathcal{C})\text{-tight} \Rightarrow (Y_n) \text{ is } \mathcal{S}_{++}(\mathcal{C})\text{-tight}.$$

The $\mathcal{S}_{++}(\mathcal{R}(E_w))$-tightness condition was used in [11] to prove the measurability of $w - ls\ X_n$ (Theorem 4.4), as well as the existence of a measurable and integrable selection of this multifunction (Theorem 5.5). In Sect. 4, we shall establish other versions of the latter result under condition $\mathcal{S}_{++}$, but also under $\mathcal{S}_+$ or $\mathcal{S}$. Other tightness conditions will be also employed.

When the multifunctions X_n are single-valued, conditions $\mathcal{S}_{++}(\mathcal{R}(E_w))$ and $\mathcal{I}_{++}(\mathcal{R}(E_w))$ are equivalent. Further, the following implications also hold for any subfamily $\mathcal{C}$ of 2^E

$$\mathcal{S}_{++}(\mathcal{C}) \Rightarrow \mathcal{S}_+(\mathcal{C}) \Rightarrow \mathcal{S}(\mathcal{C})$$
$$\mathcal{I}_{++}(\mathcal{C}) \Rightarrow \mathcal{I}_+(\mathcal{C}) \Rightarrow \mathcal{I}(\mathcal{C}).$$

4. Integrability results for the sequential weak upper limit

In this section, E still denotes a separable Banach space. For an $\mathcal{I}(\mathcal{C})$-tight sequence (X_n) of multifunctions, we present first two results on the existence of an integrable selection for the multifunction $w - ls\ X_n$. The first part of the first result as well as the second result are valid for integrable multifunctions. In particular, the multifunctions can have unbounded values.

Theorem 4.1. *Let $\mathcal{C} = \mathcal{R}(E_w)$. Consider an $\mathcal{I}(\mathcal{C})$-tight sequence (X_n) in $\mathcal{M}(\mathcal{C})$ satisfying one of the following two conditions:*

(a) *The multifunction Γ involved in the $\mathcal{I}(\mathcal{C})$-tightness condition is μ-integrably bounded.*

(b) $\limsup_{n \to +\infty} |X_n| \in L^1(\mu)$.

Then, the multifunction $w - ls\ X_n$ admits at least one μ-integrable selection.

Proof. $\mathcal{I}(\mathcal{C})$-tightness implies the existence of a measurable multifunction Γ such that for all $\omega \in \Omega$ one has

$$X_n(\omega) \cap \Gamma(\omega) \neq \emptyset \qquad i.o.$$

Consequently, the inclusions $X_n(\omega) \cap \Gamma(\omega) \subseteq \Gamma(\omega)$, valid for $\omega \in \Omega$ and $n \geq 1$, permit us to invoke Lemma 5.2 of [11] which yields the inequality

$$d\,(0, w - ls\ (X_n(\omega) \cap \Gamma(\omega))) \leq \liminf_{n\to\infty} d(0, X_n(\omega) \cap \Gamma(\omega))$$

for μ-almost all $\omega \in \Omega$. Moreover, the hypothesis on Γ and Theorem 4.4 of [11] show that the multifunction $w - ls\ (X_n \cap \Gamma)$ is measurable. For each $\omega \in \Omega$ one can find an infinite subset $I(\omega)$ of $\mathbf{N}^*$ such that $X_n(\omega) \cap \Gamma(\omega) \neq \emptyset$ for all $n \in I(\omega)$, whence

$$\begin{aligned}\liminf_{n\to\infty} d(0, X_n(\omega) \cap \Gamma(\omega)) &\leq \liminf_{n\to\infty,\, n\in I(\omega)} d(0, X_n(\omega) \cap \Gamma(\omega))\\ &\leq \liminf_{n\to\infty,\, n\in I(\omega)} |X_n(\omega) \cap \Gamma(\omega)|.\end{aligned}$$

In case (a) we deduce that

$$\liminf_{n\to\infty} d(0, X_n(\omega) \cap \Gamma(\omega)) \leq |\Gamma(\omega)|$$

and in case (b)

$$\begin{aligned}\liminf_{n\to\infty} d(0, X_n(\omega) \cap \Gamma(\omega)) &\leq \liminf_{n\to\infty,\, n\in I(\omega)} d(0, X_n(\omega) \cap \Gamma(\omega))\\ &\leq \limsup_{n\to\infty,\, n\in I(\omega)} |X_n(\omega) \cap \Gamma(\omega)|\\ &\leq \limsup_{n\to\infty} |X_n(\omega)|.\end{aligned}$$

In both cases, we have shown that the function $d\,(0, w - ls\ (X_n \cap \Gamma))$ is integrable, which by Lemma 5.1 of [11] yields the existence of a μ-integrable selection of $w - ls\ (X_n \cap \Gamma)$ and, in turn, of $w - ls\ X_n$. □

Remark 4.1. If the sequence $(|X_n|)_{n\geq 1}$ is assumed to be uniformly integrable, one has by the Fatou-Vitali Lemma

$$\limsup_{n\to+\infty} \int_\Omega |X_n| d\mu \leq \int_\Omega \limsup_{n\to+\infty} |X_n|\, d\mu$$

In this case, condition (b) entails L^1-boundedness, namely

$$\sup_{n\geq 1} \int_\Omega |X_n| d\mu < +\infty.$$

Otherwise, it is not difficult to construct sequences (X_n) such that $(|X_n|)$ satisfies condition (b) of Theorem 4.1, but is not bounded in $L^1(\mu)$ (see Remark 4.3).

In the following theorem, as in Theorem 4.1a, the multifunctions X_n may have unbounded values, but we shall use Theorem 4.1b to prove it.

Theorem 4.2. *Let $\mathcal{C} = \mathcal{R}(E_w)$. Consider a sequence (X_n) of 2^E-valued, measurable multifunctions, and assume that there exists a sequence (r_n) of positive integrable functions satisfying the following two conditions* (i) *and* (ii).

(i) *the sequence $(X_n \cap r_n B)_{n\geq 1}$ is $\mathcal{I}(\mathcal{C})$-tight*
(ii) $\limsup_{n\to+\infty} r_n \in L^1(\mu)$.

Then, the multifunction $w - ls\, X_n$ admits at least one μ-integrable selection.

Proof. Consider the sequence (Y_n) given by

$$Y_n(\omega) = X_n(\omega) \cap r_n(\omega) B \qquad \omega \in \Omega \qquad n \geq 1.$$

By assumption, (Y_n) is $\mathcal{I}(\mathcal{C})$-tight. In particular, for each $\omega \in \Omega$ one can find an infinite subset $I(\omega)$ of $\mathbf{N}^*$ such that

$$Y_n(\omega) \neq \emptyset \qquad \text{for all } n \in I(\omega).$$

Further, since $|Y_n(\omega)| = 0$ when $Y_n(\omega) = \emptyset$, we have

$$\limsup_{n\to+\infty} |Y_n(\omega)| \leq \limsup_{n\in I(\omega),\, n\to+\infty} |Y_n(\omega)| \leq \limsup_{n\in I(\omega),\, n\to+\infty} r_n(\omega) \leq \limsup_{n\to+\infty} r_n(\omega).$$

It only remain to apply Theorem 4.1b to the sequence (Y_n). □

The next simple result involves condition $\mathcal{S}(\mathcal{C})$ introduced in Sect. 3. It can be seen as a variant of Theorem 5.5 of [11].

Theorem 4.3. *Let $\mathcal{C} = \mathcal{R}(E_w)$. Consider sequence (X_n) in $\mathcal{M}(2^E)$ satisfying the following two conditions:*

(i) *(X_n) is $\mathcal{S}(\mathcal{C})$-tight*
(ii) $\limsup_{n\to+\infty} d(0, X_n)$ *is μ-integrable.*

Then, the multifunction $w - ls\, X_n$ admits at least one μ-integrable selection.

Proof. Condition $\mathcal{S}(\mathcal{C})$ entails the existence of a multifunction Γ such that for μ-almost all $\omega \in \Omega$ one can find a subsequence $(X_{n_i})_{i\geq 1}$ verifying

$$X_{n_i}(\omega) \subseteq \Gamma(\omega)$$

(the subsequence $(n_i)_{i\geq 1}$ may of course depend on ω). Therefore, one has

$$\begin{aligned} d(0, w - ls\, X_n(\omega)) &\leq d(0, w - ls\, X_{n_i}(\omega)) \leq \liminf_{i\to+\infty} d(0, X_{n_i}(\omega)) \\ &\leq \limsup_{n\to+\infty} d(0, X_n(\omega)). \end{aligned}$$

where the second inequality is a consequence of Lemma 5.2 of [11]. This shows that the function $\omega \to d(0, w - ls\ X_n)$ is μ-integrable. In turn, by Lemma 5.1 of [11] this entails the existence of a μ-integrable selection of $w - ls\ X_n$. □

Remark 4.2. Theorem 4.3 is not comparable to Theorem 5.5 of [11]. Indeed, in the latter, one supposes the $\mathcal{S}_{++}(\mathcal{R}(E_w))$-tightness condition which is stronger than $\mathcal{S}(\mathcal{R}(E_w))$-tightness. Indeed, in the $\mathcal{S}_{++}(\mathcal{R}(E_w))$-tightness condition, the inclusion

$$X_n(\omega) \subseteq \Gamma(\omega) \qquad \mu\text{-a.s.}$$

is assumed to hold for all $n \geq 1$. On the other hand, the integrability condition assumed in [11], namely "$\liminf_{n\to+\infty} d(0, X_n)$ is μ-integrable", is weaker than condition (ii) above.

The following result involves the tightness conditions $\mathcal{I}_+(\mathcal{C})_\varepsilon$ and $\mathcal{D}(\mathcal{C})_\varepsilon$. As the previous ones, it asserts the existence of an integrable selection for the sequential weak upper limit of a sequence of multifunctions, but it is worthwhile to note the presence of a Mazur type condition, namely condition (iii). The proof, longer and more subtle than those of the above results, uses an appropriate truncation technique.

Theorem 4.4. *Let $\mathcal{C} = \mathcal{R}(E_w)$ and (X_n) be a sequence in $\mathcal{M}(bd(E))$, whose members are integrably bounded and which satisfies the following three conditions*

(i) *(X_n) is $\mathcal{I}_+(\mathcal{C})_\varepsilon$-tight.*
(ii) *(X_n) is $\mathcal{D}(\mathcal{C})_\varepsilon$-tight.*
(iii) *There exists a sequence (r_n) in $L^0(\mu)$ with $r_n \in co\{|X_i| : i \geq n\}$ such that for every sequence (s_n) in $L^0(\mu)$ such that $s_n \in co\{r_i : i \geq n\}$, one has* $\liminf s_n \in L^1(\mu)$.

Then the multifunction $w{-}ls\ X_n$ admits at least one integrable selection.

Proof. We shall proceed in three steps.

Step 1. For each integer $q \geq 1$, set $\varepsilon_q = \frac{1}{q2^q}$. Using conditions (i) and (ii) it is not hard to construct a non decreasing sequence $(\Gamma_q)_{q\geq 1}$ of measurable multifunctions such that if we set

$$\Omega_q = \{\omega \in \Omega : \liminf_{n\to+\infty} d(0, X_n(\omega) \cap \Gamma_q(\omega)) < +\infty\} \qquad q \geq 1$$

and

$$A_{nq} = \{\omega \in \Omega : X_n(\omega) \cap \Gamma_q(\omega)) \neq \emptyset\} \qquad n, q \geq 1$$

we have

$$\mu(\Omega_q) \geq 1 - \varepsilon_q \qquad \text{and} \qquad \inf_{n \geq 1} \mu(A_{nq}) \geq 1 - \varepsilon_q$$

After this construction, the values of multifunctions Γ_q still belong to $\mathcal{R}(E_w)$, because this family of sets is closed under finite unions. For each $q \geq 1$ define the multifunction Z_q by

$$Z_q = w - ls\,(X_n \cap \Gamma_q \cap qB)$$

and the set

$$D_q = \text{dom}\, Z_q\,.$$

The values of multifunction $\Gamma_q \cap qB$ are weakly compact and the following inclusions hold on Ω for all $n \geq 1$

$$X_n \cap \Gamma_q \cap qB \subseteq \Gamma_q \cap qB \qquad n, q \geq 1. \tag{4.1}$$

Therefore, we can invoke Proposition 4.3 of [11], which entails the measurability of multifunction Z_q and, in turn $D_q \in \mathcal{F}$. Inclusions (4.1) also imply

$$D_q = \limsup_{n \to +\infty} \text{dom}(X_n \cap \Gamma_q \cap qB).$$

In view of the definitions and the above construction, the sequence $(\Omega_q)_{q \geq 1}$ satisfies

$$\Omega = \bigcup_{q \geq 1} \Omega_q \qquad \mu - \text{a.s.}$$

and, for each $q \geq 1$

$$\Omega_q = \bigcup_{k \geq q} \limsup_{n \to +\infty} \text{dom}(X_n \cap \Gamma_q \cap kB) \subseteq \bigcup_{k \geq q} D_k,$$

whence

$$\Omega = \bigcup_{q \geq 1} D_q \qquad \mu - \text{a.s.}$$

In particular, this shows that the D_qs are nonempty for q large enough. Without loss of generality, we can assume that this holds for all $q \geq 1$.

Step 2. For every $q \geq 1$ one can find a measurable selection f_q of Z_q, defined on D_q and such that

$$|f_q(\omega)| \leq d(0, Z_q(\omega)) + 1 \qquad \omega \in D_q \tag{4.2}$$

Further, the definition of Z_q implies

$$|f_q(\omega)| \leq q \qquad \omega \in D_q \tag{4.3}$$

For each $n, q \geq 1$ let us introduce now the measurable multifunction X_{nq} defined on Ω by

$$X_{nq} = \mathbf{1}_{A_{nq}}(X_n \cap \Gamma_q \cap qB) + \mathbf{1}_{(A_{nq})^c} f_q$$

where $(A_{nq})^c = \Omega \setminus A_{nq}$, and let us set

$$F_q = \text{dom } w - ls \, X_{nq}$$

On F_q we claim that the following inclusion holds

$$w - ls \, X_{nq} \subseteq Z_q \tag{4.4}$$

Indeed, suppose $\omega \in F_q$ and $x \in w{-}ls \, X_{nq}$. There exists a sequence $(x_k)_{k\geq 1}$ such that $x = w - \lim_{k\to+\infty} x_k$ and $x_k \in X_{n_k q}(\omega)$, where $(X_{n_k q}(\omega))_{k\geq 1}$ is a subsequence of $(X_{nq}(\omega))_{n\geq 1}$. If $x = f_q(\omega)$ then $x \in Z_q(\omega)$ by the definition of f_q. Otherwise, we cannot have $x_k = f_q(\omega)$ for infinitely many indices k. Therefore, $x_k \neq f_q(\omega)$ for all $k \geq k_0$ (for some integer k_0), which yields

$$\omega \in A_{n_k q} \qquad \text{and} \qquad x_k \in X_{n_k}(\omega) \cap \Gamma_q(\omega) \cap qB$$

for all $k \geq k_0$ and, in turn, $x \in Z_q(\omega)$ as well.

From inclusion (4.4) it follows that $F_q \subseteq D_q$. It is readily seen that the converse inclusion also holds so that $F_q = D_q$. Inclusion (4.4) also shows that for all $\omega \in D_q$ one has

$$d(0, Z_q(\omega)) \leq d(0, w - ls \, X_{nq}(\omega)) \leq \liminf_{n\to+\infty} d(0, X_{nq}(\omega))$$

whence by the definition of X_{nq}

$$d(0,Z_q(\omega)) \leq \liminf_{n\to+\infty} \left(\mathbf{1}_{A_{nq}}(\omega)\, d(0,X_n(\omega)\cap\Gamma_q(\omega)\cap qB) + \mathbf{1}_{(A_{nq})^c}(\omega)\, |f_q(\omega)|\right). \tag{4.5}$$

Since for any $\omega \in A_{nq}$, the set $X_n(\omega) \cap \Gamma_q(\omega) \cap qB$ is nonempty we deduce

$$d(0, Z_q(\omega)) \leq \liminf_{n\to+\infty} \left(|X_n(\omega)| + \mathbf{1}_{(A_{nq})^c} |f_q(\omega)|\right) \tag{4.6}$$

Step 3. We construct the measurable selection f of $w - ls\, X_n$ by setting

$$f = \sum_{q\geq 1} \mathbf{1}_{G_q}\, f_q$$

where $G_1 = D_1$ and $G_q = D_q \setminus D_{q-1}$ for $q \geq 2$.

We claim that $f \in L^1_E(\mu)$. Let (r_n) be a sequence of measurable functions as in condition (iii). Each r_n has the following form

$$r_n = \sum_{i\geq n} \lambda_i^n\, |X_i|$$

where $\lambda_i^n \geq 0$ for all $i \geq n$ and $\sum_{i\geq n} \lambda_i^n = 1$, but $\lambda_i^n > 0$ only for a finite number of indices. For each $q \geq 1$ we consider the sequence $(\varphi_{nq})_{n\geq 1}$ defined by

$$\varphi_{nq} = \sum_{i\geq n} \lambda_i^n\, \mathbf{1}_{(A_{iq})^c} \qquad n \geq 1.$$

The sequence $(\varphi_{nq})_{n\geq 1}$ is weakly relatively compact in $L^1(\mu)$. Consequently, a standard diagonal extraction argument produces a subsequence, denoted similarly, such that $(\varphi_{nq})_{n\geq 1}$ converges to $\varphi_q \in L^1(\mu)$ in the weak topology of $L^1(\mu)$, also denoted $\sigma(L^1(\mu), L^\infty(\mu))$. For each $q \geq 1$ appealing to the Mazur Theorem one can show the existence of a sequence $(\psi_{nq})_{n\geq 1}$ of convex combinations of $(\varphi_{nq})_{n\geq 1}$ such that $(\psi_{nq})_{n\geq 1}$ converges μ-almost surely (and strongly in $L^1(\mu)$) to φ_q. Recalling that a convex combination of convex combinations is still a convex combination and appealing to a straightforward diagonal procedure (see e.g. Lemma 3.1 in [7]), it can be assumed without loss of generality that the equality

$$\varphi_q = \lim_{n\to+\infty} \psi_{nq} \qquad \mu - \text{a.s.} \tag{4.7}$$

holds for all $q \geq 1$. Moreover, every ψ_{nq} reads as follows

$$\psi_{nq} = \sum_{i\geq n} \mu_i^n\, \mathbf{1}_{(A_{iq})^c}$$

where $\mu_i^n \geq 0$ for all $i \geq n$ and $\sum_{i\geq n} \mu_i^n = 1$, but $\mu_i^n > 0$ only for a finite number of indices.

Integrating both sides on each G_q and invoking Fatou's Lemma we get

$$\int_{G_q} \varphi_q\, d\mu \leq \liminf_{n\to+\infty} \int_{G_q} \psi_{nq}\, d\mu = \liminf_{n\to+\infty} \sum_{i\geq n} \mu_i^n\, \mu(G_q \cap (A_{iq})^c)$$

whence by the hypothesis on the A_{iq}'s

$$\int_{G_q} \varphi_q \, d\mu \leq \varepsilon_q = \frac{1}{q 2^q}. \tag{4.8}$$

Let us define now the sequence $(s_n)_{n\geq 1}$ by

$$s_n = \sum_{i\geq n} \mu_i^n \, |X_i| \qquad n \geq 1$$

Inequalities (4.2) and (4.6) entail

$$|f_q(\omega)| \leq d(0, Z_q(\omega)) + 1 \leq \liminf_{n\to+\infty} \left\{ |X_n(\omega)| + \mathbf{1}_{(A_{nq})^c}(\omega) \, |f_q(\omega)| \right\} + 1$$

We observe that the lim inf of a sequence is not greater than the lim inf of any sequence of convex combinations of its terms. Applying this for each ω to the sequence $u_n(\omega)$ defined by

$$u_n(\omega) = |X_n(\omega)| + \mathbf{1}_{(A_{nq})^c}(\omega) \, |f_q(\omega)| \tag{4.9}$$

we get

$$|f_q(\omega)| \leq \liminf_{n\to+\infty} \sum_{i\geq n} \mu_i^n \left(|X_i(\omega)| + \mathbf{1}_{(A_{iq})^c}(\omega) \, |f_q(\omega)| \right) + 1$$

In view of the definition of (s_n), and of (4.3) and (4.7), it follows that

$$|f_q(\omega)| \leq \liminf_{n\to+\infty} s_n(\omega) \; + \; q \, \varphi_q(\omega) + 1.$$

Integrating both sides on each G_q and summing with respect to q leads to

$$\int_{\Omega} |f| \, d\mu = \sum_{q\geq 1} \int_{G_q} |f_q| \, d\mu \leq \int_{\Omega} (\liminf s_n) \, d\mu \; + \; \sum_{q\geq 1} q \int_{G_q} \varphi_q \, d\mu + 1$$

The first integral in the right-hand side is finite by condition (iii). As to the second term, inequality (4.8) entails

$$\sum_{q\geq 1} q \int_{G_q} \varphi_q \, d\mu \leq \sum_{q\geq 1} \frac{1}{2^q}.$$

Thus, we conclude that f is a member of $L^1(\mu)$ as claimed, which ends the proof. □

Corollary 4.5. *If (X_n) is a bounded, $\mathcal{I}_+(\mathcal{R}(E))_\varepsilon$-tight sequence in $\mathcal{L}^1(bd(E), \mu)$, then $w - ls\, X_n$ admits at least a μ-integrable selection.*

Proof. In view of Proposition 3.3, (X_n) is $\mathcal{D}(\mathcal{K}(E_w))_\varepsilon$-tight, so that condition (ii) of Theorem 4.4 is satisfied. Condition (iii) is also satisfied, because $(|X_n|)$ is bounded in $L^1(\mu)$. □

Corollary 4.6. *Let (f_n) be a bounded sequence in $L^1_E(\mu)$. If it is $\mathcal{S}_{++}(\mathcal{R}(E))$-tight, then $w - ls\ f_n$ is measurable and admits at least one μ-integrable selection.*

Proof. The result obviously follows from Theorem 5.5 in [11]. The existence of an integrable selection also follows from Corollary 4.5, because (X_n) is $\mathcal{D}(\mathcal{K}(E_w))_\varepsilon$-tight and $\mathcal{I}_+(\mathcal{K}(E_w))_\varepsilon$-tight. □

The following result present a version of Theorem 4.4 for multifunctions whose values may be unbounded.

Theorem 4.7. *Let $\mathcal{C} = \mathcal{R}(E_w)$ and (X_n) be a sequence in $\mathcal{M}(2^E)$, whose members are integrable and satisfy the following three conditions.*

- (i)' *(X_n) is $\mathcal{S}_+(\mathcal{C})_\varepsilon$-tight.*
- (ii) *(X_n) is $\mathcal{D}(\mathcal{C})_\varepsilon$-tight.*
- (iii)' *There exists a sequence (r_n) in $L^0(\mu)$ with $r_n \in co\{d(0, X_i) : i \geq n\}$ such that for every sequence (s_n) in $L^0(\mu)$ with $s_n \in co\{r_i : i \geq n\}$, one has* $\liminf s_n \in L^1(\mu)$.

Then the multifunction w–$ls\ X_n$ admits at least one integrable selection.

Proof. The proof is almost the same as that of Theorem 4.4 and we only explicit the arguments to be modified. First, we change the definition of the set A_{nq} by setting now

$$A_{nq} = \{\omega \in \Omega : X_n(\omega) \subseteq \Gamma_q(\omega)\}.$$

Then, returning to (4.5) we deduce for all $\omega \in D_q$

$$\begin{aligned} d(0, Z_q(\omega)) &\leq \liminf_{n\to+\infty} \left(\mathbf{1}_{A_{nq}}(\omega)\, d(0, X_n(\omega)\cap\Gamma_q(\omega)\cap qB) + \mathbf{1}_{(A_{nq})^c}(\omega)\,|f_q(\omega)|\right) \\ &\leq \liminf_{n\to+\infty} \left(d(0, X_n(\omega)\cap qB) + \mathbf{1}_{(A_{nq})^c}(\omega)\,|f_q(\omega)|\right). \end{aligned}$$

Noting that on D_q we have $X_n(\omega) \cap qB \neq \emptyset$ i.o. and invoking Lemma 5.4 of [11] (in fact, a slight extension of it) it follows

$$d(0, Z_q(\omega)) \leq \liminf_{n\to+\infty} \left(d(0, X_n(\omega)) + \mathbf{1}_{(A_{nq})^c}(\omega)\,|f_q(\omega)|\right).$$

At last, we use the same arguments as in the Step 3 of Theorem 4.4, but we consider the sequence (u_n) defined this time by

$$u_n(\omega) = d(0, X_n(\omega)) + \mathbf{1}_{(A_{nq})^c}(\omega)\,|f_q(\omega)| \qquad \omega \in \Omega$$

and we appeal to condition (iii)' instead of condition (iii). □

Corollary 4.8. *Let* $\mathcal{C} = \mathcal{K}(E_w)$ *and* (X_n) *be a* $\mathcal{S}_+(\mathcal{C})_\varepsilon$*-tight sequence in* $\mathcal{M}(2^E)$ *such that*

$$\sup_{n\geq 1} \int_\Omega d(0, X_n)\, d\mu < +\infty.$$

Then $w - ls\, X_n$ *admits at least one integrable selection.*

Proof. In view of Proposition 3.3, condition (ii) of Theorem 4.7 is satisfied, whereas (iii)' follows from the $L^1(\mu)$-boundedness hypothesis. □

The existence results of the beginning of this section allow for deriving new versions of the Fatou Lemma in infinite dimension, alias Fatou's Lemma for Mathematical Economics. This type of result, that involves a sequence (f_n) of Bochner integrable functions, is useful for proving the existence of a general equilibrium with infinitely many agents. We present a version of this result where the L^1-boundedness hypothesis is not needed. Only a weaker condition is assumed instead. Indeed, we use a Mazur type condition similar to those of Theorems 4.4 and 4.7 (conditions (iii) and (iii)', respectively).

Theorem 4.9. *Let* $(f_n)_{n\geq 1}$ *be a sequence in* $L^1_E(\mu)$*, which satisfies the following conditions.*

(i) (f_n) *is* $\mathcal{S}_{++}(\mathcal{R}_c(E_w)$*-tight, i.e. there exists a multifunction* $\Gamma : \Omega \to \mathcal{R}_c(E_w)$ *such that*

$$f_n(\omega) \in \Gamma(\omega) \qquad \omega \in \Omega \qquad n \geq 1$$

(ii) *for each* y *in* E^* *the sequence* $(< y, f_n >)_{n\geq 1}$ *is uniformly integrable in* $L^1(\mu)$

(iii) *There exists a sequence* (r_n) *in* $L^0(\mu)$ *with* $r_n \in co\{|f_i| : i \geq n\}$ *such that* $\limsup r_n \in L^1(\mu)$.

(iv) *there exists* $a \in E$ *such that*

$$a = w - \lim_{n\to+\infty} \int_\Omega f_n\, d\mu.$$

Then, there exists $f_\infty \in L^1_E(\mu)$ *such that*

(j) $a = \int_\Omega f_\infty\, d\mu$ *and*
(jj) for μ*-almost all* $\omega \in \Omega$ *one has*

$$f_\infty(\omega) \in \bigcap_{m\geq 1} \mathrm{cl}\,\mathrm{co}\{f_n(\omega) : n \geq m\}. \tag{4.10}$$

Proof. Consider the sequence (r_n) of condition (iii). For each $n \geq 1$, there exists a sequence $(\alpha_i^n)_{i \geq n}$ of reals, such that

$$r_n = \sum_{i \geq n} \alpha_i^n \, |f_i| \qquad \sum_{i \geq n} \alpha_i^n = 1 \qquad \alpha_i^n \geq 0$$

where $\alpha_i^n > 0$ only holds for a finite number of indices i. Now, consider the sequence $(g_n)_{n \geq 1}$ defined by

$$g_n = \sum_{i \geq n} \alpha_i^n \, f_i$$

Further, let D^* be a countable w^*-dense subset of E^*. From hypothesis (ii), we know that for each $y \in D^*$ the sequence $(< y, g_n >)_{n \geq 1}$ is uniformly integrable, because uniform integrability is preserved under the convex hull operation. Thus, using a standard diagonal extraction procedure, it is possible to find a subsequence of (g_n), denoted similarly, and members ψ_y of $L^1(\mu)$, such that

$$\psi_y = \lim_{n \to \infty} < y, g_n > \qquad y \in D^*$$

in the $\sigma(L^1, L^\infty)$-topology (i.e. the weak topology of $L^1(\mu)$).

Invoking Mazur's Theorem and appealing again to a diagonal procedure, one can construct a sequence (h_n) whose members are convex combinations of (g_n) and such that for all $y \in D^*$

$$\psi_y(\omega) = \lim_{n \to \infty} < y, h_n(\omega) > \qquad \mu - \text{almost surely} \tag{4.11}$$

The construction of (h_n) is easily performed by noting that if a sequence (u_n) in $L^1(\mu)$ is $\sigma(L^1, L^\infty)$-convergent to u, then any sequence (v_n) of convex combinations of (u_n) converges to u in the same topology.

For every $n \geq 1$, h_n reads as follows

$$h_n = \sum_{i \geq n} \beta_i^n g_i$$

where the reals β_i^n satisfy

$$\sum_{i \geq n} \beta_i^n = 1 \qquad \text{and} \qquad \beta_i^n \geq 0,$$

but inequality $\beta_i^n > 0$ holds only for a finite number of indices i.

Now, consider the multifunction $Y = w - ls\ h_n$. Hypothesis (i) shows that $h_n(\omega) \in \Gamma(\omega)$ for all $n \geq 1$ and μ-almost all $\omega \in \Omega$. On the other hand, we claim that lim sup $|h_n|$ is μ-integrable. Indeed, one has

$$h_n = \sum_{i\geq 1} \beta_i^n g_i = \sum_{i\geq n} \beta_i^n \left(\sum_{j\geq i} \alpha_j^i f_j \right)$$

whence

$$|h_n| \leq \sum_{i\geq n} \beta_i^n \left(\sum_{j\geq i} \alpha_j^i |f_j| \right).$$

This yields

$$\limsup_{n\to+\infty} |h_n| \leq \limsup_{n\to+\infty} \left(\sum_{i\geq n} \beta_i^n r_i \right) \leq \limsup_{n\to+\infty} r_n$$

which, by hypothesis (iii) shows the desired integrability property.

Consequently, it is possible to invoke Theorem 5.5 of [11], which shows that Y admits at least one measurable and μ-integrable selection f_∞. Hence, for every $\omega \in \Omega$, there exists a subsequence $(h_{n_k}(\omega))_{k\geq 1}$ such that

$$f_\infty(\omega) = w - \lim_{k\to+\infty} h_{n_k}(\omega).$$

Returning to (4.11), we deduce that

$$\psi_y(\omega) \ = < y, f_\infty(\omega) >$$

for all $y \in D^*$. Since for almost all $\omega \in \Omega$ the sequence $(h_n(\omega))_{n\geq 1}$ is bounded, hypothese (i) entails that it is contained in a weakly compact subset of E. Thus, we can deduce that $f_\infty(\omega)$ is the unique weak cluster point of $(h_n(\omega))$, so that the whole sequence weakly converges, namely

$$f_\infty(\omega) = w - \lim_{n\to+\infty} h_n(\omega). \tag{4.12}$$

This holds for μ-almost all $\omega \in \Omega$. Using the properties of h_n, it is not hard to show that equation (4.12) implies

$$f_\infty(\omega) \in \bigcap_{m\geq 1} w - \mathrm{cl}\,\{h_n(\omega) : n \geq m\} \subseteq \bigcap_{m\geq 1} \mathrm{cl\,co}\{f_n(\omega) : n \geq m\}.$$

As to (j), we note that, due to hypothesis (ii), the sequence $(< y, h_n >)_{n\geq 1}$ is uniformly integrable for each $y \in D^*$, which entails

$$\int_\Omega < y, f_\infty > d\mu = \lim_{n\to+\infty} \int_\Omega < y, h_n > d\mu$$
$$= \lim_{n\to+\infty} < y, \int_\Omega f_n\, d\mu > = < y, a >$$

because the sequence $(\int_\Omega h_n\, d\mu)_{n\geq 1}$ also converges to a. By the density of D^* this yields

$$a = \int_\Omega f_\infty\, d\mu.$$

□

Remark 4.3. It is readily seen that the L^1-boundedness of the sequence (f_n) implies condition (iii) of Theorem 4.9, but the converse implication does not hold. Indeed, it suffices to consider the case where $\Omega = [0, 1]$ endowed with the Lebesgue measure, $E = \mathbf{R}$ and the sequence (f_n) defined by

$$f_n(\omega) = n^2\, \mathbf{1}_{[0,1/n]}(\omega) \qquad \omega \in \Omega.$$

Clearly, (f_n) is not bounded in $L^1(\mu)$, but satisfies condition (iii), because it converges almost surely to 0.

Remark 4.4. A quick inspection of the proof of the above theorem shows that condition (i) can be replaced with the following one:

(i)' there exists a multifunction $\Gamma \in \mathcal{M}(\mathcal{R}_c(E_w))$ such that for μ-almost all ω, one can find an integer $n(\omega)$ satisfying

$$f_n(\omega) \in \Gamma(\omega) \qquad \text{for} \qquad n \geq n(\omega).$$

This means that $f_n(\omega)$ may not belong to $\Gamma(\omega)$ for a finite subset of indices depending on ω.

Remark 4.5. The integrability of f_∞ can be proved directly by using the weak semicontinuity of the norm and the classical Fatou Lemma. Indeed, the weak semicontinuity of the norm implies

$$|f_\infty(\omega)| \leq \liminf_{n\to+\infty} |h_n(\omega)|$$

for all $\omega \in \Omega$. Then, integrate both sides and apply Fatou's Lemma.

Remark 4.6. It is readily seen that condition (iii) of Theorem 4.9 implies that $\liminf |f_n|$ is μ-integrable. Consequently, hypotheses of Theorem 4.9 entail that the multifunction $w - ls f_n$ admits at least a μ-integrable, measurable selection. This is a consequence of Theorem 4.6 (or of Theorem 5.5 of [11]). Further, by Theorem 4.4 of [11], the multifunction $w - ls f_n$ is measurable.

5. The case of multifunctions with values in a dual space

As in the previous sections $(\Omega, \mathcal{F}, \mu)$ stands for a complete probability space and E for a separable Banach space. The topological dual of E is denoted by E^* and the dual norm by $\|.\|$. Given a subset C of E^*, the distance function of C is denoted by $d(., C)$ and defined by

$$d(y, C) = \inf_{z \in C} \|y - z\| \qquad y \in E^*.$$

B^* (resp rB^*) stands for the closed unit ball of E^* (resp. the closed ball of radius r centered at 0). If t is a topology on E^*, the space E^* endowed with t is denoted by E^*_t. Three topologies will be considered on E^*, namely the norm topology s^*, the weak-star topology w^* and the metrizable topology $m^* = \sigma(E^*, H)$, where H is the linear space of E generated by a countable dense subset D_1 of B, the closed unit ball of E. Put differently, if $D_1 = \{x_k : k \geq 1\}$ is a dense sequence in B, $m^* = m^*(D_1)$ can be seen as the Hausdorff locally convex topology defined by the sequence $(p_k)_{k \geq 1}$ of semi-norms such that

$$p_k(y) = \max\{| < y, x_i > | : i \leq k\} \qquad y \in E^*. \tag{5.1}$$

By construction, the topology m^* depends on the countable dense subset D_1, but we assume from now on that D_1 is held fixed. Further, relationships (5.1) show that m^* is not stronger than w^*, because w^* can be defined as the locally convex topology generated by the semi-norms p such that

$$p(y) = \max\{| < y, x > | : x \in S\} \qquad y \in E^*$$

where S ranges over the family of finite subsets of B. Thus, we have

$$m^* \subseteq w^* \subseteq s^*$$

where the inclusion relation allows for comparing two topologies on the set of all topologies of E^*. When E is infinite dimensional these inclusions are strict. On the other hand, the restrictions of m^* and w^* to any bounded subset of E^* coincide. This is a consequence of an Ascoli's Theorem, namely on an equicontinuous set of real-valued functions defined on a topological space, the topology of pointwise convergence is equivalent to the topology of pointwise convergence on a dense subset. Noting that E^* is the countable union of closed balls, namely

$$E^* = \bigcup_{k \geq 1} kB^*$$

we deduce that the space $E^*_{w^*}$ is Suslin, as well as the metrizable topological space $E^*_{m^*}$ (we recall that a Suslin space is the continuous image of a Polish space).

If $\mathcal{B}(E_t^*)$ denotes the Borel σ-field of a topology t, we clearly have

$$\mathcal{B}(E_{m^*}^*) \subseteq \mathcal{B}(E_{w^*}^*) \subseteq \mathcal{B}(E_{s^*}^*).$$

In the above relations, the rightmost inclusion is strict except when E^* is strongly separable. However, any closed ball of E^* is a member of $\mathcal{B}(E_{m^*}^*)$. This follows from the equality

$$\|y\| = \sup\{| < y, x > | : x \in D_1\} \tag{5.2}$$

valid for all $y \in E^*$. As already mentioned, the restriction of m^* and w^* to any bounded set G of E^* are equal. This obviously implies

$$\mathcal{B}(G_{m^*}) = \mathcal{B}(G_{w^*}) \tag{5.3}$$

but equality (5.3) is also valid when $G = E^*$ as the following simple result shows.

Proposition 5.1. *If E is a separable Banach space, E^* its topological dual, and w^* and m^* are the topologies defined above, then the following equality holds*

$$\mathcal{B}(E_{m^*}^*) = \mathcal{B}(E_{w^*}^*).$$

Proof. It only remains to prove inclusion $\mathcal{B}(E_{w^*}^*) \subseteq \mathcal{B}(E_{m^*}^*)$. If G is a member of $\mathcal{B}(E_{w^*}^*)$ one has

$$G = \bigcup_{k \geq 1} G \cap kB^*¥ \tag{5.4}$$

Since B^* is w^*-closed, equality (5.3) implies that for each $k \geq 1$,

$$G \cap kB^* \in \mathcal{B}((kB^*)_{w^*}) = \mathcal{B}((kB^*)_{m^*}).$$

As already noted, kB^* is a member of $\mathcal{B}(E_{m^*}^*)$. Therefore, the restriction of $\mathcal{B}(E_{m^*})$ to kB^* consists of the members of $\mathcal{B}(E_{m^*})$ contained in kB^*. This yields $G \cap kB^* \in \mathcal{B}(E_{m^*}^*)$, whence $G \in \mathcal{B}(E_{m^*}^*)$ by (5.4). □

At this point, we need a few extra definitions. Given a subset F of E, a function $f : \Omega \to E^*$ is said to be F-*scalarly measurable* if the real-valued function $\omega \to < f(\omega), x >$ is measurable (with respect to the σ-field $\mathcal{F}$) for all $x \in F$. If $F = E$ we simply say that f is scalarly measurable. In this definition E can be replaced with B, the closed unit ball of E. We denote by $L_{E^*}^1[E]$ the space of E-scalarly measurable (classes of) functions f such that the function $\omega \to \|f(\omega)\|$ is μ-integrable. Observe that by (5.2) this function is measurable for each E-scalarly measurable f.

Remark 5.1. If D_1 stands for a countable dense subset of B, it is readily seen that a function $f : \Omega \to E^*$ is D_1-scalarly measurable if and only if it is $\mathcal{B}(E^*_{m^*})$-measurable. Indeed, for each m^*-open subset W which is the finite intersection of open half spaces, namely

$$W = \bigcap_{1 \le i \le k} \{y \in E^* : < y, x_i >< \alpha_i\} \qquad (x_i \in D_1 \quad \alpha_i \in \mathbf{R} \quad m \ge 1),$$

one has $f^{-1}(W) \in \mathcal{F}$. The Lindelöf property of $E^*_{m^*}$ allows us to derive the same conclusion for an arbitrary m^*-open set, which shows that f is $\mathcal{B}(E^*_{m^*})$-measurable. Thus, Proposition 5.1 shows that f is scalarly measurable if and only if it is $\mathcal{B}(E^*_{w^*})$-measurable.

Given a subset C of E^*, the *support function* of C is denoted by $s(., C)$ and defined on E by

$$s(x, C) = \sup\{< y, x >: y \in C\} \qquad x \in E.$$

If C is nonempty, the values of $s(., C)$ lie in $(-\infty, +\infty]$, otherwise s(., C) is identically $-\infty$.

We consider multifunctions defined on Ω with values in E^*. They can be viewed as maps from Ω into the space 2^{E^*} of all subsets of E^*. Given $F \subseteq E$, a multifunction $X : \Omega \to 2^{E^*}$ is said to be *F-scalarly measurable* if the extended real-valued function $\omega \to s(x, X(\omega))$ is measurable for all $x \in F$. Let $\mathcal{K}(E^*_{w^*})$ denote the space of all w^*-compact subsets of E^*. Since every closed ball of E^* is w^*-compact, the space $\mathcal{R}(E^*_{w^*})$ of all w^*-ball compact subsets of E^* reduces to the space of all w^*-closed sets.

In this section, we do not consider the graph measurability of multifunctions with respect to the product σ-field $\mathcal{F} \otimes \mathcal{B}(E^*_{s^*})$, because we do not assume E^* to be strongly separable, so that the Projection Theorem is no longer available (for $E^*_{s^*}$ is not Suslin). We shall consider the σ-field $\mathcal{F} \otimes \mathcal{B}(E^*_{w^*})$ instead. The next proposition and its corollary will allow us to introduce the appropriate definition of measurability for multifunctions taking on values in E^*.

Proposition 5.2. *Let X be a multifunction defined on Ω whose values are m^*-closed in E^*. The following two statements are equivalent.*

(a) $X^- V \in \mathcal{F}$ *for all m^*-open subset V of E^**
(b) $Gr(X) \in \mathcal{F} \otimes \mathcal{B}(E^*_{m^*}) = \mathcal{F} \otimes \mathcal{B}(E^*_{w^*})$

Proof. (a) $\Rightarrow$ (b). As already mentioned, $E^*_{m^*}$ is a separable metrizable space. Thus, if δ denotes any compatible distance, one has

$$Gr(X) = \{(\omega, y) \in \Omega \times E^* : \delta(y, X(\omega)) = 0\}.$$

Since (a) implies the joint measurability of the function $(\omega, y) \to \delta(y, X(\omega))$. statement (b) follows. As to implication (b) ⇒ (a), since $E^*_{m^*}$ is Suslin, we can invoke the Projection Theorem. Thus, for every m^*-open set V the equality

$$X^- V = \text{proj}_\Omega\,[Gr(X) \cap (V \times E^*)]$$

and the completeness hypothesis on $(\Omega, \mathcal{F}, \mu)$ show that $X^- V$ is a member of $\mathcal{F}$. □

Corollary 5.3. *Let X be a multifunction defined on Ω with w^*-closed valued in E^*. The following two statements are equivalent.*

(a) $X^- V \in \mathcal{F}$ *for all w^*-open set V*
(b) $Gr(X) \in \mathcal{F} \otimes \mathcal{B}(E^*_{w^*})$

Moreover, if X takes on w^*-compact values, then each of the above statements is equivalent to

(c) $X^- C \in \mathcal{F}$ *for all w^*-closed set C*

If X takes on convex w^*-compact values, then each of the above statements is equivalent to one of the following two statements

(d) *X is E-scalarly measurable.*
(e) *X is D_1-scalarly measurable (recall that D_1 stands for a countable dense subset of B).*

Proof. If (a) holds, condition (a) of Proposition 5.2 is satisfied so that $Gr(X)$ is a member of $\mathcal{F} \otimes \mathcal{B}(E^*_{m^*}) = \mathcal{F} \otimes \mathcal{B}(E^*_{w^*})$. Conversely the completeness hypothesis on $(\Omega, \mathcal{F}, \mu)$ and the Projection Theorem, applied to the Suslin space $E^*_{w^*}$, together show that (b) implies (a). Thus (a) and (b) are equivalent.

As to statement (c), observe that a w^*-compact valued multifunction is also m^*-compact valued. We have already observed that $E^*_{m^*}$ is a separable metrizable space. In such a space it is known that, for compact valued multifunctions, conditions (a) and (c) are equivalent (see e.g. Proposition III.12 of [8] or Theorem 17.10 of [1]).

At last let us prove the equivalences (a) ⇔ (d) ⇔ (e) when the values of X are w^*-compact and convex. For proving implication (a) ⇒ (d), define for each $x \in E$ and $\alpha \in \mathbf{R}$

$$W(x, \alpha) = \{y \in E^* :< y, x > > \alpha\}$$

and note the easy equality

$$\{\omega \in \Omega : s(x, X(\omega)) > \alpha\} = X^- W(x, \alpha).$$

Since implication (d) ⇒ (e) is trivial, it only remains to prove implication (e) ⇒ (a). For this purpose, we set for each $x \in E$

$$G_x = \{(\omega, y) \in \Omega \times E^* : < y, x > \leq s(x, X(\omega))\}$$

and we note the following equalities

$$Gr(X) = \bigcap_{x \in E} G_x = \bigcap_{x \in D_1} G_x.$$

The rightmost equality is a consequence of the continuity of the support function $x \to s(x, X(\omega))$, valid for all $\omega \in \Omega$. Recall that this continuity property holds because the values of X are assumed to be w^*-compact and convex. Consequently, $Gr(X)$ is a member of $\mathcal{F} \otimes \mathcal{B}(E_{m^*}) = \mathcal{F} \otimes \mathcal{B}(E_{w^*})$. This finishes the proof because (a) and (b) are equivalent as shown in the beginning of the proof. □

In the rest of this section, it will be convenient to say that a multifunction $X : \Omega \to 2^{E^*}$ satisfying condition (b) of Corollary 5.3 is *measurable*. It is useful to note that statement (b) implies statement (a) and, as shown by the previous result, that the converse implication holds when X has w^*-closed values. Further, for any subfamily $\mathcal{C}$ of 2^{E^*}, we denote by $\mathcal{M}(\mathcal{C})$ the set of all $\mathcal{C}$-valued measurable multifunctions. The following two theorems provide measurability properties for the w^*-sequential upper limit of a sequence of multifunctions. In the first one, the multifunctions are assumed to be contained in a fixed w^*-compact valued multifunction. In the second one, the multifunctions may have unbounded values.

Theorem 5.4. *Let $(X_n)_{n \geq 1}$ be a sequence in $\mathcal{M}(2^{E^*})$, which satisfies condition (5.5) hereafter: there exists a w^*-compact valued multifunction Y such that*

$$X_n(\omega) \subseteq Y(\omega) \quad \omega \in \Omega \quad n \geq 1. \tag{5.5}$$

Then, the multifunction $X = w^* - ls\ X_n$ is w^*-compact valued and measurable.

Proof. For each $\omega \in \Omega$, the restriction of w^* to $Y(\omega)$ coincide with the metrizable topology m^*. Consequently, one has

$$X(\omega) = m^* - LS\, X_n(\omega) = \bigcap_{k \geq 1} m^* - \mathrm{cl}\left(\bigcup_{n \geq k} X_n(\omega)\right)$$

$$= \bigcap_{k \geq 1} w^* - \mathrm{cl}\left(\bigcup_{n \geq k} X_n(\omega)\right) \qquad \omega \in \Omega.$$

The rightmost equality and condition (5.5) show that X has w^*-compact values. Further, using statement (a) of corollary 5.3 it is readily seen that for each $k \geq 1$ the multifunction

$$\omega \to w^* - \mathrm{cl}\left(\bigcup_{n\geq k} X_n(\omega)\right)$$

is measurable. Hence, the measurability of X easily follows, because the graph measurability if preserved under countable intersections. □

Theorem 5.5. *If $(X_n)_{n\geq 1}$ is a sequence in $\mathcal{M}(2^{E^*})$, then the multifunction $X = w^* - ls\, X_n$ is measurable.*

Proof. Since a w^*-convergent sequence is bounded in E^*, we have for all $\omega \in \Omega$

$$X(\omega) = \bigcup_{k\geq 1} w^* - ls\, \left(X_n(\omega) \cap kB^*\right).$$

From Theorem 5.4 we know that for each $k \geq 1$ the multifunction $\omega \to w^* - ls\, (X_n(\omega) \cap kB^*)$ is measurable. Thus, X is measurable, because the graph measurability is preserved under countable unions. □

Before stating the main result of the present section, it is useful to reformulate Lemmas 5.1 and 5.2 of [11] for multifunctions with values in a dual space. The first result concerns the existence of a μ-integrable selection for a multifunction whose values lie in E^*.

Lemma 5.6. *Let $(\Omega, \mathcal{F}, \mu)$ be a complete probability space and $X : \Omega \to 2^{E^*}$ be a measurable multifunction.*

(i) *If X admits a μ-integrable selection, then $d(0, X)$ is μ-integrable.*
(ii) *Conversely, if $d(0, X)$ is μ-integrable, then X admits at least one μ-integrable (and $\mathcal{F}$-measurable) selection.*

Proof. The proof of (i) is easy and analogous to that given in [11]. As to the proof of (ii), it is enough to explain why the selection can be chosen to be E-scalarly measurable (or equivalently $\mathcal{B}(E^*_{w^*})$-measurable). It suffices to consider a measurable μ-integrable function r such that $d(0, X(\omega)) < r(\omega)$ for all $\omega \in \Omega$ and the multifunction Y defined by $Y(\omega) = X(\omega) \cap r(\omega)B^*$. This multifunction is measurable namely, $Gr(Y)$ is a member of $\mathcal{F} \otimes \mathcal{B}(E^*_{m^*})$, whence admits a $\mathcal{B}(E^*_{m^*})$-measurable selection. This selection is a member of $L^1_{E^*}[E]$. □

The first part of the following lemma present an easy adaptation of Lemma 5.2 of [11]. Its proof is similar, but involves w^*-compactness instead of w-compactness. The second part is a reformulation of Lemma 5.4 of [11] in the framework of a dual space.

Lemma 5.7. (i) *If $(C_n)_{n\geq 1}$ is a sequence in 2^{E^*}, one has*

$$d(y, w^* - ls\, C_n) \leq \liminf_{n\to+\infty} d(y, C_n) \qquad y \in E^*.$$

(ii) *Moreover, if* $\alpha > 0$ *is such that* $C_n \cap \alpha B^* \neq \emptyset$ *i.o., then*

$$\liminf_{n\to+\infty} d(y, C_n \cap \alpha B^*) = \liminf_{n\to+\infty} d(y, C_n).$$

Remark 5.2. The distance function $d(., C)$ of a subset C of E^* is identically $+\infty$ if and only if C is empty. Thus, the distance function of a nonempty set is finite at every point (or, equivalently, at one point). Consequently, Lemma 5.7(i) shows that $w^* - ls\, C_n$ is nonempty as soon as $\liminf d(0, C_n)$ is finite. The converse implication is straightforward, so that the following equivalence holds

$$w^* - ls\, C_n \neq \emptyset \qquad \Leftrightarrow \qquad \liminf_{n\to+\infty} d(0, C_n) < +\infty.$$

The next result provides a sufficient condition for the existence of integrable selections for the sequential weak* upper limit multifunction in a dual space.

Theorem 5.8. *Let* $(X_n)_{n\geq 1}$ *be a sequence of measurable multifunctions with values in* E^*. *If* $\liminf_{n\to+\infty} d(0, X_n)$ *is* μ*-integrable, then* $w^* - ls\, X_n$ *admits at least one* $\mathcal{B}(E^*_{w^*})$*-measurable,* μ*-integrable selection, i.e. a selection which is a member of* $L^1_{E^*}[E]$.

Proof. Consider a positive μ-integrable function r such that

$$\liminf_{n\to+\infty} d(0, X_n(\omega)) < r(\omega) \qquad \omega \in \Omega$$

and the multifunction Y defined by

$$Y(\omega) = w^* - ls\, \left(X_n(\omega) \cap r(\omega)B^*\right).$$

This multifunction is measurable by Theorem 5.4, namely $Gr(Y) \in \mathcal{F} \otimes \mathcal{B}(E^*_{w^*})$. It is also nonempty valued, whence admits at least one measurable selection. Further, for each ω, Lemma 5.7 applied to the sequence $(X_n(\omega))_{n\geq 1}$ (with $\alpha = r(\omega)$ for the application of part (ii) of this lemma) entails

$$d(0, Y(\omega)) \leq \liminf_{n\to+\infty} d(0, X_n(\omega) \cap r(\omega)B^*) = \liminf_{n\to+\infty} d(0, X_n(\omega)).$$

Thus, $d(0, Y)$ is μ-integrable. Any μ-integrable selection of Y is also a selection of X, which yields the desired result. □

Remark 5.3. It is not difficult to check that the integrability condition of Theorem 5.8, namely

$$\liminf_{n\to+\infty} d(0, X_n) \text{ is } \mu\text{−integrable}$$

is implied by condition (iii)' of Theorem 4.7.

As in Section 4, we provide an application to the Fatou Lemma in infinite dimension, this time for functions taking on values in a dual space. As in the primal case, the L^1-boundedness hypothesis is not needed. In the next theorem, it is replaced by a (weaker) Mazur type condition.

Theorem 5.9. *Let $(f_n)_{n\geq 1}$ be a sequence in $L^1_{E^*}[E]$, which satisfies the following conditions.*

(i) *There exists a sequence (r_n) in $L^0(\mu)$ with $r_n \in co\{\|f_i\| : i \geq n\}$ such that* $\limsup r_n \in L^1(\mu)$.
(ii) *for each x in E the sequence $(< x, f_n >)_{n\geq 1}$ is uniformly integrable in $L^1(\mu)$*
(iii) *there exists $b \in E^*$ such that*

$$b = w^* - \lim_{n\to+\infty} \int_\Omega f_n \, d\mu.$$

Under the above hypotheses, there exists $f_\infty \in L^1_{E^*}[E]$ such that

(j) $b = \int_\Omega f_\infty \, d\mu$ and
(jj) for μ-almost all $\omega \in \Omega$ one has

$$f_\infty(\omega) \in \bigcap_{m\geq 1} w^* - \operatorname{cl}\operatorname{co}\{f_n(\omega) : n \geq m\}.$$

Proof. The proof follows the same lines as those of Theorem 4.9. Consider the sequence (r_n) appearing in condition (i). For each $n \geq 1$, one can find a sequence $(\alpha_i^n)_{i\geq n}$ of reals, such that

$$r_n = \sum_{i\geq n} \alpha_i^n \, \|f_i\| \qquad \sum_{i\geq n} \alpha_i^n = 1 \qquad \alpha_i^n \geq 0$$

where $\alpha_i^n > 0$ only holds for a finite number of indices i. Also consider the sequence $(g_n)_{n\geq 1}$ defined by

$$g_n = \sum_{i\geq n} \alpha_i^n \, f_i$$

Let D be a countable dense subset of E. From hypothesis (ii), we know that for each $x \in D$ the sequence $(< g_n, x >)_{n\geq 1}$ is uniformly integrable. Indeed, the convex hull of a uniformly integrable subset of $L^1(\mu)$ is uniformly integrable too. Consequently, using a standard diagonal extraction procedure, it is possible to find a subsequence of (g_n), denoted similarly, and members ψ_x of $L^1(\mu)$, such that

$$\psi_x = \lim_{n\to\infty} < g_n, x > \qquad x \in D$$

in the $\sigma(L^1, L^\infty)$-topology. Further, invoking Mazur's Theorem and appealing again to a diagonal procedure, it is possible to construct a sequence (h_n), whose members are convex combinations of (g_n) and such that for all $x \in D$

$$\psi_x(\omega) = \lim_{n\to\infty} < h_n(\omega), x > \qquad \mu - \text{almost surely} \tag{5.6}$$

For every $n \geq 1$, h_n reads as follows

$$h_n = \sum_{i\geq n} \beta_i^n\, g_i$$

where the reals β_i^n satisfy

$$\sum_{i\geq n} \beta_i^n = 1 \qquad \text{and} \qquad \beta_i^n \geq 0,$$

but where $\beta_i^n > 0$ only holds for a finite number of indices i.

Now, consider the multifunction $Z = w^* - ls\ h_n$. As in the proof of Theorem 4.9 it is readily seen that lim sup $\|h_n\|$ satisfies

$$\limsup_{n\to+\infty} \|h_n\| \leq \limsup_{n\to+\infty} \left(\sum_{i\geq n} \beta_i^n\, r_i \right) \leq \limsup_{n\to+\infty} r_n$$

which, in view of condition (i), shows that $\liminf_{n\to+\infty} \|h_n\|$ is μ-integrable. This allows us to apply Theorem 5.8, which shows that Z admits at least one scalarly measurable selection f_∞ that is also a member of $L^1_{E^*}[E]$. Hence, for every $\omega \in \Omega$, there exists a subsequence $(h_{n_k}(\omega))_{k\geq 1}$ of $(h_n(\omega))$ such that

$$f_\infty(\omega) = w - \lim_{k\to+\infty} h_{n_k}(\omega).$$

Returning to (5.6), we deduce that

$$\psi_x(\omega) = < f_\infty(\omega), x >$$

for all $x \in D$. This proves that $f_\infty(\omega)$ is the unique w^*-cluster point of $(h_n(\omega))$. Furthermore, since for almost all $\omega \in \Omega$ the sequence $(h_n(\omega))_{n\geq 1}$ is bounded, hypothese (i) entails that it is contained in a w^*-compact subset of E^*. Consequently, the whole sequence w^*-converges, namely

$$f_\infty(\omega) = w^* - \lim_{n\to+\infty} h_n(\omega). \tag{5.7}$$

This holds for μ-almost all $\omega \in \Omega$. Using the properties of h_n, it is not hard to show that equation (5.7) implies

$$f_\infty(\omega) \in \bigcap_{m \geq 1} w^* - \mathrm{cl}\,\{h_n(\omega) : n \geq m\} \subseteq \bigcap_{m \geq 1} w^* - \mathrm{cl}\,\mathrm{co}\{f_n(\omega) : n \geq m\}.$$

As to (j), we note that, due to hypothesis (ii), the sequence $(< g_n, x >)_{n \geq 1}$ is uniformly integrable for each $x \in E$, which entails

$$\int_\Omega < f_\infty, x > d\mu \; = \lim_{n \to +\infty} \int_\Omega < h_n, x > d\mu \; = < \int_\Omega f_n \, d\mu, x > = < b, x >$$

because the sequence $(\int_\Omega g_n \, d\mu)_{n \geq 1}$ also w^*-converges to b. By the density of D this yields

$$b = \int_\Omega f_\infty \, d\mu.$$

and finishes the proof. □

Remark 5.4. From Theorem 5.5 in the present section, we know that the multifunction $w^* - ls f_n$ is measurable.

References

1. Aliprantis, C.D., Border, K.C.: Infinite Dimensional Analysis. A Hitchhiker's Guide, Springer, New York (1999)
2. Amrani, A., Castaing, C., Valadier, M.: Méthodes de troncatures appliquées à des problèmes de convergences faible ou forte dans L^1. Arch. Ration. Mech. Anal. **117**, 167–191 (1992)
3. Balder, E.J., Hess, C.: Two generalizations of Komlós theorem with Lower Closure-type applications. J. Convex Anal. **3**, 25–44 (1996)
4. Balder, E.J., Sambucini, A.R.: Fatou's Lemma for multifunctions with unbounded values in a dual space. J. Convex Anal. **12**, 383–395 (2005)
5. Benabdellah, H., Castaing, C.: Weak compactness and convergences in $L^1_{E'}[E]$. Adv. Math. Econ. **3**, 1–44 (2001)
6. Castaing, C., Raynaud de Fitte, P.: Uniform scalar integrability and strong law of large numbers for Pettis integrable functions with values in a separable locally convex space. J. Theoret. Probab. **13**(1), 93–134 (2000)
7. Castaing, C., Saadoune, M.: Dunford–Pettis–types theorem and convergences in set-valued integration. J. Nonlinear Convex Anal. **1**, 37–71 (1999)
8. Castaing, C., Valadier, M.: Convex analysis and measurable multifunctions. Lectures Notes in Math 580 (1977)
9. Cornet, B., Martins da Rocha, V.F.: Fatou's Lemma for unbounded Gelfand integrable mappings. CERNSEM, Universit Paris 1 (2002)
10. Diestel, J., Uhl, J.J. Jr.: Vector Measures. Mathematical Survey No. 15, AMS, Providence, USA (1977)
11. Hess, C.: Measurability and integrability of the weak upper limit of a sequence of multifunctions. J. Math. Anal. Appl. **153**, 226–249 (1989)
12. Hess, C.: Mesurabilité, Convergence et Approximation des Multifonctions a valeurs dans un e.l.c.s. Sém. Anal. Conv. Univ. Montpellier 2 **15**, 9.1–9.100 (1985)

13. Hiai, F., Umegaki, H.: Integrals, conditional expectations, and martingales of multivalued functions. J. Multivariate Anal. **7**, 149–182 (1977)
14. Hildenbrand, W.: Core and Equilibria of a Large Economy. Princeton University Press, Princeton (1974)
15. Khan, M.A., Majumdar, M.: Weak sequential convergence in $L_1(\mu, X)$ and an approximate version of Fatou's lemma. J. Math. Anal. Appl. **114**, 569–573 (1986)
16. Saadoune, M.: Compacité, Convergences and Approximations. Thèse de doctorat d'Etat, Université Mohamed V, Rabat (1996)

Adv. Math. Econ. 11, 45–76 (2008)

Advances in
MATHEMATICAL ECONOMICS

Core convergence in economies with bads

Chiaki Hara

Institute of Economic Research, Kyoto University, Kyoto, Japan
(e-mail: hara@kier.kyoto-u.ac.jp)

Received: September 11, 2007
Revised: December 4, 2007

JEL classification: C62, C71, D41, D43, D51, D61

Mathematics Subject Classification (2000): 28A20, 60B05, 60B10, 91A12, 91A13, 91B50, 91B76

Abstract. We investigate how the presence of bads, causing disutility to consumers, affects the emergence of the price-taking behavior. Specifically, we give two examples of sequences of increasingly populous finite economies in which the core convergence property holds and, yet, for which there is a sequence of coalitions, one from each economy, such that the size of the coalition relative to the economy converges to zero but the share of the coalition in the aggregate consumption of bads converges to one. The limit atomless economy has a Walrasian equilibrium in one of the two examples but not in the other.

Key words: bads, core convergence, equilibrium existence, perfect competition, atomless economy, uniform integrability

1. Introduction

The first welfare theorem, which states that every Walrasian equilibrium allocation is Pareto efficient, justifies the use of the market mechanism as a means to attain an efficient allocation of commodities. The theorem (and, for that matter, the second welfare theorem as well) is valid even when preference relations or utility functions are not monotone, so that some commodities are *bads*, which cause disutility to consumers, and for which the prices are negative. An impli-

* This paper combines materials in an earlier paper of the same title and another paper entitled "Example on the Core Convergence Property with Bads". I am grateful to Tomoki Inoue, Atsushi Kajii, and an anonymous referee for extremely valuable comments on an earlier version of this paper.

cation of this theorem is that the allocation of bads may also be delegated to the market mechanism.

An implicit and yet important assumption underlying the first welfare theorem is that consumers are price takers. Without this assumption, the market mechanism need not bring about an efficient allocation, and the relevance of the first welfare theorem would be lost.

The assumption of the price-taking behavior is justified in the form of the core convergence theorem or the core equivalence theorem. The core convergence theorem, a general, non-replica version of which was proved by Anderson [1], asserts that the core allocations and Walrasian equilibrium allocations are, in terms of some appropriately defined measure, close to each other in an economy consisting of a large but finite number of consumers. The core equivalence theorem, originally due to Aumann [3], asserts that the two are exactly identical to each other in an *atomless economy*, an economy consisting of infinitely many consumers, each negligible in size relative to the entire economy.

The monotonicity assumption on preference relations or utility functions plays an important role in both theorems, albeit in different manners. On the one hand, the convergence theorem may fail without the monotonicity assumption, as exemplified by Manelli [14]. On the other hand, the equivalence theorem holds even without the monotonicity assumption, but if free disposability is not assumed, there may not be any Walrasian equilibrium at all in an atomless economy, as exemplified by Hara [7]. In this case, the equivalence theorem only states that there is no core allocation either, without showing how close the core and equilibrium allocations are. In these examples, the core allocations either stay away from the equilibrium allocations or simply do not exist. It would therefore be fair to say that the emergence of the price-taking behavior is more difficult to confirm in the presence of bads.

The failure of core convergence of a sequence of finite economies and the failure of equilibrium existence in an atomless economy share a common feature. It is that a negligibly small coalition consumes almost all of a commodity in large finite economies. More specifically, the first example of Manelli [14] involves a sequence of core allocations of increasingly populous finite economies that does not have the core convergence property and along which there is a consumer in each economy who consumes all of a commodity, however large the economy may be. The second example of Hara [7] involves a sequence of equilibrium allocations of increasingly populous finite economies, of which the limit atomless economy has no Walrasian equilibrium and along which it is possible to choose a coalition in each economy so that the size of the coalition relative to the entire economy converges to zero but the share of the coalition in the aggregate consumption of the bad converges to one. In both examples, for every $\varepsilon > 0$, there exists a coalition in every sufficiently large finite economy of which the population size relative to the entire economy is less than ε and yet the consumption share of bads is greater than $1 - \varepsilon$. Hence both the sequence of core allocations and the sequence of equilibrium allocations fail to be uniformly integrable.[1] This means that the limit of the sequence of core or equilibrium allocations, in whatever way deemed as reasonable it is defined, fails to be resource-feasible in the limit economy. Hence, either there is no Walrasian equilibrium in the limit economy, or even if there is one, it is quite different from the core allocations of finite economies.

There is also an important difference between these two examples. In Hara's [7] example, unlike Manelli's [14], it is not possible to choose a consumer in each economy so that these consumers' shares in the aggregate consumption stay away from zero. As noted above, there is a sequence of coalitions which eventually becomes negligible relative to the size of the economy, and whose consumption shares converge to one. For such a sequence of coalitions, the number of members of the coalition must necessarily grow to infinity as the economy becomes more populous. Thus, while the uniform integrability condition is violated in both examples, it is, so to speak, more drastically violated in Manelli's [14] example than in Hara's [7] example.

Can the core convergence property hold when the sequence of core allocations fails to satisfy the uniform integrability condition in the less drastic way of Hara's [7] example, so that a vanishingly small coalition, consisting of an increasing number of consumers, maintains a consumption share away from zero? Since the failure of uniform integrability is tantamount to an extremely high concentration of consumption, the core convergence property seems, at first sight, incompatible with a sequence of core allocations that is not uniformly integrable. However, the conditions for the core convergence theorem (and its corollaries) of Manelli [14] are imposed only on individual consumers, which have no implication on any (vanishing or not) sequence of coalitions with the numbers of members growing to infinity.[2] In this paper, we construct two

[1] A sequence of nonnegative-valued integrable functions f^n defined on probability measure spaces $(A^n, \mathscr{A}^n, \nu^n)$ is uniformly integrable if $\int_{B^n} f^n(a)\, d\nu^n(a) \to 0$ as $n \to \infty$ whenever $B^n \in \mathscr{A}^n$ for every n and $\nu^n(B^n) \to 0$ as $n \to \infty$. When the sequence of induced probability measures $\nu^n \circ (f^n)^{-1}$ on $\boldsymbol{R}_+$ converges weakly to some probability measure μ on $\boldsymbol{R}_+$, the sequence (f^n) is uniformly integrable if and only if $\int_{A^n} f^n(a)\, d\nu^n(a) = \int_{\boldsymbol{R}_+} x\, d\left(\nu^n \circ (f^n)^{-1}\right)(x) \to \int_{\boldsymbol{R}_+} x\, d\mu(x)$ as $n \to \infty$.

[2] The condition regarding initial endowments for the core convergence theorem of Anderson [1] is imposed only on individual consumers. In contrast, to define a perfectly competitive sequence of economies, Hildenbrand [10, Chap. 2, Section 1], used a condition on the average endowments of a vanishing sequence of coalitions with the numbers of members possibly growing to infinity.

examples to show, by applying Manelli's [14] theorem, that the core convergence property may hold even when every sequence of core allocations fails to be uniformly integrable in the same way as in Hara's [7] example. These examples tell us that an extremely high concentration of consumption, which is often taken as a sign of imperfect competition, is compatible with the emergence of perfect competition. However, they do not preclude the possibility that once a more demanding notion of core convergence or perfect competition is employed, the core allocations may be deemed as quite different from the equilibrium allocations whenever the sequence of core allocations fails to be uniformly integrable. We will mention a possible notion of this sort in the conclusion.

The two examples we construct in this paper differ from each other in two respects. First, the limit atomless economy has no Walrasian equilibrium in the first example but it has one in the second. In the second example, the failure of uniform integrability does not lead to the non-existence of an equilibrium in the limit but a discontinuous change in equilibrium prices at the limit. The presence of the discontinuous change suggests that the notion of the limit (atomless) economy used here may well be less than appropriate. Indeed, we will see, when analyzing the properties of the second example, that although the sequence of the joint distributions of consumers' preference relations and initial endowments of finite economies converges weakly to the joint distribution of the atomless economy, the sequence of the supports of the joint distributions of finite economies does not converge to the support of the joint distribution of the atomless economy with respect to the Hausdorff distance. Rather, a preference relation disappears at the limit. We will suggest a related direction of future research in the conclusion.

The second respect in which our two examples differ from each other is related to the core convergence theorem that Manelli [15] proved in another paper of his. Unlike the core equivalence theorem (and its corollaries) of Manelli [14], Theorem 2 of Manelli [15] uses conditions only in terms of the sequence of finite economies, with no reference to any particular core allocations, to guarantee the convergence property for all sequences of core allocations. We will show that Condition C2 of Manelli [14] is satisfied by all sequences of core allocations of both examples, but the conditions of Theorem 2 of Manelli [15] are satisfied only by the sequences of core allocations of the example having a Walrasian equilibrium in the limit. This implies that the conditions of Manelli [15] are sufficient but not necessary for core convergence.

This paper is organized as follows. In Sect. 2, we review basic definitions and results. In Sect. 3, we give two examples to show that an almost negligibly small coalition consumes all of the bads even when the core convergence property is obtained. In Sect. 4, we conclude, suggesting some directions of future research.

2. Basic definitions and results

Let L be a positive integer, denoting the number of types of commodities. The consumption set is the nonnegative orthant $\boldsymbol{R}_+^L$ of the L-dimensional Euclidean space $\boldsymbol{R}^L$. We writhe X for $\boldsymbol{R}_+^L$. Denote by $\mathscr{P}$ the set of all binary relations on X (subsets of $X \times X$) that are complete, transitive, and continuous, endowed with the relative topology of the closed convergence topology on the set of all closed subsets of $\boldsymbol{R}_+^L \times \boldsymbol{R}_+^L$. Denote by $\mathscr{P}_{\mathrm{co}}$ the set of all binary relations in $\mathscr{P}$ that are convex; by $\mathscr{P}_{\mathrm{lns}}$ the set of all binary relations in $\mathscr{P}$ that are locally non-satiated; and by $\mathscr{P}_{\mathrm{mo}}$ the set of all binary relations in $\mathscr{P}$ that are monotone.[3]

An (exchange) *economy* is characterized by a complete probability measure space $(A, \mathscr{A}, \nu)$ of names of consumers and a measurable mapping $\chi : A \to \mathscr{P} \times \boldsymbol{R}^L$, with the coordinate mappings $\succsim : A \to \mathscr{P}$ and $e : A \to \boldsymbol{R}^L$ comprising $\chi = \succsim \times e$, such that e is integrable. When there is no ambiguity, we simply refers to the economy χ, by suppressing the probability measure space $(A, \mathscr{A}, \nu)$. We write $\succsim_a$ for $\succsim(a)$. The symmetric part of $\succsim_a$ is written as $\sim_a$ and the asymmetric part is written as $\succ_a$. The measurability is with respect to $\mathscr{A}$ and the product σ-field of the Borel σ-fields on $\mathscr{P}$ and $\boldsymbol{R}^L$. In most of the subsequent analysis (and, in fact, in our examples), we assume that $\succsim_a \in \mathscr{P}_{\mathrm{co}} \cap \mathscr{P}_{\mathrm{lns}}$ and $e(a) \in \boldsymbol{R}_{++}^L$ for every $a \in A$.

An economy is *finite* if A is a finite set, $\mathscr{A}$ is the power set of A, and ν is the uniform probability measure on A, that is, $\nu(\{a\}) = |A|^{-1}$ for every $a \in A$. An economy is *atomless* if the probability measure space $(A, \mathscr{A}, \nu)$ is atomless. Then, in particular, A is an infinite set.

For a sequence $(((A^n, \mathscr{A}^n, \nu^n), \chi^n))$ of economies and an economy $((A, \mathscr{A}, \nu), \chi)$, we consider the following two notions of convergence. In both notions, we require the sequence of the numbers of consumers, $|A^n|$, converges to the number of consumers, $|A|$, allowing them to be infinite. We also require $\int_{A^n} e^n(a)\, d\nu(a) \to \int_A e(a)\, d\nu(a)$ as $n \to \infty$, that is, the sequence of average endowment vectors of finite economies χ^n converges to the average endowment vector of χ. On the top of these requirements, the first notion of convergence is nothing but the weak convergence of the joint distributions of preference relations and initial endowments. That is, we require, for every bounded and continuous function $h : \mathscr{P} \times \boldsymbol{R}^L \to \boldsymbol{R}$, $\int_{\mathscr{P} \times \boldsymbol{R}^L} h(z)\, d\left(\nu^n \circ (\chi^n)^{-1}\right)(z) \to \int_{\mathscr{P} \times \boldsymbol{R}^L} h(z)\, d\left(\nu \circ \chi^{-1}\right)(z)$ as $n \to \infty$. We then write $\nu^n \circ (\chi^n)^{-1} \to \nu \circ \chi^{-1}$ *weakly as* $n \to \infty$. Although the weak convergence means, roughly, that the distribution $\nu \circ \chi^{-1}$ can be approximated by another distribution $\nu^n \circ (\chi^n)^{-1}$ for a sufficiently large n, its precise meaning is more restricted. It is that $\nu^n \circ (\chi^n)^{-1}$ approximates $\nu \circ \chi^{-1}$ as far as the integrals of bounded and continuous functions are concerned.

---

[3] That is, if $Q \in \mathscr{P}_{\mathrm{mo}}$, $x \in X$, $y \in X$, and $x - y \in \boldsymbol{R}_{++}^L$, then xQy but not yQx.

If we take a function $h : \mathscr{P} \times \boldsymbol{R}^L \to \boldsymbol{R}$ that is not bounded or continuous, we need not have the convergence of integrals. We will see that this is responsible for the failure of uniform integrability of sequences of core allocations in our examples. For the second notion of convergence, we additionally impose the convergence of the supports of joint distributions. More specifically, we denote by supp $\left(\nu \circ \chi^{-1}\right)$ the support of $\nu \circ \chi^{-1}$ (where, as we specified before, the topology on $\mathscr{P}$ is the closed convergence topology, which is metrizable), and analogously for supp $\left(\nu^n \circ (\chi^n)^{-1}\right)$. We assume that supp $\left(\nu \circ \chi^{-1}\right)$ and the supp $\left(\nu^n \circ (\chi^n)^{-1}\right)$ are compact. Then we require the Hausdorff distance between supp $\left(\nu^n \circ (\chi^n)^{-1}\right)$ and supp $\left(\nu \circ \chi^{-1}\right)$ to converge to zero as $n \to \infty$. This means roughly that all the characteristics (preference relations and initial endowment vectors) that are present in χ^n for a sufficiently large n are also present in χ; and that all the characteristics that are present in χ can be approximated by some characteristics in χ^n for a sufficiently large n.

The second notion is obviously stronger than the first, and in fact, we see that in both of the two examples in the next section, the sequence of finite economies converges to some atomless economy with respect to the first notion of convergence, but only in one of the two it does so with respect to the second notion.[4]

Let $(A, \mathscr{A}, \nu)$ be an economy. Each element of $\mathscr{A}$ is referred to as a *coalition*. For a coalition C, a mapping $f : C \to X$ is a *feasible allocation within* C if $\int_C f(a)\, d\nu(a) = \int_C e(a)\, d\nu(a)$. Note that the feasibility is defined by the exact equality, not weak equalities, to prevent free disposability of bads. A feasible allocation within the entire A is simply called a feasible allocation, without adding "within A". A pair (f, p) of a feasible allocation f and a price vector $p \in \boldsymbol{R}^L$ is a *Walrasian equilibrium* of the economy χ if for almost every $a \in A$, $p \cdot f(a) \leq p \cdot e(a)$ and $p \cdot x > p \cdot e(a)$ whenever $x \in X$ and $x \succ_a f(a)$. A pair (C, g) of a coalition C and a feasible allocation g within C is an *objection* to a feasible allocation $f : A \to X$ if $\nu(\{a \in C \mid f(a) \succ_a g(a)\}) = 0$ and $\nu(\{a \in C \mid g(a) \succ_a f(a)\}) > 0$. The *core* of the economy χ is the set of all allocations to which there is no objection.

There are two existence theorems relevant to our analysis. The first one is by McKenzie [12,13], which deals only with finite economies.

Theorem 1 (McKenzie [12,13]). *For every finite economy χ, if $\succsim_a \in \mathscr{P}_{\text{co}} \cap \mathscr{P}_{\text{lns}}$ and $e(a) \in \boldsymbol{R}^L_{++}$ for every $a \in A$, then there exists a Walrasian equilibrium of χ.*

---

[4] The weak convergence, compactness of supports and the convergence of supports with respect to the Hausdorff distance together imply that $\int_{A^n} e^n(a)\, d\nu^n(a) \to \int_A e(a)\, d\nu(a)$, because the latter two conditions imply that the e^n and e are essentially uniformly bounded.

The second one is a special case of the existence theorems of Hildenbrand [9] and of Hara [8] for atomless economies.[5]

Theorem 2 (Hildenbrand [9] and Hara [8]). *For every atomless economy χ, if $\nu(\{a \in A \mid \succsim_a \in \mathscr{P}_{\mathrm{mo}}\}) > 0$ and $\nu(\{a \in A \mid e(a) \in \boldsymbol{R}^L_{++}\}) = 1$, then there exists a Walrasian equilibrium of χ.*

Hara [7] gave an example to show that there may not be any Walrasian equilibrium for an atomless economy even if $\succsim_a \in \mathscr{P}_{\mathrm{co}} \cap \mathscr{P}_{\mathrm{lns}}$ and $e(a) \in \boldsymbol{R}^L_{++}$ for every $a \in A$. The virtue of atomless economies lies in the following core equivalence theorem, originally due to Aumann [3].[6]

Theorem 3 (Aumann [3]). *For every atomless economy χ, if $\nu(\{a \in A \mid \succsim_a \in \mathscr{P}_{\mathrm{lns}}\}) > 0$ and $\nu(\{a \in A \mid e(a) \in \boldsymbol{R}^L_{++}\}) = 1$, then the core of χ coincides with the set of all Walrasian equilibrium allocations of χ.*

Let P be a space of normalized price vectors. Although it is most common to take $P = \left\{p \in \boldsymbol{R}^L \mid \|p\| = 1\right\}$, where $\|p\| = \sum_{\ell=1}^{L} |p_\ell|$, we only require $\inf_{p \in P} \|p\| > 0$. In fact, since there are only two types of commodities, of which the first one is a good and the second one a bad, in our examples, we will take $P = \{p \in \boldsymbol{R}^L \mid p_1 = 1\}$. For each $z \in \boldsymbol{R}$, denote $\max\{z, 0\}$ by z^+. Define $\psi : \mathscr{P} \times \boldsymbol{R}^L \times X \times P \to \boldsymbol{R}_+$ by

$$\psi(Q, w, x, p) = |p\cdot(x-w)| + (\sup\{p \cdot (x-y) \mid y \in X,\ yQx,\ \text{but not } xQy\})^+. \tag{1}$$

Thus $\psi(Q, w, x, p)$ measures, in monetary terms, the gap between the given consumption vector $x \in X$ and the demand of the consumer with the preference relation Q and the initial endowment vector w under the price vector $p \in P$, where the first term penalizes the violation of the budget-balancing condition and the second term penalizes the violation of the utility maximization condition.

For an economy $((A, \mathscr{A}, \nu), \chi)$, a feasible allocation f, and a price vector $p \in P$, define

[5] Hildenbrand's theorem establishes the existence of a free-disposal equilibrium, but if every member of some coalition with positive measure has a monotone preference relation, then a free-disposal equilibrium can be easily modified to a Walrasian equilibrium (where the feasibility constraint is satisfied with an equality rather than a weak inequality), by assigning excess supply to these consumers. On the other hand, Aumann's [4] and Schmeidler's [16] theorems assume that almost every consumer's preference relation is monotone. Hara [8] showed that there exists a Walrasian equilibrium of an exchange economy under the assumption that for every commodity there is a coalition with positive measure for whom the commodity is a good (that is, it increases their utility). This assumption is met if, as stated below, there is a coalition with positive measure who have monotone preference relations.

[6] Kim [11] provided two examples in which the core equivalence does not hold. One is based on the fact that the initial endowment vectors lie on the boundary of $\boldsymbol{R}^L_+$. The other is based on the fact that the preference relations are incomplete.

$$\psi(\chi, f, p) = \int_A \psi(\succsim_a, e(a), f(a), p)\, d\nu(a). \tag{2}$$

Thne $\psi(\chi, f, p) \geq 0$ for every (χ, f, p), and $\psi(\chi, f, p) = 0$ if and only if (f, p) is a Walrasian equilibrium of χ. Thus $\psi(\chi, f, p)$ is the average gap from (f, p) being a Walrasian equilibrium of χ. If $((A, \mathscr{A}, \nu), \chi)$ is a finite economy, then (2) can be rewritten as

$$\psi(\chi, f, p) = \frac{1}{|A|} \sum_{a \in A} \psi(\succsim_a, e(a), f(a), p)$$

Anderson [1] proved a core convergence theorem for a general, non-replica sequence of increasingly populous finite economies.[7,8]

Theorem 4 (Anderson [1]). *Let (χ^n) be a sequence of finite economies such that $\succsim_a^n \in \mathscr{P}_{\text{mo}}$ for every n and $a \in A^n$, $|A^n| \to \infty$ as $n \to \infty$, and if (a^n) is a sequence such that $a^n \in A^n$ for every n, then $|A^n|^{-1} e^n(a^n) \to 0$ as $n \to \infty$. Then, for every n and for every core allocation f^n of χ^n, there exists a sequence (p^n) of price vectors in P such that $\psi(\chi^n, f^n, p^n) \to 0$ as $n \to \infty$.*

Besides presenting two counterexamples, Manelli [14] provided sufficient conditions for core convergence. They are joint conditions on the sequence of finite economies and the sequences of particular choices of core allocations of these economies. We make use of them when establishing the core convergence property for our examples. On the other hand, Manelli [15] provided sufficient conditions for core convergence only in terms of the sequence of finite economies, independent of any particular choices of core allocations. We investigate whether these conditions are satisfied by our examples. Since, as we will see in the next section, all consumers have the identical endowment vector and convex preference relations in our examples, the critical condition among those of his theorem is the *No Peculiar Individuals Condition*, which involves the Hausdorff distance between two preference relations. The definition of the Hausdorff distance can be found in Hildenbrand [10, B.II] and we denote the distance by d.[9] We can then state a weaker version of the No Peculiar Individuals in Remark 1 of Section 3 of Manelli [15], which is imposed on a sequence (χ^n) of finite economies, as follows.

Condition 1 (No peculiar individuals). There exists a sequence of positive numbers, (t^n), such that $t^n/|A^n| \to 0$ and

---

7 Anderson [1] used a slightly different gap measure but the core convergence property with respect to the gap measure we are using here can be derived from his theorem.

8 Anderson [2] gave a taxonomy of types of core convergence. We will later touch on some of them.

9 Since the consumption set $\boldsymbol{R}_+^L$ is not bounded, the Hausdorff distance may be infinite.

$$\min_{a \in A^n} \left| \left\{ a' \in A^n \mid d\left(\succsim_a^n, \succsim_{a'}^n\right) \leq t^n \right\} \right| \to \infty$$

as $n \to \infty$.

In the analysis of the core convergence property for monotone preference relations, the No Peculiar Individuals Condition (and its variants) is often defined using the metric of the closed convergence topology in place of the Hausdorff distance. The Hausdorff distance measures the difference between two preference relations that is applicable uniformly, regardless of the choice of consumption vectors at which the difference is measured, while (the metric of) the closed convergence topology allows the difference between the two to depend on the norm (length) of such consumption vectors. A sequence (Q^n) of preference relations may converge to a preference relation Q with respect to the closed convergence topology while $d(Q^n, Q)$ does not converge to zero, or even when $d(Q^n, Q) = \infty$ for every n; and this happens when the Q^n eventually become the same as Q as far as the consumption vectors of some finite length or less are concerned, but there are many pairs of consumption vectors of unboundedly large norms over which the rankings are opposite between Q^n and Q.

As we will see in Sect. 3, the validity of the core convergence property hinges on whether the (sequences of) consumers having consumption vectors of unboundedly large norms at core allocations retain the market power. It is for this reason that to guarantee the core convergence property in the presence of bads without reference to any particular choice of core allocations, it is necessary to define the No Peculiar Individuals Condition using the Hausdorff distance, rather than the closed convergence topology.

3. Examples

In this section, we give an example of the failure of the core convergence property, and two examples to show that an almost negligible coalition may consume almost all bads in an economy even when the core convergence property is obtained. These examples share some common ingredients, which we present in the first subsection. We then turn to the specifics of each of the three.

3.1. Common ingredients

Let $L = 2$. We define preference relations for which the first commodity is a good and the second is a bad, and which is quasi-linear with respect to the good. The disutility from consuming the bad is defined by the following function.

Let $\underline{q}$ and $\overline{q}$ be such that $0 \leq \underline{q} < \overline{q} < \infty$. Define $r : (0, 1] \to \boldsymbol{R}_{++}$ by $r(b) = \left(\overline{q} - \underline{q}\right) / 4b$. Then, for each $b \in (0, 1]$, define $q_b : \boldsymbol{R}_+ \to \boldsymbol{R}_+$ by

$$q_b(x_2) = \begin{cases} \underline{q} + 2bx_2 & \text{for } x_2 \le r(b), \\ \overline{q} - \dfrac{\overline{q} - \underline{q}}{2} \exp\left(1 - \dfrac{x_2}{r(b)}\right) & \text{for } x_2 > r(b). \end{cases} \tag{3}$$

Then q_b is continuously differentiable, $q_b(r(b)) = \widehat{q}$, where $\widehat{q} = \left(\overline{q} + \underline{q}\right)/2$, and $\underline{q} < q_b(x_2) < \overline{q}$ and $q_b'(x_2) > 0$ for every $b \in (0, 1]$ and every $x_2 \in \boldsymbol{R}_{++}$. In fact, q_b is defined for $x_2 > r(b)$ so that it is strictly increasing, strictly concave, and is differentiable at $x_2 = r(b)$ with the derivative continuous at the point, and converges to $\overline{q}$ as $x_2 \to \infty$. Then define $s_b : \boldsymbol{R}_+ \to \boldsymbol{R}_+$ by

$$s_b(x_2) = \int_0^{x_2} q_b(t)\, dt,$$

then s_b is twice continuously differentiable. Moreover, $s_b'(r(b)) = \widehat{q}$, and $\underline{q} < s_b'(x_2) < \overline{q}$ and $s_b''(x_2) > 0$ for every $x_2 \in \boldsymbol{R}_{++}$.

For each $b \in (0, 1]$, we define the utility function $u_b : X \to \boldsymbol{R}$ by $u_b(x) = x_1 - s_b(x_2)$. Let $Q_b \in \mathscr{P}_{\text{co}} \cap \mathscr{P}_{\text{lns}}$ be the binary relation represented by u_b. Note that the marginal disutilities from the bad are given by q_b and hence range from $\underline{q}$ to $\overline{q}$. Thus, in particular, Q_b is proper in the sense of Manelli [14,15]. The mapping $b \mapsto Q_b$ is continuous with respect to the closed convergence topology.

Write

$$w = (w_1, w_2) = \left(\frac{\overline{q} - \underline{q}}{4} \frac{\overline{q} + \underline{q}}{2}, \frac{\overline{q} - \underline{q}}{4}\right) \in \boldsymbol{R}^L_{++}.$$

This is the endowment vector for every consumer. There is thus no market power for any consumer arising from unequal endowments.

We let $P = \{p \in \boldsymbol{R}^2 \mid p_1 = 1\}$ be the space of normalized price vectors.

3.2. Example of the failure of core convergence

To give the idea of how the presence of bads may prevent the emergence of the price-taking behavior, we first give an example of a sequence of increasingly populous finite economies along which the core convergence property fails. Manelli [14] also gave an example of the failure of core convergence with convex preference relations, but the following example is simpler and easier to analyze.

Example 1. Let $A = (0, 1]$, $\mathscr{A}$ be the set of all Lebesgue measurable subsets of A, and ν be the Lebesgue measure restricted on $\mathscr{A}$. Then $(A, \mathscr{A}, \nu)$ is an atomless complete probability measure space. Define $\succsim: A \to \mathscr{P}_{\text{co}} \cap \mathscr{P}_{\text{lns}}$ by $\succsim_a = Q_1$ for every $a \in A$. Define $e : A \to \boldsymbol{R}^L_{++}$ by $e(a) = w$ for every $a \in A$.

Letting $\chi = \succsim \times e : A \to (\mathscr{P}_{\text{co}} \cap \mathscr{P}_{\text{lns}}) \times \boldsymbol{R}^L_{++}$ defines an atomless economy $((A, \mathscr{A}, \nu), \chi)$. This economy, therefore, consists of a single type.

For each positive integer n, let $A^n = \{0, 1, \ldots, n\}$, $\mathscr{A}^n$ be the power set of A^n, and ν^n be the uniform probability measure on A^n. Define $\succsim^n : A^n \to \mathscr{P}_{\text{co}} \cap \mathscr{P}_{\text{lns}}$ by $\succsim^n_a = Q_1$ for every n and $a \in A^n$ with $a \geq 1$, and $\succsim^n_0 = Q_{1/(n+2)}$ for every n. Define $e^n(a) = w$ for every n and $a \in A^n$ Letting $\chi^n = \succsim^n \times e^n : A^n \to (\mathscr{P}_{\text{co}} \cap \mathscr{P}_{\text{lns}}) \times \boldsymbol{R}^L_{++}$ defines a finite economy $((A^n, \mathscr{A}^n, \nu^n), \chi^n)$ for each n.

Proposition 5. *In Example* 1:

1. $|A^n| \to \infty$ *and* $\nu^n \circ (\chi^n)^{-1} \to \nu \circ \chi^{-1}$ *weakly as* $n \to \infty$.
2. *For every n, there is a unique Walrasian equilibrium* (g^n, p^n) *with* $p^n \in P$ *of* χ^n, *given by*

$$p^n = \left(1, -\frac{\overline{q} + 3\underline{q}}{4}\right),$$

$$g^n(a) = \begin{cases} \left(w_1 + \frac{n}{8}\left(\overline{q} + 3\underline{q}\right) w_2, \left(\frac{n}{2} + 1\right) w_2\right) & \textit{if } a = 0, \\ \left(w_1 - \frac{1}{8}\left(\overline{q} + 3\underline{q}\right) w_2, \frac{1}{2} w_2\right) & \textit{if } a \geq 1, \end{cases}$$

3. *There is a unique Walrasian equilibrium* (g, p) *with* $p \in P$ *of* χ, *given by* $g(a) = w$ *for almost every* $a \in A$ *and*

$$p = \left(1, -\frac{\overline{q} + \underline{q}}{2}\right).$$

4. *For every sequence* (f^n) *consisting of core allocations* f^n *of* χ^n *for each* n,

$$\frac{f_2^n(0)}{|A^n|} \to \frac{w_2}{2}$$

as $n \to \infty$.

5. *For each n, define another feasible allocation* f^n *of* χ^n *by*

$$f^n(a) = \begin{cases} g^n(0) + \left(\frac{n}{8} w_2^2, 0\right) & \textit{if } a = 0, \\ g^n(a) - \left(\frac{1}{8} w_2^2, 0\right) & \textit{if } a \geq 1. \end{cases}$$

Then f^n *is a core allocation of* χ^n *for every n. Moreover, there exists a* $\delta > 0$ *such that for every sequence* (p^n) *in* P,

$$\frac{1}{|A^n|} |\{a \in A^n \mid \psi(\succsim^n_a, w, f^n(a), p^n) \geq \delta\}| \to 1 \tag{4}$$

as $n \to \infty$.

We shall not give a formal proof of this proposition, but explain its idea. Part 1 follows from the fact that the weight of consumer 0 in terms of the population in A^n is $1/(1+n)$, which converges to zero as $n \to \infty$. The support of the distribution of the atomless economy, $\nu \circ \chi^{-1}$, is of course the singleton $\{(Q_0, w)\}$, but the support of $\nu^n \circ (\chi^n)^{-1}$ is equal to $\{Q_{1/(n+2)}, Q_1\} \times \{w\}$, and the sequence of these supports converges to $\{Q_0, Q_1\} \times \{w\}$ with respect to the Hausdorff distance. Therefore, the sequence of finite economies converges to the atomless economy in the first notion of convergence explained in Sect. 2, but not in the second. Given the specification of w, at every feasible allocation that is individually rational and Pareto-efficient, every consumer consumes strictly positive quantities of both commodities. Moreover, for every consumer $a \in A^n$ with $a \geq 1$, the quantity of the bad consumed is less than $r(1)$, and for $a = 0$, the quantity of the bad consumed is less than $r(1/(n+2))$. Part 2 follows from this fact and the first-order condition of the utility maximization problem. Part 3 merely states that the Walrasian equilibrium of the atomless economy, consisting only of a single type, is the no-trade equilibrium. We should, however, note that there is a discontinuous change in equilibrium prices: $|p_2^n| = \left(\overline{q} + 3\underline{q}\right)/4$ for every n, while $|p_2| = \left(\overline{q} + \underline{q}\right)/2$. Since the consumer of type Q_0 disappears at the limit, this discontinuous change is indicative of the market power of the consumer of type $Q_{1/(n+2)}$ in χ^n. Indeed, part 4 shows that the consumer of type $Q_{1/(n+2)}$ alone consumes about half of the total endowment of the bad in a sufficiently populous economy.

Part 5 is the main result of this proposition. Note that for every n and $a \geq 1$, $u_1(g^n(a)) = (5/4)w_2^2$, while $u_1(w) = w_2^2$. Thus a transfer of $(1/8)w_2^2$ units of the good, with respect to which u_1 is quasi-linear, from each of the consumers $a \geq 1$ to $a = 0$ at the Walrasian equilibrium allocation g^n does not violate the individual rationality condition. Part 5 claims that the allocation f^n obtained from this profile of transfers is a core allocation. To see this, note first that since f^n is individually rational, no coalition consisting only of consumers $a \geq 1$ can object to f^n. Second, since the utility functions are quasi-linear with respect to the good, and since the equilibrium allocation g^n is Pareto-efficient, so is f^n. This means that the grand coalition cannot object to f^n. Third, no coalition consisting of consumer 0 and some, but not all, of $a \geq 1$ can object to f^n either, because the members $a \geq 1$ would not be able to afford the transfer to $a = 0$ to keep him as well as at g^n, while they are themselves as well as at g^n. Part 5 also claims that the core convergence property fails in a rather drastic way: There is a positive number δ such that for any choice of normalized price vectors p^n, the individual gap measure $\psi\left(\succsim_a^n, w, f^n(a), p^n\right)$ stays away from δ for almost every consumer. Thus, in particular, the sequence of the average gap measures $\psi(\chi^n, f^n, p^n)$ stays almost at least as large as δ and does not converge to zero.

The convergence (4) can be proved as follows. Since $f^n(a)$ does not depend on n or a as long as $a \geq 1$, we denote it by x. Since $\underset{\sim a}{\succ}^n = Q_1$ for every n and $a \geq 1$ and it is locally non-satiated, we can consider the problem of minimizing

$$\psi(Q_1, w, x, p) = |p \cdot (x - w)| + (\sup\{p \cdot (x - y) \mid y \in X \text{ and } y\, Q_1 x\})^+$$

by choosing a $p \in P$. The second term on the right-hand side is zero if and only if $p = \left(1, -\left(\overline{q} + 3\underline{q}\right) / 4\right)$, but then the first term is equal to $(1/8)w_2^2$. Hence $\psi(Q_1, w, x, p) > 0$ for every $p \in P$. Moreover, since each of the two terms on the right-hand side is a convex function of p attaining its minimum (zero) at some unique point, the sum of the two, $\psi(Q_1, w, x, p)$, attains its minimum. Denote it by δ, which is what we needed, because $n/(1+n) \to 1$ as $n \to \infty$.

One of the conditions for core convergence for the core convergence theorem of Manelli [14] is that $|A^n|^{-1} f^n(a^n) \to 0$ as $n \to \infty$ for every sequence (f^n) consisting of core allocations f^n of χ^n and for every sequence (a^n) consisting of $a^n \in A^n$. Part 4 of Proposition 5 shows that this property is violated by a consumer ($a^n = 0$), just as in the first example of Manelli [14]. Also, by Lemma 10 to be presented in the appendix,

$$d\left(Q_{1/(n+2)}, Q_1\right) \geq \frac{\left(\overline{q} - \underline{q}\right)^2}{8\left(1 + \overline{q}\right)}(n+1).$$

Thus, if a sequence of positive numbers, (t^n), satisfies

$$\min_{a \in A^n} \left|\left\{a' \in A^n \mid d\left(\underset{\sim a}{\succ}^n, \underset{\sim a'}{\succ}^n\right) \leq t^n\right\}\right| \to \infty$$

as $n \to \infty$, then

$$\liminf_{n \to \infty} \frac{t^n}{|A^n|} \geq \frac{\left(\overline{q} - \underline{q}\right)^2}{8\left(1 + \overline{q}\right)} > 0.$$

Thus Condition 1 is violated, where consumer 0 is the peculiar consumer.

3.3. Example with no Walrasian equilibrium in the limit

In this subsection, we give an example of the core convergence property in which the sequence of core allocations must necessarily fail to be uniformly integrable and the limit atomless economy has no Walrasian equilibrium. The example is quite similar to Example 2 of Hara [7] but differs from it in that the preference relations in the present example are proper.

Example 2. Let $A = (0, 1]$, $\mathscr{A}$ be the set of all Lebesgue measurable subsets of A, and ν be the Lebesgue measure restricted on $\mathscr{A}$. Then $(A, \mathscr{A}, \nu)$ is an atomless complete probability measure space. Define $\succsim : A \to \mathscr{P}_{\text{co}} \cap \mathscr{P}_{\text{lns}}$ by

$\succsim_a = Q_a$ for every $a \in A$. Define $e : A \to \boldsymbol{R}^L_{++}$ by $e(a) = w$ for every $a \in A$. Letting $\chi = \succsim \times e : A \to (\mathscr{P}_{\text{co}} \cap \mathscr{P}_{\text{lns}}) \times \boldsymbol{R}^L_{++}$ defines an atomless economy $((A, \mathscr{A}, \nu), \chi)$.

For each positive integer n, let $A^n = \{1, 2, \dots, n\}$, $\mathscr{A}^n$ be the power set of A^n, and ν^n be the uniform probability measure on A^n. Define $\succsim^n : A^n \to \mathscr{P}_{\text{co}} \cap \mathscr{P}_{\text{lns}}$ by $\succsim^n_a = Q_{a/n}$ for every n and $a \in A^n$. Define $e^n : A^n \to \boldsymbol{R}^L_{++}$ by $e^n(a) = w$ for every $a \in A^n$. Letting $\chi^n = \succsim^n \times e^n : A^n \to (\mathscr{P}_{\text{co}} \cap \mathscr{P}_{\text{lns}}) \times \boldsymbol{R}^L_{++}$ defines a finite economy $((A^n, \mathscr{A}^n, \nu^n), \chi^n)$ for each n.

Proposition 6. *In Example* 2:

1. $|A^n| \to \infty$ *and* $\nu^n \circ (\chi^n)^{-1} \to \nu \circ \chi^{-1}$ *weakly as* $n \to \infty$. *The supports,* $\operatorname{supp}\left(\nu^n \circ (\chi^n)^{-1}\right)$ *and* $\operatorname{supp}\left(\nu \circ \chi^{-1}\right)$, *are compact and the Hausdorff distance between* $\operatorname{supp}\left(\nu^n \circ (\chi^n)^{-1}\right)$ *and* $\operatorname{supp}\left(\nu \circ \chi^{-1}\right)$ *converges to zero as* $n \to \infty$.
2. *For every* n, *there is a unique Walrasian equilibrium* (g^n, p^n) *with* $p^n \in P$ *of* χ^n, *given by*
$$p^n = \left(1, -\left(\underline{q} + \frac{2w_2}{S^n}\right)\right),$$
$$g^n(a) = \left(w_1 + \left(\underline{q} + \frac{2w_2}{S^n}\right)\left(\frac{n}{aS^n} - 1\right) w_2, \frac{nw_2}{aS^n}\right),$$
where $S^n = 1 + 1/2 + \cdots + 1/n$.
3. *There is no Walrasian equilibrium of* χ.
4. *There exists a sequence* (B^n) *consisting of* $B^n \in \mathscr{A}^n$ *for each* n *such that* $|B^n| / |A^n| \to 0$ *and*
$$\frac{1}{|A^n|} \sum_{a \in B^n} f^n_2(a) \to w_2$$
as $n \to \infty$ *for every sequence* (f^n) *consisting of core allocations* f^n *of* χ^n *for each* n.
5. *For every sequence* (f^n) *consisting of core allocations* f^n *of* χ^n *for each* n *and for every sequence* (a^n) *consisting of* $a^n \in A^n$ *for each* n, $|A^n|^{-1} f^n(a^n) \to 0$ *as* $n \to \infty$.
6. *For every sequence* (f^n) *consisting of core allocations* f^n *of* χ^n *for each* n, $\psi(\chi^n, f^n, p^n) \to 0$ *as* $n \to \infty$, *where* p^n *is the equilibrium price vector of* χ^n *identified in part* 2.
7. *The sequence* (χ^n) *does not satisfy Condition* 1.

Part 1 of this proposition states that the sequence of finite economies χ^n converge to the atomless economy χ in the second notion of convergence introduced in Sect. 2, that is, the convergence is not only in distribution, but also in support. Part 2 and 3 require no comment, but note that the combination of these two facts implies that there is no reasonably defined limit of the sequence of equilibrium allocations of finite economies. Part 4 implies that in a very populous finite economy, almost all of the bads are consumed by an almost negligible coalition B^n at every core allocation. In particular, it implies that the sequence (f^n) of core allocations is not uniformly integrable. Part 5 implies that nevertheless, no single consumer can retain a strictly positive fraction of goods or bads. Part 6 is the core convergence property, but note that we can use the equilibrium price vectors p^n to make the sequence of gap measures $\psi(\chi^n, f^n, p^n)$ to converge to zero. Since the utility functions are quasi-linear with respect to the good, and since all core allocations are individually rational and Pareto-efficient, they can be obtained from the equilibrium allocation g^n by transferring goods among consumers without changing the allocation of bads.[10] Moreover, the equilibrium price vectors p^n are supporting price vectors of core allocations, and the second term on the right-hand side of (1) is equal to zero. Part 6, therefore, implies that the sequence of gap measures converges to zero even when the choice of price vectors is restricted to supporting price vectors. Furthermore, since $\psi\left(\succsim_a^n, w, f^n(a), p^n\right) = \|f_n(a) - g_n(a)\|$,

$$\psi\left(\chi^n, f^n, p^n\right) = \frac{1}{|A^n|} \sum_{a \in A^n} \|f_n(a) - g_n(a)\|.$$

Thus, part 6 implies that the core convergence property can be obtained in terms of the distances from the Walrasian equilibrium allocations. Part 7 implies that the conditions of Manelli's [15] theorem are, while sufficient, not necessary for core convergence.

Remark 1. The difference in economic contents between parts 4 and 5 can be understood by applying two inequality measures to the core allocations of bads, $f_2^n(a)$. Part 4 implies that the Gini coefficient for $f_2^n = \left(f_2^n(1), \ldots, f_2^n(n)\right)$, which measures the area, multiplied by 2, between the 45-degree line and the Lorenz curve, converges to 1 as $n \to \infty$. This property can be interpreted as asymptotically perfect inequality. Part 5, on the other hand, implies that the Herfindahl index, which is the sum of the squares of consumption shares,

$$\sum_{a=1}^{n} \left(\frac{f_2^n(a)}{n w_2}\right)^2,$$

converges 0 as $n \to \infty$. This fact can be interpreted as asymptotically perfect equality.

It is interesting to see that the two most commonly used measures of inequality gives rise to the completely opposite verdicts on the degree of asymptotic

[10] This will be proved later in Lemma 8.

inequality. The discrepancy arises partly from the fact that the Gini coefficient depends only on the percentage shares of bads in terms of the sizes of coalitions relative to the entire economy, while the Herfindahl index depends, in addition, on the number of consumers in the economy. As an example, think of replicating an exchange economy and an allocation of the economy by n times, while satisfying the equal treatment property. Although the Gini coefficient of the replicated allocation is equal to the Gini coefficient of the original allocation, the Herfindahl index of the n-times replicated allocation is one nth of the Herfindahl index of the original allocation. Given the core convergence property (part 5), it is probably fair to say that the Herfindahl index is more appropriate than the Gini coefficient when it comes to measuring the degree of competitiveness of core allocations. This observation is also consistent with the standard usage of the two: the Gini coefficient is used to measure income inequality, while the Herfindahl index is used to measure competitiveness in a market or industry in which a small number of firms are active and there is a room for strategic interaction.[11]

The proof of Proposition 7 is given in Appendix B.

3.4. Example with a Walrasian equilibrium in the limit

In our second example, the limit atomless economy has a Walrasian equilibrium. While our first example did not have this property, the second example is a modification of the first, in that there is a consumer having the utility function $u_{a/n}$ for every $a < n$ in the n-th economy χ^n, but the number of those having u_1, denoted by T^n, grows at a rate faster than n. The crux of the construction of this example lie in choosing appropriate values of T^n to guarantee the core convergence property and the existence of a Walrasian equilibrium in the limit.

Example 3. Let $A = (0, 1]$, $\mathscr{A}$ be the set of all Lebesgue measurable subsets of A, and ν be the Lebesgue measure restricted on $\mathscr{A}$. Then $(A, \mathscr{A}, \nu)$ is an atomless complete probability measure space. Define $\succsim : A \to \mathscr{P}_{\text{co}} \cap \mathscr{P}_{\text{lns}}$ by

[11] The fact that we are dealing with exchange economies while the Herfindahl index is used for firms' outputs seems to suggest that the use of the Herfindahl index in our context is inappropriate. But such a concern is unwarranted. Indeed, we could think of the function $s_b : \boldsymbol{R}_+ \to \boldsymbol{R}_+$ as the cost function for the disposal of bads, by which $s_b(x_2)$ is the amount of goods necessary to dispose of x_2 units of bads. Then a consumer having the utility function $u_b(x) = x_1 - s_b(x_2)$ could be thought of as a firm-owner whose disposal technology is given by s_b and who only consumes goods. Then every Walrasian equilibrium of the original exchange economy is a Walrasian equilibrium of the production economy just defined, at which all the firms, by definition, satisfies the profit maximization condition. Every core allocation of the exchange economy could analogously be thought of as a core allocation of the corresponding coalitional production economy.

$\succsim_a = Q_1$ for every $a \in A$. Define $e : A \to \boldsymbol{R}^L_{++}$ by $e(a) = w$ for every $a \in A$. Letting $\chi = \succsim \times e : A \to (\mathscr{P}_{\text{co}} \cap \mathscr{P}_{\text{lns}}) \times \boldsymbol{R}^L_{++}$ defines an atomless economy $((A, \mathscr{A}, \nu), \chi)$. This economy, therefore, consists of a single type.

For each positive integer n, let $S^n = \sum_{a=1}^{n} 1/a$ and T^n be the positive integer such that

$$n\left(S^n\right)^{1/2} \leq T^n < n\left(S^n\right)^{1/2} + 1. \tag{5}$$

Let $A^n = \{1, 2, \ldots, n, n+1, n+2, \ldots, n+T^n\}$, $\mathscr{A}^n$ be the power set of A^n, and ν^n be the uniform probability measure on A^n.

Define $\succsim^n : A^n \to \mathscr{P}_{\text{co}} \cap \mathscr{P}_{\text{lns}}$ by

$$\succsim^n_a = \begin{cases} Q_{a/n} & \text{for every } a \leq n, \\ Q_1 & \text{for every } a \geq n+1, \end{cases}$$

which can be more succinctly written as $\succsim^n_a = Q_{\min\{a/n,1\}}$ for every $a \in A^n$. Define $e^n : A^n \to \boldsymbol{R}^L_{++}$ by $e^n(a) = w$ for every $a \in A^n$. Letting $\chi^n = \succsim^n \times e^n : A^n \to (\mathscr{P}_{\text{co}} \cap \mathscr{P}_{\text{lns}}) \times \boldsymbol{R}^L_{++}$ defines a finite economy $((A^n, \mathscr{A}^n, \nu^n), \chi^n)$ for each n.

Proposition 7. *In Example* 3:

1. $|A^n| \to \infty$ *and* $\nu^n \circ (\chi^n)^{-1} \to \nu \circ \chi^{-1}$ *weakly as* $n \to \infty$.
2. *For every* n, *there is a unique Walrasian equilibrium* (g^n, p^n) *with* $p^n \in P$ *of* χ^n, *given by*

$$p^n = \left(1, -\left(\underline{q} + 2w_2 \frac{n + T^n}{nS^n + T^n}\right)\right),$$

$$g^n(a) = \left(w_1 + \left(\underline{q} + 2w_2 \frac{n+T^n}{nS^n+T^n}\right)\left(\frac{n + T^n}{nS^n + T^n} \max\left\{\frac{n}{a}, 1\right\} - 1\right) w_2, \right.$$
$$\left. \frac{n + T^n}{nS^n + T^n} w_2 \max\left\{\frac{n}{a}, 1\right\}\right).$$

3. *There is a unique Walrasian equilibrium* (g, p) *of* χ, *given by* $g(a) = w$ *for almost every* $a \in A$ *and*

$$p = \left(1, -\frac{\overline{q} + \underline{q}}{2}\right).$$

4. *For every* n, *let* $B^n = \{1, \ldots, n\}$, *then* $|B^n| / |A^n| \to 0$ *and*

$$\frac{1}{|A^n|} \sum_{a \in B^n} f_2^n(a) \to w_2$$

as $n \to \infty$ *for every sequence* (f^n) *consisting of core allocations* f^n *of* χ^n *for each* n.

5. *For every sequence* (f^n) *consisting of core allocations* f^n *of* χ^n *for each* n *and for every sequence* (a^n) *consisting of* $a^n \in A^n$ *for each* n, $|A^n|^{-1} f^n(a^n) \to 0$ *as* $n \to \infty$.
6. *For every sequence* (f^n) *consisting of core allocations* f^n *of* χ^n *for each* n, $\psi(\chi^n, f^n, p^n) \to 0$ *as* $n \to \infty$, *where* p^n *is the equilibrium price vector of* χ^n *identified in part* 2.
7. *The sequence* (χ^n) *satisfies Condition* 1.

This proposition is quite analogous to Proposition 6 and, as such, we comment only on the difference between the two. In part 1, we claim the convergence in distribution but not in supports. In fact, the sequence of supports of $\nu^n \circ (\chi^n)^{-1}$ converges, with respect to the Hausdorff distance, to $\{Q_b \mid b \in [0, 1]\} \times \{w\}$, while the support of the atomless economy is the singleton $\{(Q_1, w)\}$. This non-convergence seems to be responsible for a discontinuous change in equilibrium prices. Indeed, according to part 2 and a result in the proof of this proposition, $p^n \to \left(1, -\underline{q}\right)$ as $n \to \infty$, but, according to part 3, this limit is different from the equilibrium price vector of χ. Part 7 shows that unlike the previous examples, this example satisfies the No Peculiar Individuals Condition of Manelli [15].

The proof of Proposition 7 is given in Appendix B.

4. Conclusion

We have given two examples of sequences of increasingly populous finite economies to show that the core convergence property may be obtained even when a vanishingly small coalition consumes almost all bads in the economy. This result can be interpreted as saying that the price-taking behavior may emerge even when the consumption of bads is concentrated on a relatively small coalitions. The crucial aspect of the examples is that if there are sufficiently many consumers in an economy, even a relatively small coalition may consist of many consumers, and the competition among them may well be sufficiently intense to make a core allocations very close to equilibrium allocations.

Although there is already an extensive literature on the core convergence property in economies where the preference relations are monotone, there are relatively few contributions on it with non-monotone preference relations. There seem to be, at least, two aspects of our examples that need to be elaborated on.

First, in Example 2, the sequence of finite economies converges to the atomless economy in distribution and also in supports, but in Example 3, the sequence of finite economies does so only in distribution. These two examples differ also in that the limit economy of Example 2 has no Walrasian equilibrium but the limit economy of Example 3 has one. In the presence of bads, it is quite legitimate to require the convergence in support as part of the definition of the convergence of finite economies, because, as we have seen in the examples, a vanishingly small coalition may play a non-negligible role in the determination of equilibrium prices and allocations. Yet, we do not know to what extent the convergence in supports is (in-)compatible with the existence of an equilibrium in the limit economy, while the sequences of core allocations (and, in particular, equilibrium allocations) fail to be uniformly integrable. It will be important to thoroughly clarify the relationship between the two.

Second, although we have defined the core convergence property in terms of the convergence of the gap measures in the average over the consumers, the same property has been defined in some contributions (such as Bewley [5] and Cheng [6], assuming monotone preference relations) in term of the convergence of the gap measures uniformly across the consumers. That is, we say that the core convergence property holds if for every sequence of core allocations f^n of χ^n, there exists a sequence of price vectors p^n such that

$$\operatorname*{ess\,sup}_{a \in A^n} \psi\left(\succsim_a^n, e^n(a), f^n(a), p^n\right) \to 0$$

as $n \to \infty$. If χ^n is a finite economy, then we can of course replace ess sup by max. This notion of core convergence is stronger than the notion of core convergence we have used, and it is not clear whether the core convergence property can hold relative to this stronger notion when the sequences of core allocations fail to be uniformly integrable.

Appendix A. Proof of Proposition 6

Proof of part 1 of Proposition 6. Define $Q_0 \in \mathscr{P}$ as the preference relation represented by the utility function $u_0(x) = x_1 - \underline{q}x_2$. It is then easy to show that the mapping $b \mapsto Q_b$ from the closed unit interval $[0, 1]$ to $\mathscr{P}$ is continuous (even at $b = 0$). Since $[0, 1]$ is compact, its image, $\{Q_b \mid b \in [0, 1]\}$, is compact and, hence, closed. Thus $\operatorname{supp}\left(\nu \circ \chi^{-1}\right) = \{Q_b \mid b \in [0, 1]\} \times \{w\}$. Since $\operatorname{supp}\left(\nu^n \circ (\chi^n)^{-1}\right) = \left\{Q_{1/n}, \ldots, Q_{(n-1)/n}, Q_1\right\} \times \{w\}$, it is easy to show that the Hausdorff distance between $\operatorname{supp}\left(\nu^n \circ (\chi^n)^{-1}\right)$ and $\operatorname{supp}\left(\nu \circ \chi^{-1}\right)$ converges to zero as $n \to \infty$. To show that $\nu^n \circ (\chi^n)^{-1} \to \nu \circ \chi^{-1}$ weakly, we can apply the same method as in the proof of part (ii) of Proposition 2 of Hara [7]. □

To prove other parts of Proposition 6, we need the following lemma.

Lemma 8. *For every n, if f^n is a core allocation of χ^n of Example 2, then*

$$f_1^n(a) \geq w_2^2, \tag{6}$$

$$f_2^n(a) = \frac{n w_2}{a S^n}. \tag{7}$$

Moreover, f^n is supported by a unique price vector p^n in P,[12] *given by*

$$p^n = \left(1, -\left(\underline{q} + \frac{2w_2}{S^n}\right)\right). \tag{8}$$

Proof of Lemma 8. By definition,

$$u_{a/n}(w) \geq u_1(w) = w_1 - \left(\underline{q}w_2 + w_2^2\right) = w_2^2.$$

for every n and $a \in A^n$. Since $u_{a/n}$ is quasi-linear and $f^n(a)$ is individually rational,

$$f_1^n(a) \geq u_{a/n}\left(f_1^n(a)\right) \geq u_{a/n}(w).$$

Thus (6) follows.

As for (7), since f^n is Pareto efficient, by the second welfare theorem, there is a non-zero price vector p^n such that (f^n, p^n) is a price quasi-equilibrium.[13] We shall first prove that $p_1^n > 0$ and $p_2^n/p_1^n < -\underline{q}$.

Note first that if $p_2^n < 0$, then $p_1^n > 0$. Indeed, if $p_2^n < 0$, then every consumer in A^n satisfies the minimum income condition and, since the first commodity is a good, the utility maximization condition implies that $p_1^n > 0$.

Note second that it is impossible that $p_1^n = 0$ and $p_2^n > 0$. Indeed, if this were the case, then every consumer a with $f_2^n(a) > 0$ would satisfy the minimum income condition. But then they would choose zero consumption for bads, contradicting $f_2^n(a) > 0$.

Of course, we cannot have $p_1^n < 0$ because, then, every consumer in A^n would satisfy the minimum income condition but the utility maximization condition would then be violated.

Since at least one of p_1^n and p_2^n must not be zero, the remaining possibility is that $p_1^n > 0$. We can therefore assume that $p_1^n = 1$.

Since $f_1^n(a) > 0$ for every $a \in A^n$, the minimum income condition is satisfied by every $a \in A^n$. Thus, if $p_2^n \geq -\underline{q}$, then the utility maximization condition would imply that $f_2^n(a) = 0$ for every $a \in A^n$, which is a contradiction. Hence $p_2^n < -\underline{q}$. Then $f_2^n(a) > 0$ for every $a \in A^n$. Since $f_1^n(a) > 0$ for every $a \in A^n$, this implies that $f^n(a) \in \boldsymbol{R}_{++}^2$.

Since $r(a/n) = (n/a)w_2$,

$$\sum_{a \in A^n} r\left(\frac{a}{n}\right) = nS^n w_2 \geq nw_2.$$

Thus, there is an $a \in A^n$ such that $f^n(a) \leq r(a/n)$. Then the first-order condition for utility maximum implies that $|p_2^n| = \underline{q} + 2(a/n)f_2^n(a) \leq \left(\overline{q} + \underline{q}\right)/2$.

[12] That is, for every $a \in A^n$, if $x \in X$ and $x \succ_{a/n} f^n(a)$, then $p^n \cdot x > p^n \cdot f^n(a)$.
[13] That is, for every $a \in A^n$, if $x \in X$ and $x \succ_{a/n} f^n(a)$, then $p^n \cdot x \geq p^n \cdot f^n(a)$.

Hence $f^n(a) \leq r(a/n)$ for *every* $a \in A^n$. Then (7) and (8) follow again from the first-order condition. □

Since an equilibrium allocation is a core allocation, part 2 of Proposition 6 can be derived from Lemma 8 using the budget constraint $p^n \cdot g^n(a) = p^n \cdot w$. Part 3 can be proved in the same way as Proposition 1 of Hara [7].

Proof of part 4 of Proposition 6. For each n define $a^n \in A^n$ so that

$$n^{1-(\log n)^{-1/2}} \leq a^n < n^{1-(\log n)^{-1/2}} + 1.$$

Then define $B^n = \{1, \ldots, a^n\} \in \mathscr{A}^n$. Just as in the proof of part (iii) of Proposition 6 of Hara [7], it is possible to show that $|B^n| / |A^n| \to 0$ and

$$\frac{1}{|A^n|} \sum_{a \in B^n} f_2^n(a) \to w_2$$

as $n \to \infty$. □

Lemma 9. *For every n, if f^n is a core allocation of χ^n of Example 2, then*

$$u_{a/n}(f^n(a)) \leq \left(w_1 - \underline{q} w_2\right) + n w_2^2 \left(\frac{(1 - 1/n)^2}{S^n - 1} - \frac{1}{S^n} \right) \tag{9}$$

for every $a \in A^n$.

Proof of Lemma 9. By Lemma 8,

$$\begin{aligned} &\sum_{a \in A^n} u_{a/n}(f^n(a)) \\ &= \sum_{a \in A^n} f_1^n(a) - \sum_{a \in A^n} \left(\underline{q} w_2 \frac{n}{a S^n} + \frac{a}{n} \left(\frac{n w_2}{a S^n} \right)^2 \right) \\ &= n \left(w_1 - \underline{q} w_2 \right) - \frac{n w_2^2}{S^n}. \end{aligned} \tag{10}$$

It is thus sufficient to prove that for every $a \in A^n$,

$$\sum_{b \in A^n \setminus \{a\}} u_{b/n}(f^n(b)) \geq (n-1) \left(w_1 - \underline{q} w_2 \right) - n w_2^2 \frac{(1 - 1/n)^2}{S^n - 1}. \tag{11}$$

because (9) can be obtained by subtracting (11) from (10).

We shall now show that if (11) did not hold, then there would be a feasible allocation g^n within $A^n \setminus \{a\}$ such that $(A^n \setminus \{a\}, g^n)$ is an objection to f^n. Indeed, then, define a feasible allocation g_2^n of the bad within $A^n \setminus \{a\}$ by

$$g_2^n(b) = \frac{n-1}{S^n - 1/a}\frac{w_2}{b} \tag{12}$$

for every $b \in A^n \setminus \{a\}$. Then, just as we derived (23), we can show that

$$\begin{aligned}
&\sum_{b\in A^n\setminus\{a\}} u_{b/n}(0, g_2^n(b)) \\
&= -(n-1)\underline{q}w_2 - (n-1)\left(\frac{1-1/n}{S^n - 1/a}w_2^2\right) \\
&\geq -(n-1)\underline{q}w_2 - nw_2^2\frac{(1-1/n)^2}{S^n - 1}.
\end{aligned} \tag{13}$$

Thus, by the contradiction hypothesis,

$$\sum_{b\in A^n\setminus\{a\}} u_{b/n}(f^n(b)) < (n-1)w_1 + \sum_{b\in A^n\setminus\{a\}} u_{b/n}(0, g_2^n(b)).$$

On the other hand, by (19),

$$u_{b/n}(f^n(b)) \geq w_2^2 > 0 > u_{b/n}(0, g_2^n(b)).$$

for every $b \in A^n \setminus \{a\}$. Thus, there is a feasible allocation g_1^n of the good within $A^n \setminus \{a\}$ such that

$$g_1^n(b) + u_{b/n}(0, g_2^n(b)) > u_{b/n}(f^n(b))$$

for every $b \in A^n \setminus \{a\}$. Let $g^n = (g_1^n, g_2^n)$, then, by the quasi-linearity of $u_{b/n}$, this is equivalent to $g^n(b) \succ_{b/n} f^n(b)$. Thus $(A^n \setminus \{a\}, g^n)$ is an objection. □

Proof of part 5 of Proposition 6. Let (a^n) be a sequence such that $a^n \in A^n$ for every n. It suffices to show that

$$\frac{f_1^n(a^n)}{n} \to 0, \tag{14}$$

$$\frac{f_2^n(a^n)}{n} \to 0 \tag{15}$$

as $n \to \infty$. Indeed, by (7),

$$\frac{f_2^n(a^n)}{n} \leq \frac{w_2}{S^n} \to 0$$

as $n \to \infty$. This proves (15). As for (14), since the utility functions are quasi-linear with respect to the first commodity and $f_2(a) \leq r(a/n)$,

$$\begin{aligned}
f_1\left(a^n\right) &= u_{a^n/n}\left(f^n\left(a^n\right)\right) + \left(\underline{q}f_2^n(a) + \frac{a}{n}\left(f_2^n(a)\right)^2\right) \\
&\leq (w_1 - \underline{q}w_2) + nw_2^2\left(\frac{(1-1/n)^2}{S^n - 1} - \frac{1}{S^n}\right) + \frac{nw_2}{S^n}\left(\underline{q} + \frac{w_2}{S^n}\right)
\end{aligned}$$

by (7). Since $1/S^n \to 0$ as $n \to \infty$, this proves (14). □

Proof of part 5 of Proposition 6. By Condition C2″ of Manelli [14], it suffices to show that

$$\frac{1}{|A^n|}\max_{a\in A^n}\left\|f^n(a)+(1,0)-e^n(a)\right\|\to 0 \tag{16}$$

as $n\to\infty$. Here, $|A^n|=n$ and $\|f^n(a)+(1,0)-e^n(a)\|\le\|f^n(a)\|+1+\|w\|$. By part 4 of this proposition, $|A^n|^{-1}\,\|f^n(a)\|\to 0$ as $n\to\infty$. Thus (16) is proved. □

Remark 2. Although we assumed throughout the above argument that f^n is a core allocation, we needed only its individual rationality and Pareto efficiency for the proof of parts 3 and 4. As for the proof of parts 5 and 6, the only additional property we needed was that there is no objection by any coalition consisting all but one consumer in the economy.

The following lemma is concerned with the Hausdorff distance between two preference relations.

Lemma 10. *For every* $b\in(0,1]$ *and every* $b'\in(0,1]$,

$$d\left(Q_b,Q_{b'}\right)\ge\frac{\left(\overline{q}-\underline{q}\right)^2}{8\left(1+\overline{q}\right)}\left|\frac{1}{b}-\frac{1}{b'}\right|.$$

Proof of Lemma 10. Let's now prove the first inequality. We assume without loss of generality that $b<b'$, and show that there exists an $(x,y)\in Q_b$ such that

$$\max\left\{\left\|x'-x\right\|_\infty,\left\|y'-y\right\|_\infty\right\}>\frac{\left(\overline{q}-\underline{q}\right)^2}{8\left(1+\overline{q}\right)}\left(\frac{1}{b}-\frac{1}{b'}\right)$$

for every $(x',y')\in Q_{b'}$. To do so, note first that for every $x_2>r(b)$,

$$s_b(x_2)=\overline{q}x_2+\frac{(\overline{q}-\underline{q})^2}{8b}\exp\left(1-\frac{x_2}{r(b)}\right)-\frac{5(\overline{q}-\underline{q})^2}{16b}. \tag{17}$$

The analogous equality holds for b' as well. Hence, for every $x_2>r(b)$,

$$\begin{aligned}s_{b'}\left(x_2\right)-s_b\left(x_2\right)=&\frac{5(\overline{q}-\underline{q})^2}{16}\left(\frac{1}{b}-\frac{1}{b'}\right)\\&+\frac{(\overline{q}-\underline{q})^2}{8}\left(\frac{1}{b'}\exp\left(1-\frac{x_2}{r(b')}\right)-\frac{1}{b}\exp\left(1-\frac{x_2}{r(b)}\right)\right).\end{aligned}$$

Since

$$\frac{1}{b'}\exp\left(1-\frac{x_2}{r(b')}\right)-\frac{1}{b}\exp\left(1-\frac{x_2}{r(b)}\right)\to 0$$

as $x_2 \to \infty$, there exists an $\underline{x}_2 > r(b)$ such that

$$\left|\frac{1}{b'}\exp\left(1-\frac{x_2}{r(b')}\right)-\frac{1}{b}\exp\left(1-\frac{x_2}{r(b)}\right)\right| < \frac{1}{2}\left(\frac{1}{b}-\frac{1}{b'}\right)$$

for every $x_2 \geq \underline{x}_2$. Thus

$$s_{b'}(x_2) - s_b(x_2) > \frac{(\overline{q}-\underline{q})^2}{4}\left(\frac{1}{b}-\frac{1}{b'}\right)$$

for every $x_2 \geq \underline{x}_2$. Since $u_{b'}(s_b(x_2), x_2) = -(s_{b'}(x_2) - s_b(x_2))$,

$$u_{b'}(s_b(x_2), x_2) < -\frac{(\overline{q}-\underline{q})^2}{4}\left(\frac{1}{b}-\frac{1}{b'}\right)$$

for every $x_2 \geq \underline{x}_2$.

Since $\left|s_{b'}(x_2') - s_{b'}(x_2)\right| < \overline{q}|x_2' - x_2|$ for every $x_2 \in \boldsymbol{R}_+$ and $x_2' \in \boldsymbol{R}_+$,

$$\left|u_{b'}(x') - u_{b'}(x)\right| \leq |x_1' - x_1| + \left|s_{b'}(x_2') - s_{b'}(x_2)\right| \leq (1+\overline{q})\|x' - x\|_\infty$$

for every $x \in X$ and $x' \in X$. Let $x = \left(s_b\left(\underline{x}_2\right), \underline{x}_2\right)$ and $y = (0, 0)$. Then, for every $x' \in X$ and every $y' \in X$, if

$$\max\left\{\left\|x'-x\right\|_\infty, \left\|y'-y\right\|_\infty\right\} \leq \frac{(\overline{q}-\underline{q})^2}{8(1+\overline{q})}\left(\frac{1}{b}-\frac{1}{b'}\right)$$

then

$$\begin{aligned}
&u_{b'}(x') - u_{b'}(y') \\
&= (u_{b'}(x') - u_{b'}(x)) + (u_{b'}(x) - u_{b'}(y) + (u_{b'}(y) - u_{b'}(y')) \\
&< \frac{(\overline{q}-\underline{q})^2}{8}\left(\frac{1}{b}-\frac{1}{b'}\right) - \frac{(\overline{q}-\underline{q})^2}{4}\left(\frac{1}{b}-\frac{1}{b'}\right) + \frac{(\overline{q}-\underline{q})^2}{8}\left(\frac{1}{b}-\frac{1}{b'}\right) = 0.
\end{aligned}$$

Thus $(x', y') \notin Q_{b'}$. This is equivalent to saying that

$$\max\left\{\left\|x'-x\right\|_\infty, \left\|y'-y\right\|_\infty\right\} > \frac{(\overline{q}-\underline{q})^2}{8(1+\overline{q})}\left(\frac{1}{b}-\frac{1}{b'}\right)$$

for every $(x', y') \in Q_{b'}$. This completes the proof. □

Proof of part 7 of Proposition 6. Let (t^n) be a sequence such that

$$\min_{a \in A^n}\left|\left\{a' \in A^n \mid d\left(\succsim_a^n, \succsim_{a'}^n\right) < t^n\right\}\right| \to \infty$$

as $n \to \infty$. Since $\succsim_a^n = Q_{a/n}$ for every n and $a \in A^n$,

$$\begin{aligned}
&\min_{a\in A^n} \left|\left\{a' \in A^n \mid d\left(\succsim_a^n, \succsim_{a'}^n\right) < t^n\right\}\right| \\
&\leq \left|\left\{a \in A^n \mid d\left(Q_{a/n}, Q_1\right) < t^n\right\}\right| \\
&\leq \left|\left\{a \in A^n \mid \frac{\left(\overline{q} - \underline{q}\right)^2}{8\left(1+\overline{q}\right)} \left|\frac{1}{a/n} - \frac{1}{1/n}\right| < t^n\right\}\right| \\
&\leq \left|\left\{a \in A^n \mid \frac{\left(\overline{q} - \underline{q}\right)^2}{8\left(1+\overline{q}\right)} \left(1 - \frac{1}{a}\right) < \frac{t^n}{n}\right\}\right|
\end{aligned}$$

by Lemma 10. For each n, define a^n as the largest $a \in A^n$ that satisfies

$$\frac{\left(\overline{q} - \underline{q}\right)^2}{8\left(1+\overline{q}\right)} \left(1 - \frac{1}{a}\right) < \frac{t^n}{n}. \tag{18}$$

Then

$$\left|\left\{a \in A^n \mid \frac{\left(\overline{q} - \underline{q}\right)^2}{8\left(1+\overline{q}\right)} \left(1 - \frac{1}{a}\right) < \frac{t^n}{n}\right\}\right| = a^n$$

and hence $a^n \to \infty$ as $n \to \infty$. Thus, if we take the liminf of both sides of (18) with $a = a^n$ as $n \to \infty$, then

$$\frac{\left(\overline{q} - \underline{q}\right)^2}{8\left(1+\overline{q}\right)} \leq \liminf_{n\to\infty} \frac{t^n}{|A^n|}$$

because $|A^n| = n$. Since the left-hand side is strictly positive, this means that Condition 1 is not met. □

Appendix B. Proof of Proposition 7

Part 1 of Proposition 7 follows from

$$\nu^n(\{n+1, n+2, \ldots, n+T^n\}) = \frac{T^n}{n+T^n} \geq \frac{(S^n)^{1/2}}{2+(S^n)^{1/2}} \to 1$$

and, thus, $\nu^n(\{n+1, n+2, \ldots, n+T^n\}) \to 1$. Part 2 follows from the next lemma, which can be proved in the same way as Lemma 8. We omit its proof.

Lemma 11. *For each n, if f^n is a core allocation of χ^n of Example 3, then*

$$f_1^n(a) \geq w_2^2, \tag{19}$$

$$f_2^n(a) = \frac{n + T^n}{nS^n + T^n} w_2 \max\left\{\frac{n}{a}, 1\right\}, \tag{20}$$

for every $a \in A^n$.

Part 3 can be easily proved.

Proof of part 4 of Proposition 7. For each n, let f^n be a core allocation of the finite economy χ^n. Since

$$\nu^n(B^n) = \frac{n}{n + T^n} = \frac{1}{1 + T^n/n} \leq \frac{1}{1 + (S^n)^{1/2}} \to 0$$

as $n \to \infty$, it suffices to show that

$$\frac{1}{n + T^n} \sum_{a=1}^{n} f_2^n(a) \to w_2 \tag{21}$$

as $n \to \infty$. Indeed, by (20),

$$\begin{aligned}
w_2 > \frac{1}{n + T^n} \sum_{a=1}^{n} f_2^n(a) &= \frac{1}{n + T^n} w_2 \frac{n + T^n}{nS^n + T^n} nS^n \\
&= w_2 \frac{nS^n}{nS^n + T^n} \\
&= w_2 \frac{S^n}{S^n + T^n/n} \\
&> w_2 \frac{S^n}{S^n + (S^n)^{1/2} + 1} \to w_2
\end{aligned}$$

as $n \to \infty$. □

To prove parts 5 and 6 of Proposition 7, we need another lemma.

Lemma 12. *For each n, if f^n belongs to the core of the finite economy χ^n of Example 3, then*

$$u_{\min\{a/n, 1\}}(f^n(a)) \leq (w_1 - \underline{q} w_2) + w_2^2 \left(\frac{(n + T^n - 1)^2}{nS^n - n + T^n} - \frac{(n + T^n)^2}{nS^n + T^n} \right) \tag{22}$$

for every $a \in A^n$.

Proof of Lemma 12. By Lemma 11,

$$\begin{aligned}
&\sum_{a \in A^n} u_{\min\{a/n,1\}}(f^n(a)) \\
&= \sum_{a \in A^n} f_1^n(a) - \sum_{a \in A^n} \left(\underline{q} w_2 \frac{n+T^n}{nS^n+T^n} \max\left\{\frac{n}{a}, 1\right\} \right. \\
&\qquad \left. + \min\left\{\frac{a}{n}, 1\right\} \left(w_2 \frac{n+T^n}{nS^n+T^n} \max\left\{\frac{n}{a}, 1\right\}\right)^2 \right) \\
&= (n+T^n)\left(w_1 - \underline{q} w_2 - \frac{n+T^n}{nS^n+T^n} w_2^2 \right). \qquad (23)
\end{aligned}$$

It is thus sufficient to prove that for every $a \in A^n$,

$$\sum_{b \in A^n \setminus \{a\}} u_{\min\{b/n,1\}}(f^n(b)) \geq (n+T^n-1)\left(w_1 - \underline{q} w_2 - \frac{n+T^n-1}{nS^n-n+T^n} w_2^2 \right). \qquad (24)$$

because (22) can be obtained by subtracting (24) from (23).

We shall now show that if (24) did not hold, then there would be a feasible allocation g^n within $A^n \setminus \{a\}$ such that $(A^n \setminus \{a\}, g^n)$ is an objection to f^n. Indeed, then, define a feasible allocation g_2^n of the bad within $A^n \setminus \{a\}$ by

$$g_2^n(b) = w_2 \frac{n+T^n-1}{nS^n+T^n-\max\{n/a, 1\}} \max\left\{\frac{n}{b}, 1\right\} \qquad (25)$$

for every $b \in A^n \setminus \{a\}$. Then, just as we derived (23), we can show that

$$\begin{aligned}
&\sum_{b \in A^n \setminus \{a\}} u_{\min\{b/n,1\}}(0, g_2^n(b)) \\
&= -(n+T^n-1)\left(\underline{q} w_2 + \frac{n+T^n-1}{nS^n+T^n-\max\{n/a, 1\}} w_2^2 \right) \\
&\geq -(n+T^n-1)\left(\underline{q} w_2 + \frac{n+T^n-1}{nS^n+T^n-n} w_2^2 \right). \qquad (26)
\end{aligned}$$

Thus, by the contradiction hypothesis,

$$\sum_{b \in A^n \setminus \{a\}} u_{\min\{b/n,1\}}(f^n(b)) < (n+T^n-1)w_1 + \sum_{b \in A^n \setminus \{a\}} u_{\min\{b/n,1\}}(0, g_2^n(b)).$$

On the other hand, by (19),

$$u_{\min\{b/n,1\}}(f^n(b)) \geq w_2^2 > 0 > u_{\min\{b/n,1\}}(0, g_2^n(b)).$$

for every $b \in A^n \setminus \{a\}$. Thus, there is a feasible allocation g_1^n of the good within $A^n \setminus \{a\}$ such that

$$g_1^n(b) + u_{\min\{b/n,1\}}(0, g_2^n(b)) > u_{\min\{b/n,1\}}(f^n(b))$$

for every $b \in A^n \setminus \{a\}$. Let $g^n = (g_1^n, g_2^n)$, then, by the quasi-linearity of $u_{\min\{b/n,1\}}$, this is equivalent to $g^n(b) \succ_{\min\{b/n,1\}} f^n(b)$. Thus $(A^n \setminus \{a\}, g^n)$ is an objection. □

Proof of part 5 of Proposition 7. Let (a^n) be a sequence such that $a^n \in A^n$ for every n. It suffices to show that

$$\frac{f_1(a^n)}{n + T^n} \to 0, \tag{27}$$

$$\frac{f_2(a^n)}{n + T^n} \to 0 \tag{28}$$

as $n \to \infty$. Indeed, by (20),

$$\frac{f_2(a^n)}{n + T^n} \le w_2 \frac{n}{nS^n + T^n} = \frac{w_2}{S^n + T^n/n} \le \frac{w_2}{S^n + (S^n)^{1/2}} \to 0$$

as $n \to \infty$. This proves (28). As for (27), since the utility functions are quasi-linear with respect to the first commodity and $f_2(a) \le r\,(\min\{a/n, 1\})$,

$$\begin{aligned} f_1\left(a^n\right) &= u_{\min\{a^n/n,1\}}\left(f^n\left(a^n\right)\right) + \left(\underline{q} f_2^n(a) + \min\left\{\frac{a}{n}, 1\right\}\left(f_2^n(a)\right)^2\right) \\ &\le (w_1 - \underline{q} w_2) + w_2^2 \left(\frac{(n + T^n - 1)^2}{nS^n - n + T^n} - \frac{(n + T^n)^2}{nS^n + T^n}\right) \\ &\quad + n \frac{n + T^n}{nS^n + T^n} w_2 \left(\underline{q} + \frac{n + T^n}{nS^n + T^n} w_2\right) \end{aligned}$$

by (22). It is therefore sufficient to show that

$$\frac{1}{n + T^n} \frac{(n + T^n - 1)^2}{nS^n - n + T^n} \to 0 \text{ and } \frac{n + T^n}{nS^n + T^n} \to 0 \tag{29}$$

as $n \to 0$. Indeed,

$$\begin{aligned} \frac{1}{n + T^n} \frac{(n + T^n - 1)^2}{nS^n - n + T^n} &= \frac{n + T^n - 1}{n + T^n} \frac{1 + T^n/n - 1/n}{S^n - 1 + T^n/n} \\ &\le \frac{n + T^n - 1}{n + T^n} \frac{(S^n)^{1/2} + 1}{S^n + (S^n)^{1/2} - 1}, \end{aligned}$$

and the first fraction on the far right-hand side converges to 1, while the second fraction converges to 0. Hence the far left-hand side converges to 0. Moreover,

$$\frac{n+T^n}{nS^n+T^n} = \frac{1+T^n/n}{S^n+T^n/n} \leq \frac{(S^n)^{1/2}+2}{S^n+(S^n)^{1/2}},$$

and the far right-hand side converges to 0. Hence the far left-hand side converges to 0. This completes the proof. □

It now remains to prove parts 6 and 7. The former can be proved in the same way as part 6 of Proposition 6. We thus omit its proof. The following lemma is concerned with the Hausdorff distance between two preference relations.

Lemma 13. *For every* $b \in (0, 1]$ *and every* $b' \in (0, 1]$,

$$d(Q_b, Q_{b'}) \leq \frac{\left(\overline{q}-\underline{q}\right)^2}{2} \max\left\{\frac{1}{b}, \frac{1}{b'}\right\}.$$

Proof of Lemma 13. Let $x \in X$ and $x' \in X$ be such that $u_b(x) \leq u_b(x')$ and $u_{b'}(x) \geq u_{b'}(x')$, and at least one of the two weak inequalities is satisfied with a strict inequality. Regarding Q_b and $Q_{b'}$ as subsets of $X \times X$ and writing $(x', x) \in Q_b$ if and only if $x' Q_b x$ and so forth, this is equivalent to saying that $(x', x) \in Q_b \setminus Q_{b'}$ or $(x, x') \in Q_{b'} \setminus Q_b$. In the following, we show that

$$\left(x + \left(\frac{\left(\overline{q}-\underline{q}\right)^2}{2} \max\left\{\frac{1}{b}, \frac{1}{b'}\right\}, 0\right), x'\right) \in Q_b,$$

$$\left(x' + \left(\frac{\left(\overline{q}-\underline{q}\right)^2}{2} \max\left\{\frac{1}{b}, \frac{1}{b'}\right\}, 0\right), x\right) \in Q_{b'}.$$

This implies that $Q_{b'}$ is included in the neighborhood of Q_b of radius $2^{-1}\left(\overline{q}-\underline{q}\right)^2 \max\left\{1/b, 1/b'\right\}$, and that Q_b is included in the neighborhood of $Q_{b'}$ of radius $2^{-1}\left(\overline{q}-\underline{q}\right)^2 \max\left\{1/b, 1/b'\right\}$. The second inequality of this lemma would then follows.

We can of course assume that $x \neq x'$. If one of the two coordinates of $x' - x$ is zero, or if one is strictly positive and the other is strictly negative, then neither $(x', x) \in Q_b \setminus Q_{b'}$ nor $(x, x') \in Q_{b'} \setminus Q_b$. Thus either $x' - x \in \boldsymbol{R}^2_{++}$ or $x - x' \in \boldsymbol{R}^2_{++}$.

Let's for a moment assume that $x' - x \in \boldsymbol{R}^2_{++}$. By the definition of u_b and $u_{b'}$,

$$s_b(x'_2) - s_b(x_2) \leq x'_1 - x_1 \leq s_{b'}(x'_2) - s_{b'}(x_2).$$

By the definition of $s_{b'}$,

$$s_{b'}(x_2') - s_{b'}(x_2) < \overline{q}(x_2' - x_2).$$

By the definitions of q_b,

$$q_b(t) \geq \overline{q} - \frac{\overline{q} - \underline{q}}{2} \exp\left(1 - \frac{t}{r(b)}\right)$$

for every $t \in \boldsymbol{R}_+$ (even when $t \leq r(b)$). Hence, by the definition of s_b,

$$\begin{aligned}
& s_b(x_2') - s_b(x_2) \\
& \geq \int_{x_2}^{x_2'} \left(\overline{q} - \frac{\overline{q} - \underline{q}}{2} \exp\left(1 - \frac{t}{r(b)}\right)\right) dt \\
& = \overline{q}(x_2' - x_2) + r(b)\frac{\overline{q} - \underline{q}}{2}\left(\exp\left(1 - \frac{x_2'}{r(b)}\right) - \exp\left(1 - \frac{x_2}{r(b)}\right)\right) \\
& > \overline{q}(x_2' - x_2) + r(b)\frac{\overline{q} - \underline{q}}{2}(-4) \\
& = \overline{q}(x_2' - x_2) - \frac{(\overline{q} - \underline{q})^2}{2b}.
\end{aligned}$$

Hence

$$\overline{q}(x_2' - x_2) - \frac{(\overline{q} - \underline{q})^2}{2b} < s_b(x_2') - s_b(x_2) \leq x_1' - x_1 \leq s_{b'}(x_2') - s_{b'}(x_2) < \overline{q}(x_2' - x_2).$$

Therefore

$$0 \leq u_b(x') - u_b(x) = (x_1' - x_1) - (s_b(x_2') - s_b(x_2)) < \frac{(\overline{q} - \underline{q})^2}{2b}, \tag{30}$$

$$0 \leq u_{b'}(x) - u_{b'}(x') = (s_{b'}(x_2') - s_{b'}(x_2)) - (x_1' - x_1) < \frac{(\overline{q} - \underline{q})^2}{2b}. \tag{31}$$

By quasi-linearity,

$$\begin{aligned}
u_b\left(x + \left(\frac{(\overline{q} - \underline{q})^2}{2b}, 0\right)\right) & > u_b\left(x' + \left(u_b(x) - u_b(x'), 0\right)\right) \\
& = u_b(x') + \left(u_b(x) - u_b(x')\right) = u_b(x), \\
u_{b'}\left(x' + \left(\frac{(\overline{q} - \underline{q})^2}{2b}, 0\right)\right) & > u_{b'}\left(x' + \left(u_{b'}(x) - u_{b'}(x'), 0\right)\right) \\
& = u_{b'}(x') + \left(u_{b'}(x) - u_{b'}(x')\right) = u_{b'}(x).
\end{aligned}$$

Hence

$$\left(x + \left(\frac{(\overline{q}-\underline{q})^2}{2b}, 0\right), x'\right) \in Q_b \quad \text{and} \quad \left(x' + \left(\frac{(\overline{q}-\underline{q})^2}{2b}, 0\right), x\right) \in Q_{b'}.$$

If $x - x' \in \boldsymbol{R}^2_{++}$, then by swapping the roles of x and x, and of b and b', we can show that

$$\left(x + \left(\frac{(\overline{q}-\underline{q})^2}{2b'}, 0\right), x'\right) \in Q_b \quad \text{and} \quad \left(x' + \left(\frac{(\overline{q}-\underline{q})^2}{2b'}, 0\right), x\right) \in Q_{b'}.$$

The proof is thus completed. □

Proof of part 7 of Proposition 7. Define (t^n) by letting $t^n = 2^{-1}\left(\overline{q}-\underline{q}\right)^2 n$ for every n. Then

$$\frac{t^n}{|A^n|} = \frac{1}{1 + T^n/n} \leq \frac{1}{1 + (S^n)^{1/2}} \to 0$$

as $n \to \infty$. By Lemma 13,

$$\begin{aligned} & d\left(\succsim^n_a, \succsim^n_{a'}\right) \\ & = d\left(Q_{\min\{a/n,1\}}, Q_{\min\{a'/n,1\}}\right) \\ & \leq \frac{\left(\overline{q}-\underline{q}\right)^2}{2} \max\left\{\frac{1}{\min\{a/n, 1\}}, \frac{1}{\min\{a'/n, 1\}}\right\} \\ & = \frac{\left(\overline{q}-\underline{q}\right)^2}{2} \max\left\{\max\left\{\frac{n}{a}, 1\right\}, \max\left\{\frac{n}{a'}, 1\right\}\right\} \leq t^n \end{aligned}$$

for every n, $a \in A^n$, and $a' \in A^n$. That is, for every n,

$$\min_{a \in A^n} \left|\left\{a' \in A^n \mid d\left(\succsim^n_a, \succsim^n_{a'}\right) \leq t^n\right\}\right| = |A^n| = n + T^n.$$

Thus Condition 1 is met. □

References

1. Anderson, R.M.: An elementary core equivalence theorem. Econometrica **46**, 1483–1487 (1978)
2. Anderson, R.M.: The core in perfectly competitive economies, Chap. 14. In: Aumann, R.J. and Hart, S. (eds) Handbook of Game Theory with Economic Applications, vol. 1, North-Holland, Amsterdam (1992)
3. Aumann, R.J.: Markets with a continuum of traders. Econometrica **32**, 39–50 (1964)
4. Aumann, R.J.: Existence of competitive equilibria in markets with a continuum of traders. Econometrica **34**, 1–17 (1966)

5. Bewley, T.F.: Edgeworth's conjecture. Econometrica **41**, 425–454 (1973)
6. Cheng, H.-C.: A uniform core convergence result for non-convex economies. J. Econ. Theory **31**, 269–282 (1983)
7. Hara, C.: Existence of equilibria in economies with bads. Econometrica **73**, 647–658 (2005)
8. Hara, C.: An equilibrium existence theorem for an atomless economy without the monotonicity assumption. Econ. Bull. **4**(34), 1–5 (2006)
9. Hildenbrand, W.: Existence of equilibria for economies with production and a measure space of consumers. Econometrica **38**, 608–623 (1970)
10. Hildenbrand, W.: Core and Equilibria of a Large Economy. Princeton University Press, Princeton (1974)
11. Kim, S.H.: Core equivalence may fail without monotonicity. Proc. Econom. **16**, 47–62 (2005)
12. McKenzie, L.W.: On the existence of general equilibrium for a competitive market. Econometrica **27**, 54–71 (1959)
13. McKenzie, L.W.: The classical theorem on existence of competitive equilibrium. Econometrica **49**, 819–841 (1981)
14. Manelli, A.M.: Monotonic preferences and core equivalence. Econometrica **59**, 123–138 (1991)
15. Manelli, A.M.: Core convergence without monotone preferences and free disposal. J. Econ. Theory **55**, 400–415 (1991)
16. Schmeidler, D.: Competitive equilibria in markets with a continuum of traders and incomplete preferences. Econometrica **37**, 578–585 (1969)

Adv. Math. Econ. 11, 77–93 (2008)

Advances in MATHEMATICAL ECONOMICS

A distance and a binary relation related to income comparisons

Hidetoshi Komiya

Faculty of Business and Commerce, Keio University, Hiyoshi, Kohoku-ku, Yokohama 223-8521, Japan
(e-mail: hkomiya@fbc.keio.ac.jp)

Received: October 31, 2007
Revised: December 3, 2007

JEL classification: I32

Mathematics Subject Classification (2000): 15A51, 60E15, 91A05

Abstract. We define a distance and a binary relation among income distributions which is closely related to Lorenz dominance. An income distribution is represented by a vector $(x_1, x_2, \dots, x_n)$ when the society under consideration consists of n individuals or households. The component x_i denotes the income of the ith individual and the sum $\sum_{i=1}^{n} x_i$ is the total wealth of the society. The distance is defined on the n-dimensional Euclidean space R^n mathematically, and it gives indices of difference between two income distributions with not only the same total wealth but also the different total wealths. Thus, the distance might give a criterion for income distributions taking account of equity and efficiency.

Key words: Lorenz dominance, distance, binary relation, minimax theorem

1. Introduction

Lorenz dominance is a criterion when we compare two income distributions in order to judge which is more equal. Lorenz [5] introduced what has become known as the "Lorenz curve", and observed that one distribution is more equal than the other when the Lorenz curve of the former distribution lies over that of the latter. For an income distribution $(x_1, x_2, \dots, x_n)$, order the individuals from poorest to richest by a permutation π of N; thus we have

$$x_{\pi(1)} \le x_{\pi(2)} \le \cdots \le x_{\pi(n)}.$$

The n-vector

$$\pi x = (x_{\pi(1)}, x_{\pi(2)}, \ldots, x_{\pi(n)})$$

is called the *increasing rearrangement* of x and denoted by x^*. Now plot the points $(k/n, \sigma_k/\sigma_n)$, $k = 0, 1, \ldots, n$ on the plane, where $\sigma_0 = 0$ and $\sigma_k = \sum_{i=1}^{k} x_{\pi(i)}$ for $k \geq 1$. Join these points by line segments to obtain a piecewise linear curve connecting the origin and the point $(1, 1)$. The curve is called the *Lorenz curve* of the income distribution $(x_1, x_2, \ldots, x_n)$. For two income distributions $x = (x_1, x_2, \ldots, x_n)$ and $y = (y_1, y_2, \ldots, y_n)$ with equal total wealth, it is easily seen that the Lorenz curve of x lies under that of y if and only if

$$\sum_{i=1}^{k} x_i^* \leq \sum_{i=1}^{k} y_i^* \quad \text{for } k = 1, 2, \ldots, n.$$

In this case x is said to be *Lorenz dominated* by y, which means that y is more equal than x in the sense of Lorenz [5]. Although Lorenz dominance is a relation between income distributions with the same total wealth, Shorrocks [8] studied income comparisons where income distributions do not necessarily have the same total wealth. In order to include his argument in our scope, the concept of the Lorenz dominance is extended to that of generalized Lorenz dominance in the subsequent section.

Lorenz and generalized Lorenz dominance is closely related to the theory of majorization and stochastic matrices. On the other hand, the minimax theorem, the fundamental theorem of zero-sum two-person games, plays a crucial role in the argument developed in this paper. We integrate these results from different disciplines so as to obtain a distance defined on the n-dimensional Euclidean space which measures both equality and efficiency of income distributions.

2. Preliminaries

We prepare notations used hereafter and observe several established theorems necessary for our arguments. Let R^n be an n-dimensional Euclidean space. For any two elements x and y of R^n, if their increasing rearrangements x^* and y^* satisfy the inequalities

$$\sum_{i=1}^{k} x_i^* \leq \sum_{i=1}^{k} y_i^* \quad \text{and} \quad \sum_{i=1}^{n} x_i^* = \sum_{i=1}^{n} y_i^*,$$

then x is said to *be Lorenz dominated* by y because of what is stated in Sect. 1. We write $x \precsim_L y$ if x is Lorenz dominated by y. An n-square matrix is said to be a *permutation matrix* if it has exactly one 1 in each row and each column, and all other components are 0. For any element x of R^n, if we operate a permutation matrix P to x, that is, if we calculate xP, then the result is a permutation of x. Conversely, for any permutation π, we can find a unique permutation matrix P such that $\pi x = xP$ for every $x \in R^n$. An n-square matrix is said to be *doubly stochastic* if it has nonnegative components and each row sum and each column sum are 1. A permutation matrix is obviously doubly stochastic and it is easily seen that any convex combination of permutation matrices is doubly stochastic. The following theorem due to Birkhoff [1] asserts that the inverse is also valid.

Theorem 1. *The set of all extreme points of the set of all doubly stochastic n-matrices consists of permutation n-matrices, and hence the convex hull of all permutation n-matrices coincides with the set of doubly stochastic n-matrices.*

The Lorenz dominance and doubly stochastic matrices are closely related, and Hardy et al. [2] established the following theorem.

Theorem 2. *For any two elements x and y of R^n, x is Lorenz dominated by y if and only if there is a doubly stochastic matrix D such that $xD = y$.*

This theorem asserts that more equal income distribution is obtained by operating a doubly stochastic matrix to an original income distribution, and conversely operating a doubly stochastic matrix to an income distribution yields a more equal income distribution.

For two elements x and y in R^n, if we remove the condition of equality of total wealth, then we reach the definition of generalized Lorenz dominance; x is said to *be generally Lorenz dominated* by y if their increasing rearrangement x^* and y^* satisfy

$$\sum_{i=1}^{k} x_i^* \leq \sum_{i=1}^{k} y_i^*, \quad k = 1, 2, \ldots, n,$$

and we write $x \precsim_{GL} y$. Similar to the relation between Lorenz dominance and doubly stochastic matrices, generalized Lorenz dominance is closely related to doubly superstochastic matrices. An n-square matrix $P = (p_{ij})$ is said to be *doubly superstochastic* if there is a doubly stochastic matrix $D = (d_{ij})$ such that $p_{ij} \geq d_{ij}$ for all i and j. Let R^n_{++} be the set $\{x \in R^n : x_i > 0,\ i = 1, 2, \ldots, n\}$ of all n-vectors whose components are all positive.

Theorem 3. *For any two elements x and y of R^n_{++}, x is generally Lorenz dominated by y if and only if there is a doubly superstochastic matrix P such that $xP = y$.*

This theorem is a version of Proposition D.2.b, Chapter 2, Marshall and Olkin [6].

The last half of this section is devoted to an introduction of the fundamental theorem for zero-sum two-person games, which is known as the minimax theorem. A finite zero-sum two-person game is described by a triplet (S, T, u): S is a finite set $\{s_1, s_2, \ldots, s_m\}$ of pure strategies of the first player; T is a finite set $\{t_1, t_2, \ldots, t_n\}$ of pure strategies of the second player; and u is a real-valued function defined on the product set $S \times T$ of S and T. The function u represents the payoff of the first player and $-u$ represents that of the second player. A mixed strategy of the first player is a probability distribution on the set S of his pure strategies, and hence the set of mixed strategies is the simplex $\Delta_S = \{\lambda \in R^m : \lambda_i \geq 0, \sum_{i=1}^m \lambda_i = 1\}$ in R^m. Similarly the set Δ_T of mixed strategies of the second player is the simplex $\{\mu \in R^n : \mu_j \geq 0, \sum_{j=1}^n \mu_j = 1\}$ in R^n. We extend the payoff function u to $\widehat{u} : \Delta_S \times \Delta_T \to R$ by

$$\widehat{u}(\lambda, \mu) = \sum_{i=1}^{m} \sum_{j=1}^{n} \lambda_i \mu_j u(s_i, t_j)$$

identifying the pure strategy s_i and t_j with e_i^m and e_j^n, where e_i^m is the m-vector whose ith component is 1 and the other components are all 0. For a zero-sum two-person game $G = (S, T, u)$, the triplet $(\Delta_S, \Delta_T, \widehat{u})$ is called the mixed extension of G, and denoted by $\widehat{G}$. The minimax theorem asserts that the mixed extension of any finite zero-sum two-person game has an equilibrium and the value of the game is uniquely determined (cf. [7]).

Theorem 4. *Let $G = (S, T, u)$ be a zero-sum two-person game and $\widehat{G} = (\Delta_S, \Delta_T, \widehat{u})$ be the mixed extension of G. Then we have the minimax equation*

$$\max_{\lambda \in \Delta_S} \min_{\mu \in \Delta_T} \widehat{u}(\lambda, \mu) = \min_{\mu \in \Delta_T} \max_{\lambda \in \Delta_S} \widehat{u}(\lambda, \mu).$$

Since the function $\mu \mapsto \widehat{u}(\lambda, \mu)$ is linear for each λ, $\min_{\mu \in \Delta_T} \widehat{u}(\lambda, \mu)$ is attained at an extreme point of Δ_T. Thus, $\min_{\mu \in \Delta_T} \widehat{u}(\lambda, \mu)$ is equal to $\min_{t \in T} \sum_{i=1}^m \lambda_i u(s_i, t)$. Similarly we have the equality of $\max_{\lambda \in \Delta_S} \widehat{u}(\lambda, \mu)$ and $\max_{s \in S} \sum_{j=1}^n \mu_j u(s, t_j)$. Therefore, the minimax equation in Theorem 4 reduces to

$$\max_{\lambda \in \Delta_S} \min_{t \in T} \sum_{i=1}^{m} \lambda_i u(s_i, t) = \min_{\mu \in \Delta_T} \max_{s \in S} \sum_{j=1}^{n} \mu_j u(s, t_j).$$

The common value of the maximin and minimax values is called the *value* of the mixed extension $\widehat{G}$ and is denoted by $v(\widehat{G})$.

3. General Lorenz dominance and zero-sum two-person games

Let x and y be any two elements of R^n. We define a zero-sum two-person game from x and y, and specify a necessary and sufficient condition for x to be generally Lorenz dominated by y in terms of the value of the game. We need some lemmas to accomplish our purpose. We denote by $\langle \cdot, \cdot \rangle$ the standard Euclidean inner product of R^n, that is, $\langle \lambda, x \rangle = \sum_{i=1}^n \lambda_i x_i$ for any elements λ and x of R^n. For an element x of R^n, x^* and x_* denote the increasing and decreasing rearrangements, respectively.

Lemma 5. *Let λ and x be elements of R^n. Then we have*

$$\langle \lambda_*, x^* \rangle \leq \langle \lambda, x \rangle \leq \langle \lambda^*, x^* \rangle.$$

Lemma 5 is found in Hardy et al. [2].

Lemma 6. *Let x, y and λ be elements of R^n satisfying*

$$\lambda_1 \geq \lambda_2 \geq \cdots \geq \lambda_n \geq 0, \quad \text{and} \quad \sum_{i=1}^k x_i \leq \sum_{i=1}^k y_i, \quad k = 1, 2, \ldots, n.$$

Then we have $\langle \lambda, x \rangle \leq \langle \lambda, y \rangle$.

Proof. Let $\xi_k = \sum_{i=1}^k x_i$ and $\eta_k = \sum_{i=1}^k y_i$ for $k = 1, 2, \ldots, n$. Then we have

$$\begin{aligned}
\langle \lambda, x \rangle &= \lambda_1 x_1 + \lambda_2 x_2 + \cdots + \lambda_n x_n \\
&= \lambda_1 \xi_1 + \lambda_2(\xi_2 - \xi_1) + \cdots + \lambda_n(\xi_n - \xi_{n-1}) \\
&= (\lambda_1 - \lambda_2)\xi_1 + (\lambda_2 - \lambda_3)\xi_2 + \cdots + (\lambda_{n-1} - \lambda_n)\xi_{n-1} + \lambda_n \xi_n \\
&\leq (\lambda_1 - \lambda_2)\eta_1 + (\lambda_2 - \lambda_3)\eta_2 + \cdots + (\lambda_{n-1} - \lambda_n)\eta_{n-1} + \lambda_n \eta_n \\
&= \langle \lambda, y \rangle.
\end{aligned}$$

□

Let x and y be two fixed elements of R^n. We define a zero-sum two-person game $G_{x,y}$ as follows: the strategy set of the first player is $N = \{1, 2, \ldots, n\}$. The first player chooses a coordinate or a position of the n-vector as his strategy. The strategy set of the second player is the set Π of all permutations of N. The second player chooses a permutation of N or a rearrangement of the n-vector as his strategy. Finally the payoff function $u_{x,y} : N \times \Pi \to R$ of the first player is defined by

$$u_{x,y}(i, \pi) = (\pi x - y)_i, \quad (i, \pi) \in N \times \Pi.$$

The setting of the game $G_{x,y} = (N, \Pi, u_{x,y})$ is inspired by the arguments in [3] and [4].

The zero-sum two-person game $G_{x,y}$ has the mixed extension $\widehat{G}_{x,y} = (\Delta_N, \Delta_\Pi, \widehat{u}_{x,y})$ as stated in the previous section, and the minimax equation holds and the value $v(\widehat{G}_{x,y})$ of the mixed extension $\widehat{G}_{x,y}$ is uniquely determined. Moreover, according to Theorem 1, we can regard the simplex Δ_Π as the set of all doubly stochastic n-matrices because an element $\sum_{\pi\in\Pi}\mu_\pi\pi$ of Δ_Π is equal to the doubly stochastic matrix $\sum_{\pi\in\Pi}\mu_\pi P_\pi$ regarded as the operator $x \mapsto x(\sum_{\pi\in\Pi}\mu_\pi P_\pi)$ on R^n, where P_π is the permutation matrix corresponding to π. Consequently, we have the equations

$$v(\widehat{G}_{x,y}) = \max_{\lambda\in\Delta_N}\min_{\pi\in\Pi}\langle\lambda, \pi x - y\rangle = \min_{D\in\Delta_\Pi}\max_{i\in N}(xD - y)_i.$$

Now we reach the main result of this section.

Theorem 7. *For any two elements x and y of R^n, $x \precsim_{GL} y$ if and only if $v(\widehat{G}_{x,y}) \leq 0$.*

Proof. At first, we assume that both x and y belong to R^n_{++}. Suppose that $x \precsim_{GL} y$. Let λ be any element of Δ_N. Then we have the following series of inequalities in virtue of Lemmas 5 and 6:

$$\begin{aligned}\langle\lambda, y\rangle &\geq \langle\lambda_*, y^*\rangle\\ &\geq \langle\lambda_*, x^*\rangle\\ &= \langle\pi'\lambda, \pi''x\rangle\\ &= \langle\lambda, \pi'^{-1}(\pi''x)\rangle,\end{aligned}$$

where π' and π'' are some permutations of N. Therefore, putting $\pi = \pi'^{-1}\circ\pi'' \in \Pi$, we have $\langle\lambda, \pi x - y\rangle \leq 0$, and hence $\min_{\pi\in\Pi}\langle\lambda, \pi x - y\rangle \leq 0$. Since $\lambda \in \Delta_N$ is arbitrary, we have

$$v(\widehat{G}_{x,y}) = \max_{\lambda\in\Delta_N}\min_{\pi\in\Pi}\langle\lambda, \pi x - y\rangle \leq 0.$$

Conversely suppose that $v(\widehat{G}_{x,y}) \leq 0$. Then we have

$$\min_{D\in\Delta_\Pi}\max_{i\in N}(xD - y)_i \leq 0,$$

and hence there is a doubly stochastic matrix D such that $(xD)_i \leq y_i$ for $i = 1, 2, \ldots, n$. Since we have assumed that x is in R^n_{++}, $(xD)_i > 0$ for $i = 1, 2, \ldots, n$. Put $\alpha_i = y_i/(xD)_i \geq 1$ for $i = 1, 2, \ldots, n$ and define an n-square matrix P by $P = (\alpha_1 d_1, \alpha_2 d_2, \ldots, \alpha_n d_n)$, where d_i denotes the i-th column of D. Then it is obvious that P is superstochastic and $xP = y$. Therefore, we have $x \precsim_{GL} y$ in virtue of Theorem 3.

We have completed the proof in case both x and y belong to R^n_{++}. Take two elements x and y of R^n generally, and find a sufficiently large $\alpha > 0$ such that

$x+\alpha e$, $y+\alpha e \in R^n_{++}$, where e denotes the vector with all components 1. Since $x \precsim_{GL} y$ if and only if $x+\alpha e \precsim_{GL} y+\alpha e$ and $v(\widehat{G}_{x,y}) = v(\widehat{G}_{x+\alpha e,y+\alpha e})$, we have the desired result and the proof is complete. □

Corollary 8. *For any two elements x and y of R^n, we have $x \precsim_L y$ if and only if $v(\widehat{G}_{x,y}) = 0$ and $\sum_{i=1}^n x_i = \sum_{i=1}^n y_i$. In particular, if $x^* = y^*$, then $v(\widehat{G}_{x,y}) = 0$.*

Proof. Suppose that $x \precsim_L y$. We have $v(\widehat{G}_{x,y}) \le 0$ by Theorem 7. If $v(\widehat{G}_{x,y}) < 0$, then we have $\min_{D\in\Delta_\Pi} \max_{i\in N}(xD - y)_i < 0$, that is, there is a doubly stochastic matrix D such that $(xD-y)_i < 0$ for $i = 1, 2, \ldots, n$. Thus we have $\sum_{i=1}^n x_i = \sum_{i=1}^n (xD)_i < \sum_{i=1}^n y_i$, but this contradicts $x \precsim_L y$.

Conversely suppose that $v(\widehat{G}_{x,y}) = 0$ and $\sum_{i=1}^n x_i = \sum_{i=1}^n y_i$. By the same argument to the above, there is a doubly stochastic matrix D such that $(xD)_i \le y_i$ for $i = 1, 2, \ldots, n$. Since $\sum_{i=1}^n (xD)_i = \sum_{i=1}^n x_i = \sum_{i=1}^n y_i$, we have $(xD)_i = y_i$ for $i = 1, 2, \ldots, n$, that is, $xD = y$, and hence $x \precsim_L y$ by Theorem 2.

The last assertion is obvious. □

The assumption $\sum_{i=1}^n x_i = \sum_{i=1}^n y_i$ in Corollary 8 is not redundant. Consider, for example, $x = (1, 1)$ and $y = (1, 2)$ in R^2.

Corollary 9. *For any two elements x and y of R^n such that $x^* \ne y^*$, we have $x \precsim_{GL} y$ if and only if $v(\widehat{G}_{x,y}) = 0 < v(\widehat{G}_{y,x})$.*

Proof. It is obvious by virtue of Theorem 7 if we note that $x^* = y^*$ if and only if $x \precsim_{GL} y$ and $y \precsim_{GL} x$. □

4. Distance and binary relation derived from values of games

We have studied the relationship between generalized Lorenz dominance and zero-sum two-person games. Define a real-valued function δ on $R^n \times R^n$ by

$$\delta(x, y) = v(\widehat{G}_{x,y}).$$

We define a complete binary relation $\precsim$ on R^n by

$$x \precsim y \quad \text{if} \quad \delta(x, y) \le \delta(y, x)$$

for any x and y in R^n. This relation is not transitive as shown in the following example and we cannot call the relation an "order", but it is closely related to the generalized Lorentz dominance shown as in Proposition 12.

Example 10. Consider three elements $x = (0, 4, 5, 5)$, $y = (1.1, 2, 3, 4)$, and $z = (0.7, 1.5, 4, 6)$ of R^4. It is easily seen that $x \precsim y$ and $y \precsim z$, but $x \not\precsim z$.

At first, we prove that the function δ satisfies the triangle inequality.

Proposition 11. *For any elements x, y, and z of R^n, we have*

$$\delta(x, z) \leq \delta(x, y) + \delta(y, z).$$

Proof. Since $\delta(x, z) = \max_{\lambda \in \Delta_N} \min_{\pi \in \Pi} \langle \lambda, \pi x - z \rangle$, there is $\lambda' \in \Delta_N$ such that $\delta(x, z) = \min_{\pi \in \Pi} \langle \lambda', \pi x - z \rangle$. Take an arbitrary permutation π' in Π and fix it. Then we have

$$\begin{aligned}
\delta(x, z) &= \min_{\pi \in \Pi} \langle \lambda', \pi x - \pi' y + \pi' y - z \rangle \\
&= \min_{\pi \in \Pi} \langle \lambda', \pi x - \pi' y \rangle + \langle \lambda', \pi' y - z \rangle \\
&= \min_{\pi \in \Pi} \langle \pi'^{-1} \lambda', (\pi'^{-1} \circ \pi) x - y \rangle + \langle \lambda', \pi' y - z \rangle \\
&= \min_{\pi \in \Pi} \langle \pi'^{-1} \lambda', \pi x - y \rangle + \langle \lambda', \pi' y - z \rangle \\
&\leq \max_{\lambda \in \Delta_N} \min_{\pi \in \Pi} \langle \lambda, \pi x - y \rangle + \langle \lambda', \pi' y - z \rangle \\
&= \delta(x, y) + \langle \lambda', \pi' y - z \rangle.
\end{aligned}$$

Since $\pi' \in \Pi$ is arbitrary, we have

$$\begin{aligned}
\delta(x, z) - \delta(x, y) &\leq \min_{\pi \in \Pi} \langle \lambda', \pi y - z \rangle \\
&\leq \max_{\lambda \in \Delta_N} \min_{\pi \in \Pi} \langle \lambda, \pi y - z \rangle \\
&= \delta(y, z)
\end{aligned}$$

Therefore, we have $\delta(x, z) \leq \delta(x, y) + \delta(y, z)$. □

Proposition 12. *Let x, y and z be three elements of R^n.*

1. *If $x \precsim_{GL} y$, then $x \precsim y$;*
2. *If ($x \precsim_{GL} y$ and $y \precsim z$) or ($x \precsim y$ and $y \precsim_{GL} z$), then $x \precsim z$.*

Proof. 1. It is obvious by virtue of Corollaries 8 and 9.
2. Suppose that $x \precsim_{GL} y$ and $y \precsim z$. We have the following inequalities

$$\begin{aligned}
\delta(x, z) &\leq \delta(x, y) + \delta(y, z) \\
&\leq \delta(x, y) + \delta(z, y) \\
&\leq \delta(x, y) + \delta(z, x) + \delta(x, y) \\
&\leq \delta(z, x) + 2\delta(x, y) \\
&\leq \delta(z, x).
\end{aligned}$$

Thus we have $x \precsim z$. The other assertion is proved similarly.

Next, we define a distance on R^n in terms of the function δ and investigate fundamental properties of the distance. Define a real-valued function d on $R^n \times R^n$ by

$$d(x, y) = \delta(x, y) \vee \delta(y, x).$$

Theorem 13 asserts that d is almost a distance and compatible with generalized Lorenz dominance.

Theorem 13. *For any elements x, y and z of R^n, the function d has the following properties:*

1. $d(x, y) \geq 0$ *and* $d(x, y) = 0$ *if and only if* $\pi x = y$ *for some permutation* π *of* N;
2. $d(x, y) = d(y, x)$;
3. $d(x, z) \leq d(x, y) + d(y, z)$;
4. *If* $x \precsim_{GL} y \precsim_{GL} z$, *then*

$$d(x, y) \leq d(x, z) \quad \text{and} \quad d(y, z) \leq d(x, z).$$

Proof. 1. It is obvious by virtue of Corollary 9.
2. It is obvious from the definition of d.
3. It is a direct consequence of Proposition 11.
4. The following sequence of inequalities shows the first conclusion:

$$d(x, y) = \delta(y, x) \leq \delta(y, z) + \delta(z, x) \leq \delta(z, x) = d(x, z).$$

Similarly we have the inequality $d(y, z) \leq d(x, z)$. □

The following proposition states fundamental properties of the distance d.

Proposition 14. *For any element x and y of R^n and a real number α, we have*

1. $d(x + \alpha e, y + \alpha e) = d(x, y)$;
2. $d(\alpha x, \alpha y) = \alpha d(x, y)$ *if* $\alpha \geq 0$;
3. $d(\pi x, \pi' y) = d(x, y)$ *for any permutations* π *and* π' *of* Π.

Proof. The proof of the first and second statements are obvious if we observe that the corresponding properties hold for the function δ. We can easily verify the last statement observing the definition of d. □

5. Distances between typical income distributions

We calculate several distances between typical income distributions. We prepare some lemmas in order to advance the calculations. Define a subset M of R^n by $M = \{\lambda \in R^n : \lambda_1 \geq \lambda_2 \geq \cdots \geq \lambda_n \geq 0\}$.

Lemma 15. *For any two elements x and y of R^n, we have*

$$\delta(x, y) = \max_{\lambda \in M \cap \Delta_N} \langle \lambda, x^* - y^* \rangle.$$

Proof. Put $\beta = \max_{\lambda \in M \cap \Delta_N} \langle \lambda, x^* - y^* \rangle$. Firstly we show $\beta \leq \delta(x, y)$. Take $\lambda' \in M \cap \Delta_N$ such that $\beta = \langle \lambda', x^* - y^* \rangle = \langle \lambda', x^* \rangle - \langle \lambda', y^* \rangle$. Take $\pi' \in \Pi$ such that $\pi' y^* = y$, then we have $\beta = \langle \lambda', x^* \rangle - \langle \pi'\lambda', y \rangle$. Since $\langle \lambda', \pi x \rangle \geq \langle \lambda', x^* \rangle$ for all $\pi \in \Pi$ by Lemma 5, we have

$$\begin{aligned} \beta &\leq \langle \lambda', \pi x \rangle - \langle \pi'\lambda', y \rangle \\ &= \langle \pi'\lambda', (\pi' \circ \pi) x \rangle - \langle \pi'\lambda', y \rangle \\ &= \langle \pi'\lambda', (\pi' \circ \pi) x - y \rangle. \end{aligned}$$

Thus we have $\beta \leq \min_{\pi \in \Pi} \langle \pi'\lambda', (\pi' \circ \pi) x - y \rangle$ because π is arbitrary, and hence $\beta \leq \min_{\pi \in \Pi} \langle \pi'\lambda', \pi x - y \rangle$. Since $\pi'\lambda' \in \Delta_N$, we have

$$\beta \leq \max_{\lambda \in \Delta_N} \min_{\pi \in \Pi} \langle \lambda, \pi x - y \rangle = \delta(x, y).$$

Next we show the reverse inequality $\delta(x, y) \leq \beta$. Take $\lambda' \in \Delta_N$ such that $\delta(x, y) = \min_{\pi \in \Pi} \langle \lambda', \pi x - y \rangle = \min_{\pi \in \Pi} \langle \lambda', \pi x \rangle - \langle \lambda', y \rangle$. Take $\pi' \in \Pi$ such that $\pi'\lambda'$ belongs to M, then $\langle \pi'\lambda', y^* \rangle \leq \langle \lambda', y \rangle$ by Lemma 5, and hence we have $\delta(x, y) \leq \min_{\pi \in \Pi} \langle \lambda', \pi x \rangle - \langle \pi'\lambda', y^* \rangle$. Let $\pi'' \in \Pi$ be the permutation such that $\pi'' x^* = x$. Then we have the following series of inequalities:

$$\begin{aligned} \delta(x, y) &\leq \min_{\pi \in \Pi} \langle \lambda', (\pi \circ \pi'') x^* \rangle - \langle \pi'\lambda', y^* \rangle \\ &= \min_{\pi \in \Pi} \langle (\pi \circ \pi'')^{-1} \lambda', x^* \rangle - \langle \pi'\lambda', y^* \rangle \\ &\leq \langle \pi'\lambda', x^* \rangle - \langle \pi'\lambda', y^* \rangle \\ &= \langle \pi'\lambda', x^* - y^* \rangle \\ &\leq \max_{\lambda \in M \cap \Delta_N} \langle \lambda, x^* - y^* \rangle \\ &= \beta. \end{aligned}$$

□

Lemma 16. *If $\lambda \in M \cap \Delta_N$ and $0 \leq x_1 \leq x_2 \leq \cdots \leq x_n$, then we have*

$$\sum_{i=1}^{k} \lambda_i x_i \leq \frac{1}{k} \sum_{i=1}^{k} x_i, \quad k = 1, 2, \ldots, n.$$

Proof. Fix any integer k with $1 \leq k \leq n$. If $\lambda_k > 1/k$, then it follows $\sum_{i=1}^{k} \lambda_i > 1$, which contradicts our hypothesis, and hence $\lambda_k \leq 1/k$. Let i_0 be the minimum index such that $\lambda_i \leq 1/k$. Then we have $1 \leq i_0 \leq k$. If $i_0 = 1$, then $1/k \geq \lambda_1 \geq \cdots \geq \lambda_k$, and hence we have the conclusion $\sum_{i=1}^{k} \lambda_i x_i \leq (\sum_{i=1}^{k} x_i)/k$. Thus we assume that $1 < i_0 \leq k$ hereafter. Then $\lambda_i > 1/k$ for $i = 1, \ldots, i_0 - 1$ and $\lambda_i \leq 1/k$ for $i = i_0, \ldots, k$, and hence we have $1/k - \lambda_i < 0$ for $i = 1, \ldots, i_0 - 1$ and $1/k - \lambda_i \geq 0$ for $i = i_0, \ldots, k$. Thus we have

$$\begin{aligned} \frac{1}{k}\sum_{i=1}^{k} x_i - \sum_{i=1}^{k} \lambda_i x_i &= \sum_{i=1}^{i_0-1}\left(\frac{1}{k} - \lambda_i\right) x_i + \sum_{i=i_0}^{k}\left(\frac{1}{k} - \lambda_i\right) x_i \\ &\geq x_{i_0-1}\sum_{i=1}^{i_0-1}\left(\frac{1}{k} - \lambda_i\right) + x_{i_0}\sum_{i=i_0}^{k}\left(\frac{1}{k} - \lambda_i\right). \end{aligned}$$

On the other hand, since

$$\sum_{i=1}^{i_0-1}\left(\frac{1}{k} - \lambda_i\right) + \sum_{i=i_0}^{k}\left(\frac{1}{k} - \lambda_i\right) = \sum_{i=1}^{k}\left(\frac{1}{k} - \lambda_i\right) = 1 - \sum_{i=1}^{k}\lambda_i \geq 0,$$

we have

$$\sum_{i=1}^{i_0-1}\left(\frac{1}{k} - \lambda_i\right) \geq -\sum_{i=i_0}^{k}\left(\frac{1}{k} - \lambda_i\right).$$

Therefore, we have

$$\begin{aligned} \frac{1}{k}\sum_{i=1}^{k} x_i - \sum_{i=1}^{k} \lambda_i x_i &\geq -x_{i_0-1}\sum_{i=i_0}^{k}\left(\frac{1}{k} - \lambda_i\right) + x_{i_0}\sum_{i=i_0}^{k}\left(\frac{1}{k} - \lambda_i\right) \\ &= \left(x_{i_0} - x_{i_0-1}\right)\sum_{i=i_0}^{k}\left(\frac{1}{k} - \lambda_i\right) \geq 0. \end{aligned}$$

□

We denote by e the element of R^n whose components are all 1, and by e_n the element of R^n whose components are all 0 except for the last component whose value is 1. Then e and ne_n has nonnegative components and the total sums of the components are n. We denote by F_n the set of all elements having such properties, that is, $F_n = \{x \in R^n : x_i \geq 0, i = 1, 2, \ldots, n \text{ and } \sum_{i=1}^{n} x_i = n\}$. We use the similar notation F_r even if the subscript r is not necessarily equal to n, that is, for any $r \geq 0$, $F_r = \{x \in R^n : x_i \geq 0, i = 1, 2, \ldots, n \text{ and } \sum_{i=1}^{n} x_i = r\}$. The following proposition asserts that distance between any elements in F_n is at most 1 and distance 1 is achieved by pairs of these extreme elements with respect to Lorenz dominance.

Proposition 17. 1. *$d(x, y) \leq 1$ for any $x, y \in F_n$.*

2. *$d(ne_n, x) = \dfrac{1}{n-1}(n - \max_{i \in N} x_i)$ for any $x \in F_n$; therefore, for $x \in F_n$, $d(ne_n, x) = 1$ if and only if $x = e$.*
3. *$d(e, x) = 1 - \min_{i \in N} x_i$ for any $x \in F_n$; therefore, for $x \in F_n$, $d(e, x) = 1$ if and only if $\min_{i \in N} x_i = 0$.*

Proof. 1. Suppose $x, y \in F_n$. Note that $\delta(x, y) = \min_{D \in \Delta_\Pi} \max_{i \in N}(xD - y)_i$. It is easily seen that $x \precsim_L e$, and hence there is a doubly stochastic matrix D such that $xD = e$ by Theorem 2. Thus we have $\delta(x, y) \leq \max_{i \in N}(e - y)_i$. Since $(e - y)_i \leq 1$ for $i = 1, 2, \ldots, n$, we have $\delta(x, y) \leq 1$. Exchanging the roles of x and y, we also have $\delta(y, x) \leq 1$. Therefore, we have $d(x, y) \leq 1$.

2. Note that $d(ne_n, x) = \delta(x, ne_n)$ because $ne_n \precsim_L x$. Then we have a series of equations:

$$\begin{aligned}\delta(x, ne_n) &= \max_{\lambda \in M \cap \Delta_N} \langle \lambda, x^* - ne_n \rangle \\ &= \max_{\substack{\lambda \in M \cap \Delta_N \\ \lambda_n = 0}} \sum_{i=1}^{n-1} \lambda_i x_i^* \\ &= \frac{1}{n-1} \sum_{i=1}^{n-1} x_i^* \\ &= \frac{1}{n-1}\left(n - \max_{i \in N} x_i\right).\end{aligned}$$

The first and third equations hold in virtue of Lemmas 15 and 16, respectively.

3. By Lemma 15, we have

$$\begin{aligned}d(e, x) &= \delta(e, x) \\ &= \max_{\lambda \in D \cap \Delta_N} \langle \lambda, e - x^* \rangle \\ &= \max_{\lambda \in D \cap \Delta_N} \sum_{i=1}^{n} \lambda_i (1 - x_i^*).\end{aligned}$$

Because $1 - x_1^* \geq 1 - x_2^* \geq \cdots \geq 1 - x_n^*$, the last maximum is attained at $\lambda = (1, 0, \ldots, 0)$, and we have $d(e, x) = 1 - x_1^* = 1 - \min_{i \in N} x_i$. □

Proposition 20 below refines the first assertion of Proposition 17. We first show two lemmas used in proving the proposition. The proof of the first lemma is similar to that of the first statement of Proposition 17 and we omit it.

Lemma 18. *For any elements x and y of F_r, we have $d(x, y) \leq r/n$.*

Let Z_n be the set of all elements of F_n that have at least one element of zero, that is, $Z_n = \{x \in F_n : \min_{i \in N} x_i = 0\}$.

Lemma 19. *If $x \notin \{e\} \cup Z_n$, then $d(x, y) < 1$ for all $y \in F_n$.*

Proof. Suppose $y \notin Z_n$. Since $x \precsim_L e$, there is a doubly stochastic matrix D such that $e = xD$. Thus, we have

$$\delta(x, y) = \min_{D \in \Delta_\Pi} \max_{i \in N} (xD - y)_i \leq \max_{i \in N} (e - y)_i < 1.$$

Similarly we have $\delta(y, x) < 1$, and hence $d(x, y) < 1$.

Suppose $y \in Z_n$. We can show $\delta(y, x) < 1$ with the same reason as above, and we only need show $\delta(x, y) < 1$. Note that $0 < x_1^* < 1$ and $y_1^* = 0$. Take any element λ in $M \cap \Delta_N$ and put $\alpha = \sum_{i=1}^n \lambda_i (x_i^* - y_i^*)$. If $\lambda_1 = 1$, then we have $\alpha = x_1^* < 1$. If $\lambda_1 = 1/n$, then $\lambda_2 = \cdots = \lambda_n = 1/n$, and hence $\alpha = 0$. If $1/n < \lambda_1 < 1$, then put $\mu = \sum_{i=2}^n \lambda_i = 1 - \lambda_1 > 0$. By virtue of Lemma 18, we have

$$\frac{n - x_1^*}{n - 1} \geq \sum_{i=2}^n \frac{\lambda_i}{\mu} \left(x_i^* - \frac{n - x_1^*}{n} y_i^* \right) \geq \sum_{i=2}^n \frac{\lambda_i}{\mu} (x_i^* - y_i^*),$$

and hence

$$\sum_{i=2}^n \lambda_i (x_i^* - y_i^*) \leq \frac{\mu(n - x_1^*)}{n - 1}.$$

Thus, we have

$$\begin{aligned} \alpha &< \lambda_1 x_1^* + (1 - \lambda_1) \frac{n - x_1^*}{n - 1} \\ &= \lambda_1 \frac{n}{n - 1} (x_1^* - 1) + \frac{n - x_1^*}{n - 1} \\ &< \frac{1}{n} \frac{n}{n - 1} (x_1^* - 1) + \frac{n - x_1^*}{n - 1} \\ &= 1. \end{aligned}$$

Therefore, we have $\alpha < 1$ for all $\lambda \in M \cap \Delta_N$, and hence $\delta(x, y) < 1$. □

Proposition 20. *For any two elements x and y of F_n, $d(x, y) = 1$ if and only if $(x, y) \in (\{e\} \times Z_n) \cup (Z_n \times \{e\})$.*

Proof. The "if" part is direct consequence of the third statement of Proposition 17, and hence we proceed to the proof of the "only if" part.

Suppose that $d(x, y) = 1$. Then we have $x = e$ or $x \in Z_n$ by virtue of Lemma 19. If $x = e$ then we have $y \in Z_n$ by the third statement of Proposition 17, and hence $(x, y) \in \{e\} \times Z_n$. Thus we proceed to the case $x \in Z_n$. If $y \notin \{e\} \cup Z_n$, then we have $d(x, y) < 1$ by virtue of Lemma 19 again. If $y \in Z_n$, then take any element λ in $M \cap \Delta_N$. If $\lambda_1 = 1/n$, then $\lambda_2 = \cdots = \lambda_n = 1/n$, and hence

$$\sum_{i=1}^{n} \lambda_i (x_i^* - y_i^*) = \frac{1}{n} \left(\sum_{i=1}^{n} x_i^* - \sum_{i=1}^{n} y_i^* \right) = 0.$$

If $\lambda_1 > 1/n$, then we put $\mu = \sum_{i=2}^{n} \lambda_i < (n-1)/n$ and have

$$\begin{aligned} \sum_{i=1}^{n} \lambda_i (x_i^* - y_i^*) &= \sum_{i=2}^{n} \lambda_i (x_i^* - y_i^*) \\ &= \mu \sum_{i=2}^{n} \frac{\lambda_i}{\mu} (x_i^* - y_i^*) \\ &\leq \mu \frac{n}{n-1} \\ &< 1, \end{aligned}$$

by virtue of Lemma 18. Thus, we have $\delta(x, y) < 1$, and hence $d(x, y) < 1$ with the symmetry of x and y. Therefore, y should be equal to e and we have $(x, y) \in Z_n \times \{e\}$. □

Now consider line segments in R^n. For two different elements x and y of R^n, the line segment $[x, y]$ joining x and y is usually defined by

$$[x, y] = \{(1-s)x + sy : 0 \leq s \leq 1\}$$

by virtue of the linear structure of R^n. The following characterization of $[x, y]$ by the Euclidean distance d_E, where $d_E(x, y) = \sqrt{\langle x - y, x - y \rangle}$, is easily proved:

$$z \in [x, y] \text{ if and only if } d_E(x, z) + d_E(z, y) = d_E(x, y).$$

Stimulated by this characterization, we define the *line segment* L_n in F_n joining ne_n and e by

$$L_n = \{x \in F_n : d(ne_n, x) + d(x, e) = d(ne_n, e)(= 1)\}$$

in terms of our distance d. The following proposition characterizes the set L_n.

Proposition 21. *Let L_n be the line segment in F_n joining ne_n and e defined above, and let $x \in F_n$. Then, $x \in L_n$ if and only if x has $(n-1)$ components whose values are the same and the common value is less than or equal to the value of the remaining component.*

Proof. In case $n = 2$, it follows that $F_2 = L_2$ and we have nothing to prove, so we assume that $n \geq 3$. By virtue of Proposition 17, we have

$$\begin{aligned} d(ne_n, x) + d(x, e) &= \frac{1}{n-1}\left(n - \max_{i \in N} x_i\right) + 1 - \min_{i \in N} x_i \\ &= 1 + \frac{1}{n-1}\left(n - \max_{i \in N} x_i - (n-1)\min_{i \in N} x_i\right) \end{aligned}$$

Thus note that $x \in L_n$ if and only if x satisfies the equation $\max_{i \in N} x_i + (n-1)\min_{i \in N} x_i = n$.

Suppose that x satisfies the equation $\max_{i \in N} x_i - (n-1)\min_{i \in N} x_i = n$. Take different two indices i_1 and i_2 such that $x_{i_1} = \min_{i \in N} x_i$ and $x_{i_2} = \max_{i \in N} x_i$. Since $x_{i_2} + (n-1)x_{i_1} = n = \sum_{i=1}^n x_i$, we have $\sum_{i \neq i_1, i_2}(x_i - x_{i_1}) = 0$, and hence $x_i = x_{i_1}$ for $i \neq i_2$. Thus we have $x_i = \min_{i \in N} x_i \leq x_{i_2}$ for $i \neq i_2$.

Conversely suppose that there is an index i_0 such that $x_{i_0} \geq x_i$ for all $i \neq i_0$ and there is α such that $x_i = \alpha$ for all $i \neq i_0$. Then we have $\max_{i \in N} x_i + (n-1)\min_{i \in N} x_i = x_{i_0} + (n-1)\alpha = \sum_{i=1}^n x_i = n$. □

Takahashi [9] introduced an abstract convex structure in metric spaces and developed fixed point theory for nonexpansive mappings. Let (X, d) be a metric space and W be a mapping from $X \times X \times [0, 1]$ to X. A triple (X, d, W) is said to be a *convex metric space* if it follows that

$$d(u, W(x, y, \lambda)) \leq (1-\lambda)d(u, x) + \lambda d(u, y)$$

for $(x, y, \lambda) \in X \times X \times [0, 1]$ and $u \in X$.

Proposition 22. *Let L_n be the line segment in F_n joining ne_n and e defined above. Define a mapping $W : L_n \times L_n \times [0, 1] \to L_n$ by*

$$W(x, y, \lambda) = (1-\lambda)x^* + \lambda y^*.$$

Then (X, d, W) is a convex metric space.

Proof. For an element x of the line segment L_n, put $l(x) = \min_{i \in N} x_i$. Then it is easily seen that, for any two elements x and y of L_n, $l(x) \leq l(y)$ if and only if $x \precsim_L y$, and

$$d(x, y) = \frac{1}{n-1}|l(x) - l(y)|,$$

by virtue of Proposition 21. Moreover, we have $l(W(x, y, \lambda)) = (1-\lambda)l(x) + \lambda l(y)$. Observing these results, it is easily seen that the inequality

$$d(u, W(x, y, \lambda)) \leq (1-\lambda)d(u, x) + \lambda d(u, y)$$

holds for any $u, x, y \in L_n$ and $\lambda \in [0, 1]$. □

Next we calculate the distance between income distributions when some transfer takes place between adjacent two individuals with respect to income level, and the distance when the total wealth increases but the rate of the distribution is unaltered.

Proposition 23. *Let x be an element of F_n.*

1. *Suppose that $x_k^* < x_{k+1}^*$, and take $t > 0$ with $x_k^* + t \leq x_{k+1}^* - t$. Let $x' \in F_n$ be a distribution defined by $x_i' = x_i^*$ for i with $i \neq k$ and $i \neq k+1$, $x_k' = x_k^* + t$ and $x_{k+1}' = x_{k+1}^* - t$. Then we have*

$$d(x, x') = \frac{t}{k}.$$

2. *Take $r > 0$. Then we have*

$$d(x, (1+r)x) = r.$$

Proof. 1. We have $d(x, x') = d(x^*, x') = \delta(x', x^*) = \max_{\lambda \in M \cap \Delta_N} \langle \lambda, x' - x^* \rangle$ by 3 of Proposition 14 and Lemma 15. Since

$$x' - x^* = (0, \ldots, 0, t, -t, 0, \ldots, 0),$$

the λ's in $M \cap \Delta_N$ can be restricted to λ's such that $\lambda_{k+1} = \cdots = \lambda_n = 0$. Hence, by Lemma 16, $\max_{\lambda \in D \cap \Delta_N} \langle \lambda, x' - x^* \rangle = t/k$ and we have $d(x, x') = t/k$.

2. Note that $d(x, (1+r)x) = \delta((1+r)x, x) = \max_{\lambda \in M \cap \Delta_N} \langle \lambda, rx^* \rangle = r \max_{\lambda \in M \cap \Delta_N} \langle \lambda, x^* \rangle = r$. The second equation is due to Lemma 15 and the last equation is due to Lemma 16. □

According to Proposition 23, if we measure the reduction of inequality by our distance, then the reduction of inequality with transfer of t from $(k+1)$th ranked individual to kth ranked individual can be compensated by the increase of total wealth with the rate $r = t/k$ without changing the distribution ratio.

Acknowledgments The author would like to express his gratitude to Professor Jean-Michel Grandmont for his valuable comments on this paper he made during his visit to Keio University.

References

1. Birkhoff, G.: Tres Observasiones sobre el Álgebra Lineal. Univ. Nac. Tucumán Rev. Ser. A **5**, 147–151 (1946)
2. Hardy, G.H., Littlewood, J.E., Pólya, G.: Inequalities, 2nd edn. Cambridge Univ. Press, London (1952)
3. Komiya, H.: On infinite doubly substochastic matrices. Z. Wahrscheinlichkeistheorie verw. Gebiete **61**, 119–128 (1982)
4. Komiya, H.: Necessary and sufficient conditions for multivariate majorization. Linear Algebra **55**, 147–154 (1983)
5. Lorenz, M.O.: Methods of measuring concentration of wealth. J. Am. Stat. Assoc. **9**, 209–219 (1905)
6. Marshall, A.W., Olkin, I.: Inequalities: Theory of Majorization and its Applications. Academic Press, New York (1979)
7. von Neumann, J., Morgenstern, O.: Theory of Games and Economic Behavior, 2nd edn. Princeton Univ. Press, Princeton (1947)
8. Shorrocks, A.F.: Ranking income distributions. Economica **50**, 3–17 (1983)
9. Takahashi, W.: A Convexity in metric space and nonexpansive mappings, I. Kōdai Math. Sem. Rep. **22**, 142–149 (1970)

Adv. Math. Econ. 11, 95–104 (2008)

Advances in
MATHEMATICAL
ECONOMICS

On preference relations that admit smooth utility functions

Vladimir L. Levin*

Central Economics and Mathematics Institute of the Russian Academy of Sciences, Nakhimovskii Prospect 47, 117418 Moscow, Russia
(e-mail: vl_levin@cemi.rssi.ru)

Received: February 9, 2007
Revised: August 21, 2007

JEL classification: C65

Mathematics Subject Classification (2000): 91B16

Abstract. We prove the existence of smooth utility functions for a class of preferences (closed preorders) on a subset X in $\mathbb{R}^n$ which satisfies $X = X + \mathbb{R}^n_+$. This class of preferences is given by the condition that adding one and the same positive vector to each of two comparable alternatives cannot affect the preference relation between them. Moreover, some its subclass consisting of total preferences admits linear utility functions. Also, we prove the existence of universal smooth utilities for preferences depending on a parameter. Our approach relies on our earlier results on continuous utilities for closed (non-total) preorders on metrizable spaces along with a particular device that enable to pass from a continuous utility to a smooth one.

Key words: closed preorder, utility function, stability with respect to shifts in positive directions, smooth utility function, linear utility, universal utility theorem.

1. Introduction

This paper is concerned with preference relations admitting smooth utility functions on subsets of $\mathbb{R}^n$. Conditions for the existence of a smooth utility function based on manifold theory may be found in [13][1] for the case where the corresponding preference relation is a locally non-satiated closed total preorder $\preceq$ on an open subset X of $\mathbb{R}^n$. Unlike this, we do not assume the preorder to

* Supported in part by Russian Foundation for Basic Research (grant 07-01-00048) and by the Russian Leading Scientific School Support Programme (grant NSh-6417.2006.6).

[1] In this connection, see also [1,4,5].

be total (or locally non-satiated) and consider open or closed sets X satisfying $x \in X, z \in \mathbb{R}^n_+ \Rightarrow x + z \in X$. Our approach relies on our earlier results on continuous utilities for closed (non-total) preorders [8–10] combined with a particular device that enables us to pass from a continuous utility to a smooth one.[2] We show that if $\preceq$ is closed and stable with respect to shifts in positive directions, i.e. $x \preceq y \Rightarrow (x + z) \preceq (y + z)$ whenever $z \in \mathbb{R}^n_+$, then there exists a smooth utility function for $\preceq$ (Theorem 3.1). A condition imposed on preorder by this implication seems rather specific, however, in many cases, it proves to be natural and justified from the economic viewpoint. See, in that connection, [6, 14] and other papers on collective choice devoted to interpersonal comparability and utilitarian social welfare functions.[3] In Theorem 3.2 and Corollary 3.1, we consider some subclass of closed preorders that are total and stable with respect to shifts in positive directions, and establish their representability by linear utility functions.

Theorem 3.3 and Corollary 3.2 are concerned with the following question arising in various parts of mathematical economics. Given a closed preorder $\preceq_\omega$ depending on a parameter ω, when is there a jointly continuous real-valued function $u(\omega, x)$ such that, for every ω, $u(\omega, \cdot)$ is a smooth utility function for $\preceq_\omega$? We show that the answer is affirmative when all $\preceq_\omega$ are stable with respect to shifts in positive directions and the set $\{(\omega, x, y) : x \preceq_\omega y\}$ is closed in $\Omega \times X \times X$.

The main results are formulated in Sect. 3 and proved in Sect. 4. Section 2 contains basic notions and auxiliary results.

2. Preliminary notions and results

A *preorder* on a set X is a binary relation $\preceq$ which is reflexive ($x \preceq x$ for all $x \in X$) and transitive ($x, y, z \in X$, $x \preceq y$, $y \preceq z \Rightarrow x \preceq z$). Any preorder $\preceq$ can be treated as a preference relation: $x \preceq y$ means that y is preferred to x. Every preorder $\preceq$ determines two binary relations on X: the strict preference relation $\prec$,

$$x \prec y \iff x \preceq y \quad \text{but not } y \preceq x,$$

and the equivalence relation $\sim$,

$$x \sim y \iff x \preceq y \quad \text{and} \quad y \preceq x.$$

[2] The same device in a different context was used earlier when proving Theorems 3 and 4 in [12].

[3] In these papers, a similar translation-invariance assumption $x \preceq y \Rightarrow (x + z) \preceq (y + z)$ is considered for $X = \mathbb{R}^n$ and all $z \in \mathbb{R}^n$.

A real-valued function u on X is said to be an *utility function* for a preorder $\preceq$ if for any $x, y \in X$ two conditions are satisfied as follows:

$$x \preceq y \;\Rightarrow\; u(x) \leq u(y), \tag{1}$$

$$x \prec y \Rightarrow u(x) < u(y). \tag{2}$$

Clearly, it follows from (1) that $x \sim y \Rightarrow u(x) = u(y)$.

The pair of conditions (1) and (2) is equivalent to the single condition

$$x \preceq y \Leftrightarrow u(x) \leq u(y)$$

if and only if the preorder $\preceq$ is *total* that is any two elements of X, x and y, are comparable ($x \preceq y$ or $y \preceq x$). Moreover, if $\preceq$ is total, then $x \prec y \Leftrightarrow u(x) < u(y)$ and $x \sim y \Leftrightarrow u(x) = u(y)$, that is, the preference relation is completely determined by its utility function.

A preorder $\preceq$ on a topological space X is called *closed* if its graph,

$$gr(\preceq) := \{(x, y) : x \preceq y\},$$

is a closed subset in $X \times X$. One of fundamental results in the mathematical utility theory is a celebrated theorem due to Debreu [2,3], which asserts the existence of a continuous utility function for every total closed preorder on a separable metrizable space. Some generalizations of that theorem to the case where the preorder is not assumed to be total were obtained in [8–10].[4] In particular, the following theorems hold true.

Theorem 2.1. *Every closed preorder on a separable locally compact metrizable space admits a continuous utility function.*

Theorem 2.2. ([9,10]). *Suppose Ω and X are metrizable topological spaces, and X, in addition, is separable locally compact. Suppose also that for every $\omega \in \Omega$ a preorder $\preceq_\omega$ is given on X, and that the set $\{(\omega, x, y) : x \preceq_\omega y\}$ is closed in $\Omega \times X \times X$. Then there exists a continuous function $u : \Omega \times X \to [0, 1]$ such that, for every $\omega \in \Omega$, $u(\omega, \cdot)$ is a utility function for $\preceq_\omega$.*

Remark 2.1. It is easily seen that if all $\preceq_\omega$ are total, then the condition that the set $\{(\omega, x, y) : x \preceq_\omega y\}$ is closed in $\Omega \times X \times X$ is *necessary* (as well as sufficient) for the existence of a continuous function $u : \Omega \times X \to [0, 1]$ such that, for every $\omega \in \Omega$, $u(\omega, \cdot)$ is a utility function for $\preceq_\omega$.

We denote by $\mathcal{P}$ the set of all closed preorders on X. By identifying a preorder $\preceq \in \mathcal{P}$ with its graph in $X \times X$, we consider in $\mathcal{P}$ the topology t which is induced by the exponential topology on the space of closed subsets in the one-point compactification of $X \times X$ (for the definition and properties of the exponential topology, see [7]). Obviously $(\mathcal{P}, t)$ is a metrizable space. The next result is obtained by applying Theorem 2.2 to $\Omega = (\mathcal{P}, t)$.

[4] See also [11, Corollary 2.3].

Corollary 2.1. (Universal Utility Theorem [9, 10]). *There exists a continuous function $u : (\mathcal{P}, t) \times X \to [0, 1]$ such that $u(\preceq, \cdot)$ is a utility function for $\preceq$ whenever $\preceq \in \mathcal{P}$.*

3. Main results

In what follows, X is a subset in $\mathbb{R}^n$ which is open or closed and satisfies $X = X + \mathbb{R}^n_+$. Clearly, such a set is a domain or a closed domain.[5] Notice that generally X is not convex, and its boundary is not smooth. In particular, one can take $X = F + \mathbb{R}^n_+$ where F is a finite subset in $\mathbb{R}^n$.

For every positive integer r, we denote by $C^r(X)$ the class of all r times continuously differentiable real-valued functions on X: $u \in C^r(X)$ if and only if, for every $x = (x_1, \dots, x_n) \in int\, X$, all the partial derivatives

$$\frac{\partial^k u(x)}{\partial x_1^{k_1} \dots \partial x_n^{k_n}}, \qquad k_1 + \dots + k_n = k, \quad k \le r$$

exist and each of them is uniquely continued with preserving continuity to the whole of X. Also we will consider the class of infinitely differentiable functions on X, $C^\infty(X) = \bigcap_r C^r(X)$.

Theorem 3.1. *Suppose $\preceq$ is a closed preorder on X satisfying*

$$x, y \in X, \quad z \in \mathbb{R}^n_+, \quad x \preceq y \Rightarrow (x + z) \preceq (y + z), \tag{3}$$

then $\preceq$ admits an utility function $u \in C^\infty(X)$.

We shall need an additional assumption as follows:

(**A**) For every $y \in int\, X$ there exists $\varepsilon = \varepsilon(y) > 0$ such that the ball $B_\varepsilon(y) := \{x \in \mathbb{R}^n : \|x - y\| \le \varepsilon\}$ is contained in $int\, X$ and

$$x \preceq y \Leftrightarrow (x + z) \preceq (y + z)$$

whenever $z \in \mathbb{R}^n_+$, $x \in B_\varepsilon(y)$.

Theorem 3.2. *Suppose $\preceq$ is a closed total preorder on X satisfying (3) and* **A**, *the following statements are then equivalent: (a)for some $y^* \in int\, X$, $\{x \in B_{\varepsilon(y^*)}(y^*) : x \preceq y^*\} = cl\{x \in B_{\varepsilon(y^*)}(y^*) : x \prec y^*\}$; (b) there exists a vector $a \in \mathbb{R}^n$, $a \ne 0$, such that $u_1(x) = a \cdot x$ is a utility function for $\preceq$.*

The following *translation-invariance assumption* (cf. [14]) strengthens (3):

---

[5] A closed domain is a connected closed set coinciding with the closure of its interior.

(**TIA**) For every $x, y \in X$,

$$x \preceq y \Rightarrow (x+z) \preceq (y+z)$$

whenever $z \in \mathbb{R}^n$, $x+z, y+z \in X$.

Clearly, **TIA** may be equivalently rewritten as

$$x \preceq y \Leftrightarrow (x+z) \preceq (y+z)$$

whenever $z \in \mathbb{R}^n$, $x, y, x+z, y+z \in X$; therefore it implies both (3) and **A**. The next result is derived from Theorem 3.2.

Corollary 3.1. *Suppose $\preceq$ is a closed total preorder on X satisfying* **TIA**, *then it is represented by a linear utility function.*

For $X = \mathbb{R}^n$, a close result was obtained by Neuefeind and Trockel [14].[6]

Theorem 3.3. *Suppose Ω is a metrizable topological space, for every $\omega \in \Omega$ a preorder $\preceq_\omega$ is given on X satisfying (3), and the set $\{(\omega, x, y) : x \preceq_\omega y\}$ is closed in $\Omega \times X \times X$. Then there exists a continuous function $u : \Omega \times X \to [0, 1]$ such that, for every $\omega \in \Omega$, $u(\omega, \cdot)$ belongs to the class $C^\infty(X)$ and is a utility function for $\preceq_\omega$.*

Let $\mathcal{P}_1(X)$ be the set of all closed preorders on X satisfying (3) for $z \in \mathbb{R}^n_+$. Clearly, $\mathcal{P}_1(X)$ is a subset of $\mathcal{P}(X)$, and we consider it with the induced topology $t|_{\mathcal{P}_1(X)}$.

Corollary 3.2. *There is a continuous function $u : (\mathcal{P}_1(X), t|_{\mathcal{P}_1(X)}) \times X \to [0, 1]$ such that, for every $\preceq \in \mathcal{P}_1(X)$, $u(\preceq, \cdot)$ belongs to the class $C^\infty(X)$ and is an utility function for $\preceq$.*

4. Proofs

Suppose $\eta \in C^\infty(\mathbb{R}^n)$, $\int_{\mathbb{R}^n} \eta(z)\, dz_1 \dots dz_n = 1$, $\eta(z) > 0$ for $z \in int\, \mathbb{R}^n_- = \{z = (z_1, \dots, z_n) : z_1 < 0, \dots, z_n < 0\}$, and $\eta(z) = 0$ for $z \notin \mathbb{R}^n_-$. An example of such a function is as follows:

$$\eta(z) = \left(\int_0^\infty h(-t)\, dt\right)^{-n} \prod_{i=1}^n h(z_i), \quad z = (z_1, \dots, z_n),$$

where

$$h(t) = \begin{cases} 0 & \text{for } t \geq 0, \\ \exp(t - \frac{1}{t^2}) & \text{for } t < 0. \end{cases}$$

6 Although in [14] it is not explicitly supposed that a preference relation satisfying **TIA** and other hypotheses of [14, Proposition] is transitive or total (complete in other terminology), it proves, in fact, to be a closed total preorder.

Given a continuous function $v : X \to [0, 1]$, we extend it (without preserving continuity) to the whole of $\mathbb{R}^n$ by setting $v(x) = 0$ for $x \notin X$ and define a function $\Phi(v)$ on $\mathbb{R}^n$ to be the convolution of v and η: for every $x = (x_1, \dots, x_n) \in \mathbb{R}^n$,

$$\Phi(v)(x) := (v * \eta)(x) = \int_{\mathbb{R}^n} v(x - z)\eta(z)\, dz_1 \dots dz_n$$
$$= \int_X v(z)\eta(x - z)\, dz_1 \dots dz_n. \tag{4}$$

Since $\eta \in C^\infty(\mathbb{R}^n)$, it follows from (4) that $\Phi(v) \in C^\infty(\mathbb{R}^n)$, and since $\eta(-z) = 0$ for $z \notin \mathbb{R}^n_+$, we get

$$\Phi(v)(x) = \int_{\mathbb{R}^n_+} v(x + z)\eta(-z)\, dz_1 \dots dz_n. \tag{5}$$

Clearly, $\Phi(v)(X) \subset [0, 1]$.

The next lemma is a direct consequence of the above observations.

Lemma 4.1. $\Phi(v)|_X \in C^\infty(X)$ *and* $\Phi(v)|_X : X \to [0, 1]$.

Lemma 4.2. *Suppose* $\preceq$ *is a closed preorder on* X *satisfying (3), and* $v : X \to [0, 1]$ *is a continuous utility function for it. Then* $\Phi(v)|_X$ *is a (continuous) utility function for* $\preceq$, *too.*

Proof. If $x \preceq y$ then, by (3), $(x + z) \preceq (y + z)$ for all $z \in \mathbb{R}^n_+$, and as v is a utility function, we get $v(x + z) \leq v(y + z)$. It follows from (5) that $\Phi(v)(x) \leq \Phi(v)(y)$. If now $x \prec y$, then $v(x) < v(y)$ and $v(x + z) \leq v(y + z)$ for all $z \in \mathbb{R}^n_+$. Moreover, since v is continuous and $v(x) < v(y)$, there is $\delta > 0$ such that $v(x + z) < v(y + z)$ whenever $z \in \mathbb{R}^n_+$, $\|z\| < \delta$. Let $B = \{z = (z_1, \dots, z_n) \in \mathbb{R}^n_+ : \|z\| < \delta\}$. We have

$$\int_B v(x + z)\eta(-z)\, dz_1 \dots dz_n < \int_B v(y + z)\eta(-z)\, dz_1 \dots dz_n,$$
$$\int_{\mathbb{R}^n_+ \setminus B} v(x + z)\eta(-z)\, dz_1 \dots dz_n \leq \int_{\mathbb{R}^n_+ \setminus B} v(y + z)\eta(-z)\, dz_1 \dots dz_n,$$

and we deduce from (5) that $\Phi(v)(x) < \Phi(v)(y)$, that is $\Phi(v)|_X$ is a utility function. □

Proof of Theorem 3.1. Let $v : X \to \mathbb{R}$ be a continuous utility function for $\preceq$. Such a function exists according to Theorem 2.1. Taking into account that for any real numbers a, b the equivalences hold true

$$a \leq b \Leftrightarrow \frac{a}{1 + |a|} \leq \frac{b}{1 + |b|},$$
$$a < b \Leftrightarrow \frac{a}{1 + |a|} < \frac{b}{1 + |b|},$$

one can assume[7] that $v : X \to [0,1]$. We define $u = \Phi(v)|_X$. Then, by Lemma 4.1, $u \in C^\infty(X)$, $u(X) \subset [0,1]$, and, by Lemma 4.2, u is a utility function for $\preceq$. □

Proof of Theorem 3.2. $(a) \Rightarrow (b)$ Given $y \in int\, X$, we consider the set

$$M_\varepsilon(y) = \{x \in X : x \preceq y\} \cap B_\varepsilon(y), \quad 0 < \varepsilon \le \varepsilon(y).$$

Then, for every $z \in \mathbb{R}^n_+$, one has $y + z \in int\, X$, and by **A**, $M_\varepsilon(y+z) = M_\varepsilon(y) + z$. Let $u : X \to \mathbb{R}$ be a C^∞-smooth utility function for $\preceq$. Such a function exists according to Theorem 3.1. Since the preorder $\preceq$ is total, one has $\{x : x \preceq y\} = \{x : u(x) \le u(y)\}$ and $\{x : x \prec y\} = \{x : u(x) < u(y)\}$ whenever $y \in X$. It follows that $M_\varepsilon(y^*)$ is a closed domain with a smooth boundary $\{x : u(x) = u(y^*)\} \cap B_\varepsilon(y^*)$. Since y^* is a boundary point of $M_\varepsilon(y^*)$, and since the boundary of $M_\varepsilon(y^*)$ is smooth, the normal to it at y^* is well defined. We take $a = (a_1, \ldots, a_n)$ to be the unit normal vector at y^*, which is directed outside $M_\varepsilon(y^*)$; then $\nabla u(y^*) = \|\nabla u(y^*)\| a$. Now take a point $y^1 \in \mathbb{R}^n$ such that $y^1 \ge y$ and $y^1 \ge y^*$; then $y^1 \in int\, X$ and $y^1 = y + z = y^* + z^*$ where $z, z^* \in \mathbb{R}^n_+$, and we get

$$M_\varepsilon(y^1) = M_\varepsilon(y) + z = M_\varepsilon(y^*) + z^*$$

whenever ε is small enough. Thus, $M_\varepsilon(y)$ is a shift of $M_\varepsilon(y^*)$; therefore, it is a closed domain with a smooth boundary, y is its boundary point, and a is its unit normal vector at y directed outside $M_\varepsilon(y)$. Then $\nabla u(y) = \|\nabla u(y)\| a$ for any $y \in int\, X$; therefore $\lambda(y) := \|\nabla u(y)\|$ is C^∞-smooth, and

$$a_i \frac{\partial \lambda(y)}{\partial y_j} = a_j \frac{\partial \lambda(y)}{\partial y_i}, \qquad y \in int\, X, \quad i, j \in \{1, \ldots, n\}. \tag{6}$$

We will show that for any $x, y \in int\, X$ an equivalence holds as follows:

$$u(x) \le u(y) \Leftrightarrow a \cdot x \le a \cdot y. \tag{7}$$

Notice that if there exists a smooth function $h : \mathbb{R} \to \mathbb{R}$ such that

$$\lambda(x) = \frac{dh(t)}{dt}\Big|_{t = a \cdot x}, \quad x \in int\, X, \tag{8}$$

then h is increasing and $u(x) = h(a \cdot x) + const$, therefore, (7) holds. Let us prove the existence of such a function h. We assume, for the sake of definiteness, that $a_1 \ne 0$, and pass from $x = (x_1, \ldots, x_n)$ to new variables $y = (y_1, \ldots, y_n) = Ax$, where $y_1 = a_1x_1 + a_2x_2 + \cdots + a_nx_n$, $y_k = x_k$ $(k = 2, \ldots, n)$. Let $y = Ax$, and $\mu(y) := \lambda(A^{-1}(y)) = \lambda(x)$. One has

[7] By passing, if needed, from v to $\frac{1}{2} + \frac{1}{2}\frac{v}{1+|v|}$.

$$\frac{\partial\lambda}{\partial x_1} = \frac{\partial\mu}{\partial y_1}a_1, \qquad \frac{\partial\lambda}{\partial x_k} = \frac{\partial\mu}{\partial y_1}a_k + \frac{\partial\mu}{\partial y_k} \quad (k = 2, \dots, n);$$

and by taking into account (6), we derive from here

$$\frac{\partial\mu}{\partial y_k} = \frac{\partial\lambda}{\partial x_k} - \frac{a_k}{a_1}\frac{\partial\lambda}{\partial x_1} = 0 \quad \forall k \neq 1.$$

It follows that $\mu(y)$ depends on y_1 only, i.e., $\lambda(x)$ is a function of $a \cdot x$; then there is a smooth function $\lambda_0 : \mathbb{R} \to (0, \infty)$ such that $\lambda(x) = \lambda_0(a \cdot x)$, and (8) is satisfied for h being a primitive function of λ_0.

Thus (7) is established. Since u is a utility function for $\preceq$, (7) can be rewritten as $x \preceq y \Leftrightarrow a \cdot x \leq a \cdot y$ for all $x, y \in int\ X$. Let now x, y be arbitrary elements of X, and take $z \in int\ \mathbb{R}^n_+$. Then $x + tz, y + tz \in int\ X$ whenever $t > 0$, and one gets two chains of implications:

$$x \preceq y \Rightarrow (x + z) \preceq (y + z) \Rightarrow a \cdot (x + z) \leq a \cdot (y + z) \Rightarrow a \cdot x \leq a \cdot y,$$
$$a \cdot x \leq a \cdot y \Rightarrow a \cdot (x + tz) \leq a \cdot (y + tz)\ \forall t > 0$$
$$\Rightarrow u(x + tz) \leq u(y + tz)\ \forall t > 0 \Rightarrow u(x) \leq u(y) \Rightarrow x \preceq y,$$

and the result follows.

$(b) \Rightarrow (a)$ Obvious. □

Proof of Corollary 3.1. It suffices to consider only the case where statement (a) of Theorem 3.2 fails. We will show that then $y^1 \sim y^2$ for all $y^1, y^2 \in X$, hence $\preceq = \sim$ is represented by the linear function $u_1(x) \equiv 0$. Thus suppose (a) is not true, consequently, for every $y \in int\ X$ there is $y' \in B_{\varepsilon(y)}(y) \subset int\ X$ such that $y' \sim y$ and $y' \notin cl\{x \in B_{\varepsilon(y)}(y) : x \prec y\}$. Then, for some $0 < \delta \leq \varepsilon(y)$, $B_\delta(y') \subset int\ X$ and

$$B_\delta(y') \cap \{x \in B_{\varepsilon(y)}(y) : x \prec y\} = \emptyset,$$

and since $\preceq$ is total, $y \preceq x'$ whenever $x' \in B_\delta(y')$. Since $y' \sim y$, one gets $y' \preceq x'$ whenever $x' \in B_\delta(y')$, and, by **TIA**, $y \preceq x$ whenever $x \in B_\delta(y) = B_\delta(y') + (y - y')$.

Now, given two points in $int X$, y^1 and y^2, there are $0 < \delta_1 \leq \varepsilon(y^1)$ and $0 < \delta_2 \leq \varepsilon(y^2)$ such that $y^1 \preceq x^1$ and $y^2 \preceq x^2$ whenever $x^1 \in B_{\delta_1}(y^1)$, $x^2 \in B_{\delta_2}(y^2)$. Then, for $\delta = \min(\delta_1, \delta_2)$ and $z = (1 - t)y^1 + ty^2, 0 \leq t \leq 1$, one has $B_\delta(z) \subset int\ X$, and, by **TIA**, $z \preceq x$ whenever $x \in B_\delta(z)$. Let us consider the closed segment $I(y^1, y^2) := \{z = (1 - t)y^1 + ty^2 : 0 \leq t \leq 1\}$. If $\|y^1 - y^2\| \leq \delta$ then $y^1 \preceq y^2$, otherwise there is a sole point $z^1 \in I(y^1, y^2)$ such that $\|y^1 - z^1\| = \delta$, and we get $y^1 \preceq z^1$. If $\|z^1 - y^2\| \leq \delta$ then $z^1 \preceq y^2$, otherwise there is a sole point $z^2 \in I(z^1, y^2)$ such that $\|z^1 - z^2\| = \delta$, and we get $z^1 \preceq z^2$. If $\|z^2 - y^2\| \leq \delta$ then $z^2 \preceq y^2$, otherwise there is a sole point $z^3 \in I(z^2, y^2)$ such that $\|z^2 - z^3\| = \delta$, and we get $z^2 \preceq z^3$. This process ends after k steps where $\frac{\|y^1-y^2\|}{\delta} - 1 \leq k < \frac{\|y^1-y^2\|}{\delta}$, and we obtain a point $z^k \in I(z^{k-1}, y^2)$ such that $\|z^k - z^{k-1}\| \leq \delta$, therefore $z^k \preceq y^2$. Thus, we have $y^1 \preceq z^1 \preceq z^2 \preceq \cdots \preceq z^{k-1} \preceq z^k \preceq y^2$, and since y^1 and y^2 were taken arbitrarily from $intX$ and the preorder $\preceq$ is closed, it follows that $y^1 \sim y^2$ for all $y^1, y^2 \in X$. □

Proof of Theorem 3.3. According to Theorem 2.2, there exists a continuous function $v : \Omega \times X \to [0, 1]$ such that, for every $\omega \in \Omega$, $v(\omega, \cdot)$ is a utility function for $\preceq_\omega$. We consider ω as a parameter and define $u(\omega, \cdot) = \Phi(v(\omega, \cdot))$. Arguing as in the proof of Theorem 3.1 we see that, for every $\omega \in \Omega$, $u(\omega, X) \subset [0, 1]$, $u(\omega, \cdot) \in C^\infty(X)$, and $u(\omega, \cdot)$ is a utility function for $\preceq_\omega$. The theorem will be established if we prove that u is continuous as a function on $\Omega \times X$. To this end, take in $\Omega \times X$ a convergent sequence $(\omega^k, x^k) \to (\omega, x)$. Since v is continuous, we have $v(\omega, x + z) = \lim_{k\to\infty} v(\omega^k, x^k + z)$ whenever $z \in \mathbb{R}^n_+$, and as $0 \leq v \leq 1$, the Lebesgue dominant convergence theorem can be applied, and we get

$$\int_{\mathbb{R}^n_+} v(\omega, x + z)\eta(-z)\, dz_1 \ldots dz_n$$
$$= \lim_{k\to\infty} \int_{\mathbb{R}^n_+} v(\omega^k, x^k + z)\eta(-z)\, dz_1 \ldots dz_n,$$

that is $u(\omega, x) = \lim_{k\to\infty} u(\omega^k, x^k)$. □

Proof of Corollary 3.2. This is a particular case of Theorem 3.3. □

References

1. Bridges, D.S., Mehta, G.B.: Representations of Preference Orderings. LN in Economics and Mathematical Systems, vol. 422. Springer, Heidelberg (1995)
2. Debreu, G.: Representation of a preference ordering by a numerical function. In: Thrall, R., et al. (eds.) Decision Processes, pp. 159–165. Wiley (1954)
3. Debreu, G.: Continuity properties of Paretian utility. Intern. Econ. Rev. **5**, 285–293 (1964)
4. Debreu, G.: Smooth preferences. Econometrica **40**, 603–615 (1972)
5. Debreu, G.: Smooth preferences: a corrigendum. Econometrica **44**, 831–832 (1976)
6. Gevers, L.: On interpersonal comparability and social welfare orderings. Econometrica **47**, 75–89 (1979)
7. Kuratowski, K.: Topology, vol.1. Academic Press, Warsaw (1966)
8. Levin, V.L.: Some applications of duality for the problem of translocation of masses with a lower semicontinuous cost function. Closed preferences and Choquet theory. Soviet Math. Dokl. **24**(2), 262–267 (1981)
9. Levin, V.L.: A continuous utility theorem for closed preorders on a σ-compact metrizable space. Soviet Math. Dokl. **28**(3), 715–718 (1983)

10. Levin, V.L.: General Monge–Kantorovich problem and its applications in measure theory and mathematical economics. In: Leifman, L.J. (ed.) Functional Analysis, Optimization, and Mathematical Economics. A Collection of Papers Dedicated to Memory of L.V.Kantorovich. pp. 141–176. Oxford University Press, N.Y., Oxford (1990)
11. Levin, V.L.: The Monge–Kantorovich problems and stochastic preference relations. Adv. Math. Econ. **3**, 97–124 (2001)
12. Levin, V.L.: Best approximation problems relating to Monge–Kantorovich duality. Sbornik Math. **197**(9), 1353–1364 (2006)
13. Mas-Colell, A.: The Theory of General Economic Equilibrium: A Differentiable Approach. Cambridge University Press, London (1985)
14. Neuefeind, W., Trockel, W.: Continuous linear representations for binary relations. Econ. Theory **6**, 351–356 (1995)

Adv. Math. Econ. 11, 105–116 (2008)

Advances in
MATHEMATICAL
ECONOMICS

Rational expectations can preclude trades*

Takashi Matsuhisa[1] **and Ryuichiro Ishikawa**[2]

[1] Department of Natural Sciences, Ibaraki National College of Technology, 866 Nakane, Hitachinaka, Ibaraki 312-8508, Japan
(e-mail: mathisa@ge.ibaraki-ct.ac.jp)

[2] Graduate School of Systems and Information Engineering, University of Tsukuba, 1-1-1, Ten-nodai, Tsukuba, Ibaraki 305-8573, Japan
(e-mail: ishikawa@sk.tsukuba.ac.jp)

Received: June 4, 2007
Revised: October 2, 2007

JEL classification: D51, C78, D61

Mathematics Subject Classification (2000): 91A10, 91B44, 91B50

Abstract. We reconsider the no trade theorem in an exchange economy where the traders have non-partition information. By introducing a new concept, *rationality of expectations*, we show some versions of the theorem different from previous works, such as Geanakoplos (http://cowles.econ.yale.edu, 1989). We also reexamine a standard assumption of the no trade theorem: *the common prior assumption*.

Key words: no trade theorem, ex ante Pareto optimum, common knowledge, rational expectations equilibrium

1. Introduction

The no trade theorem has shown that new information will not give the traders any incentive to trade when their initial endowments are allocated ex ante Pareto-optimally. In this theorem, there are two standard assumptions: (1) the

* This article constitutes part of the second author's Ph.D. dissertation (Ishikawa [4]). He is grateful for the many conversations with Akira Yamazaki and Shin-ichi Takekuma. The authors also thank Chiaki Hara and the anonymous referees for the valuable comments. The first author is partially supported by Grants-in-Aid for Scientific Research (C) (No. 18540153) from the Japan Society for the Promotion of Sciences. The second author is partially supported by Grant-in-Aid for Young Scientists (B) (No. 19730137) from the Ministry of Education, Culture, Sports, Science and Technology.

partitional information structure, and (2) the common prior assumption. This paper explores the extent to which these two assumptions are generalized in the theorem.

In recent years, several investigators have already generalized the assumptions in this theorem. For (1), Geanakoplos [3] neatly analyzes non-partition information structure[1] with the introduction of a new concept, *positive balancedness*. With this concept, he examines several classes of non-partition information and the relations among them, and characterizes Nash equilibrium and rational expectations equilibrium in those classes.

Our paper discusses similar issues, but captures different features from his analysis with a new concept, *rationality of expectations*. This concept means that each trader knows his own expected utility. As shown later, this requirement does not necessarily imply either partitional information structure or positive balancedness. Moreover it does not require that traders are risk-neutral or risk-averse, which is usually assumed in this literature (c.f. [7,15]).

We do not need (2), the common prior assumption, although recent research shows that the common prior gives a necessary and sufficient condition for the no trader theorem (See [2,8,11,14]). Among those authors, Morris [8] explores different varieties of heterogeneous prior beliefs. We comment on heterogeneous priors in our model below.

Several variations of the no trade theorem have been developed. Neeman [10] applies it in the case of p-beliefs, Luo and Ma [5] in the non-expected utility case, Morris and Skiadas [9] in the case of rationalizable trades, and so on. Our model applies it to expected utility and rational expectations equilibrium, and therefore uses the standard setting of the original as Milgrom and Stokey [7] and Sebenius and Geanakoplos [15].

This paper is organized as follows: In Sect. 2 we define an economy with non-partition information structure and rational expectations equilibrium in our economy. The key notion, rationality of expectations, is defined in this section. In Sect. 3 we show two extended no trade theorems, and we comment on welfare of the rational expectations equilibrium in our economy. In Sect. 4, we give an example to compare with Geanakoplos [3]. In the example, we consider non-partition information different from that of Geanakoplos. Finally Sect. 5 gives comments on the common prior assumption.

[1] Brandenburger et al. [1] analyze correlated equilibrium in games with non-partition information. In addition, Samet [13], Rubinstein and Wolinsky [12], Matsuhisa and Kamiyama [6], and others show the Aumann's disagreement theorem in the non-partition information.

2. Model of an exchange economy

Let Ω be a non-empty *finite* set called a *state space* and let 2^{Ω} denote the field of all subsets of Ω. Each member of 2^{Ω} is called an *event* and each element of Ω called a *state*. We consider the set N of n traders; i.e., $N = \{1, 2, \dots, n\}$.

2.1. Information and knowledge

We define i's possible correspondence $P_i : \Omega \to 2^{\Omega} \setminus \emptyset$ where $P_i(\omega)$ is interpreted as the set of all the states that trader i thinks are possible at ω. A special class of correspondences $(P_i)_{i \in N}$ is called *RT-information structure*[2] if the following two conditions are satisfied for every $i \in N$:

Ref : $\omega \in P_i(\omega)$ for every $\omega \in \Omega$.
Trn : $\xi \in P_i(\omega)$ implies $P_i(\xi) \subseteq P_i(\omega)$ for all $\xi, \omega \in \Omega$.

The possible correspondence gives rise to i's knowledge operator K_i defined by $K_i E = \{\omega \in \Omega | \ P_i(\omega) \subseteq E\}$, which is the event that i knows E. Then P_i satisfies **Ref** if and only if K_i satisfies 'Truth':

T : $K_i E \subseteq E$ for every $E \in 2^{\Omega}$.

It satisfies **Trn** if and only if K_i satisfies "positive introspection":

4 : $K_i E \subseteq K_i K_i E$ for every $E \in 2^{\Omega}$.

The *common knowledge* operator K_C is defined by the infinite recursion of knowledge operators:

$$K_C E := \bigcap_{k=1,2,\dots} \bigcap_{\{i_1, i_2, \dots, i_k\} \subset N} K_{i_1} K_{i_2} \dots K_{i_k} E.$$

Given the RT-information structure $(P_i)_{i \in N}$, the *commonly* possible operator is the correspondence $M : \Omega \to 2^{\Omega}$ defined by

$$M(\omega) = \bigcup (P_{i_1}(P_{i_2}(\cdots P_{i_k}(\omega) \cdots))),$$

where the union ranges over all finite sequences of traders. We note that $\omega \in K_C E$ if and only if $M(\omega) \subseteq E$.[3]

[2] The *RT*-information structure stands for the *reflexive* and *transitive* information structure. Geanakoplos [3] refers the former as *nondelusion* and the latter as *knowing that you know* (KTYK).

[3] See Samet [13] for details.

2.2. Economy with RT-information structure

We define *a pure exchange economy with RT-information structure* $\mathcal{E}$ as a tuple

$$\langle N, (\Omega, (P_i, \mu_i)_{i\in N}), (e_i, U_i)_{i\in N}\rangle,$$

which consists of the following structure and interpretations: There are l commodities at each state, and it is assumed that i's consumption set at each state is $\mathbb{R}^l_+$. Each trader i has a state-dependent endowment $e_i : \Omega \to \mathbb{R}^l_+$ with $\sum_{i\in N} e_i(\omega) > 0$ for all $\omega \in \Omega$, a quasi-concave von Neumann–Morgenstern utility function $U_i : \mathbb{R}^l_+ \times \Omega \to \mathbb{R}$, and a subjective prior μ_i on Ω with *full support*[4] for every $i \in N$. In our economy $\mathcal{E}$, we assume that i's utility function $U_i(\cdot, \omega)$ for each ω is continuous and strictly quasi-concave.

The traders trade according to a profile $\boldsymbol{t} = (t_i)_{i\in N}$ of functions t_i from Ω into $\mathbb{R}^l$. A trade is said to be *feasible* if, for all $i \in N$ and for all $\omega \in \Omega$, $e_i(\omega) + t_i(\omega) \geq 0$ and $\sum_{i\in N} t_i(\omega) \leq 0$. Given initial endowments $(e_i)_{i\in N}$ and any feasible trade $\boldsymbol{t} = (t_i)_{i\in N}$, we refer to $(e_i + t_i)_{i\in N}$ as an allocation $\boldsymbol{a} = (a_i)_{i\in N}$. Note that an allocation is $\sum_{i\in N} a_i(\omega) \leq \sum_{i\in N} e_i(\omega)$ for every $\omega \in \Omega$. We denote by $\mathcal{A}$ the set of all allocations and denote by $\mathcal{A}_i$ the projection of A onto player i's allocations.

For i's allocation $a_i \in \mathcal{A}_i$, each trader i has expectations; i's *ex ante* expectation is defined by $\mathbf{E}_i[U_i(a_i)] := \sum_{\omega\in\Omega} U_i(a_i(\omega), \omega)\mu_i(\omega)$. Then we define ex ante Pareto optimality as follows:

Definition 1. *The endowments $(e_i)_{i\in N}$ are said to be* ex ante Pareto-optimal *if there is no allocation $(a_i)_{i\in N}$ such that $\mathbf{E}_i[U_i(a_i)] \geq \mathbf{E}_i[U_i(e_i)]$ for every trader $i \in N$ with at least one strict inequality.*

For i's allocation $a_i \in \mathcal{A}_i$, we define i's interim expectation at $\omega \in \Omega$ as $\mathbf{E}_i[U_i(a_i)|P_i](\omega) := \sum_{\xi\in\Omega} U_i(a_i(\xi), \xi)\mu_i(\xi|P_i(\omega))$. Then we define the acceptability of i's trade as:

Definition 2. *Given a feasible trade $\boldsymbol{t} = (t_i)_{i\in N}$, t_i is* acceptable *for trader $i \in N$ at state $\omega \in \Omega$ if $\mathbf{E}_i[U_i(e_i + t_i)|P_i](\omega) \geq \mathbf{E}_i[U_i(e_i)|P_i](\omega)$.*

We denote by $Acp_i(t_i)$ the set of all the states in which t_i is acceptable for i, and denote $Acp(\boldsymbol{t}) := \bigcap_{i\in N} Acp_i(t_i)$. Furthermore we set the event of i's interim expectation for the trade t_i at ω:

$$[\mathbf{E}_i[U_i(e_i + t_i)|P_i](\omega)] := \{\xi \in \Omega \mid \mathbf{E}_i[U_i(e_i + t_i)|P_i](\xi) = \mathbf{E}_i[U_i(e_i + t_i)|P_i](\omega)\}.$$

Given the event $[\mathbf{E}_i[U_i(e_i + t_i)|P_i](\omega)]$, we denote $R_i(t_i) = \{\omega \in \Omega \mid P_i(\omega) \subseteq [\mathbf{E}_i[U_i(e_i + t_i)|P_i](\omega)]\ \}$ and $R(\boldsymbol{t}) = \bigcap_{i\in N} R_i(t_i)$.

---

[4] I.e., $\mu_i(\omega) > 0$ for every $\omega \in \Omega$.

Definition 3. *A trader i is* rational about his expectation *for his trade t_i at ω if $\omega \in R_i(t_i)$; that is, $\omega \in K_i([\mathbf{E}_i[U_i(e_i + t_i)|P_i](\omega))$. A trader i is rational* everywhere *about his expectation for t_i if $R_i(t_i) = \Omega$.*

The event $R_i(t_i)$ means that trader i knows his expected gain from t_i at ω. Trader i is interpreted as knowing his interim expected utility at ω. If we consider the standard information structure of a partition on Ω, trader i is necessarily rational everywhere; i.e., $R_i(t_i) = \Omega$.

2.3. Price system and rational expectations equilibrium

A *price system* is a positive function $p : \Omega \to \mathbb{R}^l_{++}$. The *budget set* of a trader i at a state ω for a price system p is defined by $B_i(\omega, p) = \{a \in \mathbb{R}^l_+ \mid p(\omega) \cdot a \leqq p(\omega) \cdot e_i(\omega)\}$.

We denote $\Delta(p)(\omega) := \{\xi \in \Omega | \ p(\xi) = p(\omega)\}$ and $\Delta(p)$ the partition induced by p i.e., $\Delta(p) = \{\Delta(p)(\omega)| \ \omega \in \Omega\}$. When trader i learns from prices, his new information is represented by a mapping $\Delta(p) \cap P_i : \Omega \to 2^\Omega$ defined by $(\Delta(p) \cap P_i)(\omega) := \Delta(p)(\omega) \cap P_i(\omega)$. Note that $(\Delta(p) \cap P_i)_{i \in N}$, as well as $(P_i)_{i \in N}$, is *RT*-information structure.

Definition 4 (Geanakoplos [3]). *A* rational expectations equilibrium *for an economy $\mathcal{E}$ is a pair $(p, \boldsymbol{x})$, in which p is a price system and $\boldsymbol{x} = (x_i)_{i \in N}$ is an allocation satisfying the following conditions:*

RE 1 *For every $\omega \in \Omega$, $\sum_{i \in N} x_i(\omega) = \sum_{i \in N} e_i(\omega)$.*
RE 2 *For every $\omega \in \Omega$ and each $i \in N$, $x_i(\omega) \in B_i(\omega, p)$.*
RE 3 *If $P_i(\omega) = P_i(\xi)$ and $p(\omega) = p(\xi)$, then $x_i(\omega) = x_i(\xi)$ for trader $i \in N$ for any $\xi, \omega \in \Omega$.*
RE 4 *For each $i \in N$ and any mapping $y_i : \Omega \to \mathbb{R}^l_+$ with $y_i(\omega) \in B_i(\omega, p)$ for all $\omega \in \Omega$,*

$$\mathbf{E}_i[U_i(x_i)|\Delta(p) \cap P_i](\omega) \geqq \mathbf{E}_i[U_i(y_i)|\Delta(p) \cap P_i](\omega).$$

The profile $\boldsymbol{x} = (x_i)_{i \in N}$ is called a rational expectations equilibrium allocation.

For i's trade t_i, we set

$$R_i(p, t_i) := \{\omega \in \Omega | \ (\Delta(p) \cap P_i)(\omega) \subseteq [\mathbf{E}_i[U_i(e_i + t_i)|\Delta(p) \cap P_i](\omega)]\},$$

and denote $R(p, \boldsymbol{t}) = \bigcap_{i \in N} R_i(p, t_i)$. The set $R_i(p, t_i)$ is interpreted as the event that i knows his interim expectation for his trade t_i when he receives some new information from the price system p, and $R(p, \boldsymbol{t})$ is interpreted as the event that everyone knows his interim expectation for his trade with the price system p.

Definition 5. *A trader i is said to be* rational *about his expectation for t_i* with a price system *p at ω if $\omega \in R_i(p, t_i)$. All traders are* rational everywhere *about their expectations for $\boldsymbol{t}$ with p if $R(p, \boldsymbol{t}) = \Omega$.*

3. No trade theorems

In this section we shall give two extensions of the no trade theorem of Milgrom and Stokey [7]. In addition, we show the welfare of the rational expectations equilibrium.

3.1. No trade theorem with RT-information structure

The following is a direct extension of Milgrom and Stokey's theorem to an economy with RT-information structure, which will be proved in Appendix.

Theorem 1. *Let $\mathcal{E}$ be an economy with RT-information structure, and let $\boldsymbol{t} = (t_i)_{i\in N}$ be a feasible trade. Suppose that the initial endowments $(e_i)_{i\in N}$ are ex ante Pareto optimal. Then the traders can never agree to any non-null trade at each state where they commonly know both the acceptable trade $\boldsymbol{t} = (t_i)$ and where they are rational about their expectations for the trade; that is,*

$$\boldsymbol{t}(\omega) = \mathbf{0} \text{ at every } \omega \in K_C(Acp(\boldsymbol{t}) \cap R(\boldsymbol{t})).$$

To state this in a different way, we introduce the knowledge operator $K_i^{(p)}$ *associated with a price system p*, which is defined by $K_i^{(p)}E = \{\omega \in \Omega | (\Delta(p) \cap P_i)(\omega) \subseteq E\}$. The common knowledge operator $K_C^{(p)}$ associated with p is also defined by

$$K_C^{(p)}E := \bigcap_{k=1,2,\dots} \bigcap_{\{i_1,i_2,\dots,i_k\}\subset N} K_{i_1}^{(p)}K_{i_2}^{(p)}\dots K_{i_k}^{(p)}E.$$

Then we obtain another no trade theorem with a price system p in the same way as Theorem 1.

Corollary 1. *Let $\mathcal{E}$ be an economy with RT-information structure. If $\boldsymbol{e} = (e_i)_{i\in N}$ is a rational expectations equilibrium allocation relative to some price system p with which all traders are rational everywhere about their expectations for the trade $\boldsymbol{t} = (t_i)_{i\in N}$, then the traders can never agree to any non-null trade at each state where they commonly know the acceptable feasible trade; that is,*

$$\boldsymbol{t}(\omega) = \mathbf{0} \text{ at every } \omega \in K_C^{(p)}(Acp(\boldsymbol{t})).$$

3.2. Welfare in an economy with knowledge

We examine the welfare of the rational expectations equilibrium in our economy. It is characterized from the viewpoint of ex ante optimality. This will be proved in Appendix as well as Theorem 1.

Proposition 1. *In an economy with RT-information structure $\mathcal{E}$, let an allocation $\boldsymbol{x} = (x_i)_{i \in N}$ be a rational expectations equilibrium allocation relative to some price system p with which all the traders are rational everywhere about their expectations with respect to $(x_i - e_i)_{i \in N}$. Then $\boldsymbol{x}$ is ex ante Pareto optimal.*

4. Example

We give an example to make clear the difference with Geanakoplos [3]. In our model, we impose reflexivity and transitivity on traders' information structure while Geanakoplos imposes reflexivity and positive balancedness as follows:

Definition 6. *The information structure (Ω, P) is called* positively balanced *with respect to $E \subset \Omega$ if there is a function $\lambda : \underline{P} \to \mathbb{R}_+$ such that*

$$\sum_{\substack{C \in \underline{P} \\ C \subset E}} \lambda(C)\chi_C(\omega) = \chi_E \text{ for all } \omega \in \Omega,$$

where $\underline{P} := \{F \in 2^{\Omega} \mid F = P(\omega) \text{ for some } \omega\}$, and χ_A is the characteristic function of any set $A \subset \Omega$.

Although positively balanced information structure is weaker than partitional structure, it does not necessarily imply RT-information structure.[5] Therefore our theorem under RT-information structure is obtained under a different setting in which the information structure is reflexive and transitive but not positively balanced. The following example illustrates a consequence of our theorem.

Example 1. Consider an economy $\mathcal{E}$ with RT-information structure where there is a single contingent commodity. The economy consists of: $N = \{1, 2\}$, $\Omega = \{\omega_1, \omega_2, \omega_3, \omega_4\}$. The endowments, information structure, traders' priors and utilities, and their trades are given as Table 1:

In this example, the RT-information structure is not positively balanced and the endowments are allocated ex ante Pareto-optimally. In addition, we do not specify the traders' attitudes toward risk like Geanakoplos [3], but unlike several other papers such as Milgrom and Stokey [7], or Sebenius and Geanakoplos [15]. This means that the crucial character of utility is strict quasi-concavity or monotonicity.

For the feasible trade $\boldsymbol{t} = (t_i)_{i \in N}$, $Acp(\boldsymbol{t}) = \Omega$ and then $K_C(Acp(\boldsymbol{t})) = \Omega$. Non-zero trades, however, occur at ω_1, ω_2, and ω_3. This is because $R(\boldsymbol{t}) = \{\omega_4\}$. That is, $K_C(Acp(\boldsymbol{t}) \cap R(\boldsymbol{t})) = \{\omega_4\}$. In this case, zero trade occurs at the state ω_4.

[5] See Geanakoplos [3, p.19] for these relations.

Table 1. Example 1

	Trader 1	Trader 2
(e_i)	$e_1(\omega) := \begin{cases} 5/2 & \text{for } \omega_1 \\ 1/3 & \text{for } \omega_2 \\ 1 & \text{for } \omega_3 \\ 2 & \text{for } \omega_4 \end{cases}$	$e_2(\omega) := \begin{cases} 1 & \text{for } \omega_1, \omega_2 \\ 5/2 & \text{for } \omega_3 \\ 1 & \text{for } \omega_4 \end{cases}$
(U_i)	$U_1(x, \omega) := \begin{cases} x & \text{for } \omega_1, \omega_2 \\ x^{\frac{4}{5}} & \text{for } \omega_3 \\ x^2 & \text{for } \omega_4 \end{cases}$	$U_2(x, \omega) := \begin{cases} x^{\frac{6}{5}} & \text{for } \omega_1 \\ x^2 & \text{for } \omega_2 \\ x & \text{for } \omega_3 \\ x^2 & \text{for } \omega_4 \end{cases}$
(P_i)	$P_1(\omega) := \begin{cases} \{\omega_1, \omega_3\} & \text{for } \omega_1 \\ \{\omega_2, \omega_3\} & \text{for } \omega_2 \\ \{\omega_3\} & \text{for } \omega_3 \\ \{\omega_4\} & \text{for } \omega_4 \end{cases}$	$P_2(\omega) := \begin{cases} \{\omega_1, \omega_2\} & \text{for } \omega_1 \\ \{\omega_2\} & \text{for } \omega_2 \\ \{\omega_2, \omega_3\} & \text{for } \omega_3 \\ \{\omega_4\} & \text{for } \omega_4 \end{cases}$
(μ_i)	$\mu_1(\omega) := \begin{cases} 1/2 & \text{for } \omega_1 \\ 1/3 & \text{for } \omega_2 \\ 1/12 & \text{for } \omega_3, \omega_4 \end{cases}$	$\mu_2(\omega) := \begin{cases} 1/6 & \text{for } \omega_1 \\ 1/2 & \text{for } \omega_2 \\ 1/6 & \text{for } \omega_3, \omega_4 \end{cases}$
(t_i)	$t_1(\omega) := \begin{cases} 3/5 & \text{for } \omega_1 \\ -2/15 & \text{for } \omega_2 \\ 4/5 & \text{for } \omega_3 \\ 0 & \text{for } \omega_4 \end{cases}$	$t_2(\omega) := \begin{cases} -3/5 & \text{for } \omega_1 \\ 2/15 & \text{for } \omega_2 \\ -4/5 & \text{for } \omega_3 \\ 0 & \text{for } \omega_4 \end{cases}$

On the whole, what role does the rationality of expectations play in our model? Since, under this concept, each trader knows his expected utility of a given trade, a relationship is stipulated between traders' information structure and expected gains. This approach is similar to the non-partition information technique of Aumann's disagreement theorem.

The technique is made clear by Rubinstein and Wolinsky [12] and Matsuhisa and Kamiyama [6], whose analyses are based on the decomposition of information structure of Samet [13]. However, their two analyses are slightly different from each other. Rubinstein and Wolinsky give a result relating two functions of 2^{Ω} between players, whereas Matsuhisa and Kamiyama analyze each player's function of 2^{Ω} with the same assumption as our rationality of expectations (Lemma 1 in Appendix). The latter approach enables us to analyze trader's interim expected utility from the ex ante viewpoint (Lemma 2 in our Appendix). Therefore we prove our no trade theorem with the rationality of expectations as an application of Samet's decomposition à la Matsuhisa and Kamiyama.

5. Concluding remarks

This paper has examined the no trade theorem under RT-information structure by introducing the concept of rationality of expectations. Although this situation has been investigated by Geanakoplos [3], our no trade theorem is shown under a slightly different setting as illustrated above, i.e., not positively balanced but RT-information structure. As stated in the Introduction, the common prior assumption is another standard assumption in the no trade theorem. Finally we comment on the relation between this assumption and our model.

Recent research shows that a common prior is a necessary and sufficient condition of the no trade result [2,8,11,14]. Among these authors, Morris shows the no trade result with heterogeneous priors in a general belief system ([8, p. 1336]).

In our framework, Morris's belief condition, called *the public consistent concordance*, means that, for any trader $i, j \in N$, $\mu_i(\xi|P_i(\omega)) = \mu_j(\xi|P_j(\omega))$ for any ξ, ω in a common knowledge event. Referencing to our example again, although $Acp(\boldsymbol{t})$ is a common knowledge event, any state except ω_4 is not public consistent concordant. Therefore, as shown by Morris [8, Corollary 3.2], there exists a common knowledge event that non-zero trade occurs from ex ante Pareto efficient endowments. Our result is consistent with Morris's under non-partition information structure.[6]

Appendix

Basic lemmas

In a decision set Ω, a function f of 2^{Ω} is said to be *preserved under difference* provided that, if $f(S) = f(T) = d$, then $f(T \setminus S) = d$ for all events S and T

[6] See Ng [11, Remark 2, p. 46].

with $S \subseteq T$. Furthermore the function f is said to satisfy the *sure thing principle* if $f(S \cup T) = d$ for two disjoint events S and T with $f(S) = f(T) = d$. When we consider the function $f_i(a_i) : 2^\Omega \to \mathbb{R}$ for $a_i \in \mathcal{A}_i$, which is defined by

$$f_i(a_i)(X) := \mathbf{E}_i[U_i(a_i)|X] = \sum_{\xi \in \Omega} U_i(a_i(\xi), \xi)\mu_i(\xi|X),$$

it is preserved under difference and satisfies the sure thing principle. Then we show the first lemma proved as the Fundamental lemma in Matsuhisa and Kamiyama [6].

Lemma 1. *Let P_i be i's RT-information structure and Π_i be the partition induced by P_i such that $\Pi_i(\omega) := \{\xi \in \Omega |\ P_i(\xi) = P_i(\omega)\}$. Then, if $P_i(\omega) \subseteq \{\xi \in \Omega |\ f(a_i)(P_i(\xi)) = f(a_i)(P_i(\omega))\}$ for $\omega \in \Omega$ and $a_i \in \mathcal{A}_i$, $f_i(a_i)(P_i(\omega)) = f_i(a_i)(\Pi_i(\xi))$ for every $\xi \in P_i(\omega)$.*

Let M be the common possible operator associated with K_C.

Lemma 2. *Let $\mathcal{E}$ be an economy with RT-information structure and $\boldsymbol{t} = (t_i)_{i \in N}$ be a feasible trade. If $\omega \in K_C(Acp_i(t_i) \cap R_i)$ for each $i \in N$ then the following equality is true:*

$$\mathbf{E}_i[U_i(t_i^* + e_i)|P_i](\omega) = \mathbf{E}_i[U_i(e_i)|P_i](\omega), \tag{1}$$

where the trade $\boldsymbol{t}^* = (t_i^*)_{i \in N}$ is defined by

$$t_i^*(\xi) := \begin{cases} t_i(\xi) & \text{if } \xi \in M(\omega), \\ 0 & \text{otherwise}. \end{cases} \tag{2}$$

Proof. We specify $\Pi_i(\omega) = \{\xi \in \Omega |\ P_i(\xi) = P_i(\omega)\}$ for every $\omega \in \Omega$. We can observe the two points: First $\boldsymbol{t}^* = (t_i^*)_{i \in N}$ is feasible because so is $\boldsymbol{t}$, and secondly $M(\omega) = \Pi_i(\xi_1) \cup \Pi_i(\xi_2) \cup \cdots \cup \Pi_i(\xi_K)$ for $\xi_k \in M(\omega)$ $(1 \leq k \leq K)$. We notice by Lemma 1 that, given $a_i \in \mathcal{A}_i$,

$$\mathbf{E}_i[U_i(a_i)|\ P_i)](\xi) = \mathbf{E}_i[U_i(a_i)|\ \Pi_i](\xi) \quad \text{for all } \xi \in M(\omega). \tag{3}$$

Then, it follows that

$$\begin{aligned}\mathbf{E}_i[U_i(t_i^* + e_i)] = &\sum_{k=1}^{K} \sum_{\xi \in \Pi_i(\xi_k)} U_i(t_i(\xi) + e_i(\xi), \xi)\mu_i(\xi) \\ &+ \sum_{\xi \in \Omega \setminus M(\omega)} U_i(e_i(\xi), \xi)\mu_i(\xi)\end{aligned}$$

$$
\begin{aligned}
&= \sum_{k=1}^{K} \mu_i(\Pi(\xi_k))\mathbf{E}_i[U_i(t_i + e_i)|P_i](\xi_k) \\
&\quad + \sum_{\xi \in \Omega \setminus M(\omega)} U_i(e_i(\xi), \xi)\mu_i(\xi) \\
&\geqq \sum_{k=1}^{K} \mu_i(\Pi_i(\xi_k))\mathbf{E}_i[U_i(e_i)|P_i](\xi_k) \\
&\quad + \sum_{\xi \in \Omega \setminus M(\omega)} U_i(e_i(\xi), \xi)\mu_i(\xi) \qquad (4) \\
&= \mathbf{E}_i[U_i(e_i)].
\end{aligned}
$$

Inequality (4) is owing to $\xi_k \in M(\omega) \subseteq Acp(t_i)$ for all k. That is, $P_i(\xi_k) \subseteq M(\omega) \subseteq Acp(t_i)$ for every $\xi_k \in M(\omega)$ $(1 \leq k \leq K)$.

Therefore, if equation (1) does not hold, inequality (4) holds strictly. This means that $\mathbf{E}_i[U_i(t_i^* + e_i)] \gneqq \mathbf{E}_i[U_i(e_i)]$, in contradiction to the assumption that $(e_i)_{i \in N}$ is ex ante Pareto optimal. □

Proof of Theorem 1

Suppose to the contrary that $t_i(\omega) \neq \mathbf{0}$ at some $\omega \in K_C(Acp(\boldsymbol{t}) \cap R(\boldsymbol{t}))$. We set $A_i := \{\omega \in K_C(Acp(\boldsymbol{t}) \cap R(\boldsymbol{t}))|\ t_i(\omega) \neq 0\}$. Then we define the trade $\boldsymbol{t}^* = (t_i)_{i \in N}$ in Lemma 2 as follows:

$$
t_i^*(\xi) := \begin{cases} \frac{t_i(\xi)}{2} & \text{if } \xi \in A_i, \\ 0 & \text{otherwise.} \end{cases} \qquad (5)
$$

Since $t_i(\xi)$ is feasible, so is t_i^*. Noting that $e_i + \frac{1}{2}t_i$ is a convex combination between e_i and $e_i + t_i$, it follows from $\omega \in A_i \subseteq K_C(Acp(t_i))$ and the quasi concavity of U_i that

$$
\mathbf{E}_i\left[U_i\left(e_i + \frac{1}{2}t_i\right)|P_i\right](\omega) \gneqq \mathbf{E}_i[U_i(e_i + t_i)|P_i](\omega) \geq \mathbf{E}_i[U_i(e_i)|P_i](\omega),
$$

in contradiction to the ex ante Pareto optimality of $(e_i)_{i \in N}$ for the same reason as Lemma 2. □

Proof of Proposition 1

We set $\Pi_i(p)(\omega) := \{\xi \in \Omega|\ (\Delta(p) \cap P_i)(\xi) = (\Delta(p) \cap P_i)(\omega)\}$ for each $\omega \in \Omega$. Then $\Omega = \cup_{k=1}^{K} \Pi_i(p)(\omega_k)$. Since $\Delta(p) \cap P_i$ is i's information structure and $R_i(p, x_i) = \Omega$, it follows from Lemma 1 and **RE 4** that, for all $\xi \in \Pi_i(p)(\omega) \subseteq (\Delta(p) \cap P_i)(\omega)$,

$$\mathbf{E}_i[U_i(x_i)|(\Delta(p) \cap P_i)](\xi) = \mathbf{E}_i[U_i(x_i)|\Pi_i(p)](\xi)$$
$$\geq \mathbf{E}_i[U_i(e_i)|(\Delta(p) \cap P_i)](\xi) = \mathbf{E}_i[U_i(e_i)|\Pi_i(p)](\xi).$$

By adding up the above inequality over $\Pi_i(p)$, we obtain that, for all $i \in N$,

$$\begin{aligned} E_i[U_i(x_i)] &= \sum_{k=1}^{K} \mu_i(\Pi_i(p)(\omega_k))\mathbf{E}_i[U_i(x_i)|\Pi_i(p)](\omega_k) \\ &\geq \sum_{k=1}^{K} \mu_i(\Pi_i(p)(\omega_k))\mathbf{E}_i[U_i(e_i)|\Pi_i(p)](\omega_k) \\ &= E_i[U_i(e_i)]. \end{aligned}$$

□

References

1. Brandenburger, B., Dekel, E., Geanakoplos, J.: Correlated equilibrium with generalized information structures. Games Econ. Behav. **4**, 182–201 (1992)
2. Feinberg, Y.: Characterizing common priors in the form of posteriors. J. Econ. Theory **91**(2), 127–179 (2000)
3. Geanakoplos, J.: Game theory without partitions, and applications to speculation and consensus. Cowles Foundation Discussion Paper No. 914 (Available on http://cowles.econ.yale.edu) (1989)
4. Ishikawa, R.: Belief, Rationality, and Equilibrium in Game Theory, Ph. D. Dissertation, Hitotsubashi University (2003)
5. Luo, X., Ma, C.: Agreeing to disagree type results: a decision-theoretic approach. J. Math. Econ. **39**, 849–861 (2003)
6. Matsuhisa, T., Kamiyama, K.: Lattice structure of knowledge and agreeing to disagree. J. Math. Econ. **27**, 389–410 (1997)
7. Milgrom, P., Stokey, N.: Information, trade and common knowledge. J. Econ. Theory. **26**, 17–27 (1982)
8. Morris, S.: Trade with heterogeneous prior beliefs and asymmetric information. Econometrica **62**, 1327–1347 (1994)
9. Morris, S., Skiadas, C.: Rationalizable trade. Games Econ. Behav. **31**, 311–323 (2000)
10. Neeman, Z.: Common beliefs and the existence of speculative trade. Games Econ. Behav. **16**, 77–96 (1996)
11. Ng, M.-C.: On the duality between prior beliefs and trading demands. J. Econ. Theory **109**, 39–51 (2003)
12. Rubinstein, A., Wolinsky, A.: On the logic of "Agreeing to Disagree" type results. J. Econ. Theory **51**, 184–193 (1990)
13. Samet, D.: Ignoring ignorance and agreeing to disagree. J. Econ. Theory **52**, 190–207 (1990)
14. Samet, D.: Common priors and separation convex sets. Games Econ. Behav. **24**, 172–174 (1998)
15. Sebenius, J.K., Geanakoplos, J.: Don't bet on it: contingent agreements with asymmetric information. J. Am. Stat. Assoc. **78**(382), 424–426 (1983)

Adv. Math. Econ. 11, 117–145 (2008)

Advances in
MATHEMATICAL ECONOMICS

The Le Chatelier Principle in dynamic models of the firm*

Robert J. Rossana

Department of Economics, 2074 FAB, Wayne State University, Detroit, MI 48202, USA
(e-mail: r.j.rossana@wayne.edu)

Received: August 16, 2007
Revised: December 5, 2007

JEL classification: D21, E22

Mathematics Subject Classification (2000): 49K30

Abstract. This study examines the Le Chatelier Principle in intertemporal models of the firm with a delivery lag for capital. Adjustment costs are attached to labor and capital. Dynamic demands for labor and capital investment obey the principle when short-run and delivery-period factor price responses are compared. If own-adjustment parameters for quasi-fixed inputs are between zero and minus unity, a form of the principle holds when comparing delivery-period and steady-state factor price responses. Adding variable factors, the principle arises for quasi-fixed and variable factors in response to quasi-fixed factor prices but not to variable factor demands and variable factor input prices.

Key words: Le Chatelier principle, adjustment costs, Marshallian short run, dynamic demands, investment

1. Introduction

The Le Chatelier Principle, introduced into the economics literature in [16, pp. 36–39], provides one possible explanation for the inertia that is evident in economic systems. This principle asserts that, while a subset of choice variables are fixed, optimal decision rules for the remaining choice variables, available

* I am indebted to Adrian R. Fleissig, Boris S. Mordukhovich, and Peter J. Schmidt for helpful discussions and to Eric W. Bond, Louis D. Johnston, and John J. Seater for comments on a previous draft of this paper. I received useful comments from the members of the informal afternoon workshop in the Department of Economics at Wayne State University and from seminar participants at Michigan State University. The usual disclaimer applies regarding responsibility for errors and omissions.

to an economic agent, will display price elasticities that are less elastic when compared to their counterparts arising when all choice variables can be set optimally. Thus the short run in an economy is frequently described as having inelastic demands when compared to their full equilibrium versions, thereby providing one possible explanation of why economies display inertia with economic magnitudes responding sluggishly to shifts in economic incentives.[1]

This principle has been studied by a number of authors. Silberberg [18] established that Le Chatelier effects were a consequence of envelope relationships involving the indirect objective functions that arise in static optimization problems and later generalized the principle in a comparative statics context [19]. The principle has been studied where there are nondifferentiable demands and nonconcave maximization problems [11] and when discrete price changes are permitted [11,20]. While these studies have generalized the principle in a number of directions, demonstrating its applicability in wider contexts, the Le Chatelier Principle remains essentially intact as it was first discussed by Samuelson [16].

All of these analyses, as well as others that have examined the Le Chatelier Principle, are confined to a static setting.[2] However, it would seem to be natural to study the existence of the Le Chatelier Principle in a dynamic framework where economic behavior could be studied with one or more choice (state) variables fixed for a finite time as part of a broader optimizing framework, and where these fixed economic choice variables can be rationalized in an intuitive way. In this setting, one could derive factor price elasticities when subsets of state variables are fixed and when they are not while ensuring that such results are rigorously consistent with optimal behavior for all time.

In this paper, the existence of the Le Chatelier Principle is studied in a series of intertemporal models of the firm facing a finite delivery lag attached to one or more capital goods.[3] If a firm faces unanticipated changes in any of the determinants of its capital stock, causing it to desire a capital stock different from what it currently has installed, then the existence of a delivery lag implies

[1] A considerable amount of research effort in macroeconomics has been devoted to the search for explanations of the inertia in aggregate economies. Adjustment costs [9,23], among others is the idea most frequently used in macroeconomic models, an idea that can explain the serial persistence in output and other variables, but delivery lags [10,13] and the time to build [8] are other examples of economic assumptions that can rationalize sluggish movements in various economic magnitudes.

[2] Epstein [3] has examined the Le Châtelier Principle in a dynamic setting but did so in a framework different from the analysis in this paper. For example, the analysis in this paper looks at optimal decision rules when one or more state variables are fixed, an approach that is not contained in Epstein [3].

[3] The firm will be assumed in this paper to produce a nonstorable output without any delay in the delivery of it's output. But there could be a delivery lag associated with the production of the firm's output. For an analysis of this case when there is also a finite delay associated with increasing the capital stock, see [14].

that the firm will be capacity-constrained until it can take delivery of (or dispose of) capital goods. This quite naturally gives rise to the Marshallian short run embedded within an intertemporal model of the firm. It is clear that, over the period when the capital stock is fixed, demands for other factors of production may well display factor price elasticities that are consistent with the Le Chatelier Principle. This possibility is investigated here.

The models examined in this paper are conventional in the sense that they are neoclassical models of the firm using ordinary factor inputs in production to produce a nonstorable output. There are costs of adjustment attached to both labor and capital in these models. But the models differ in a number of their details so that we can study how various features of these models might affect the existence of the Le Chatelier Principle.

The first model will assume that production occurs using two quasi-fixed factor inputs in production, thereby omitting variable factor inputs (those not subject to adjustment costs) from production. The fact that labor is quasi-fixed allows us to determine if the dynamic demand for labor, arising over the fixed-capacity period, displays factor price responses consistent with the Le Chatelier Principle, an issue not addressed previously in the literature. A second model will be specified where the role of variable factor inputs can be studied, allowing us to see if the presence of variable factors affects the results derived in the first model and to permit us to observe if there are Le Chatelier effects evident in the demands for variable factor inputs. The final model that is presented will assume that there are two capital goods used in production along with labor and each capital good is subject to the same finite delivery lag. The reason for studying this model is to see if the existence of the second fixed state variable reduces factor price elasticities from what they would be in the case of one fixed capital good. The static literature studying the Le Chatelier Principle has established that adding more fixed choice variables reduces factor price elasticities in the demands for those factors that can be varied. We will want to see if this result carries over to a dynamic setting.

Factor price response comparisons can be made in these models in a way that is different from the static literature on this topic. One difference is that, because there will be installation costs attached to labor and capital, we will compare factor price responses in dynamic, as opposed to static, demand schedules. Such comparisons will be made in this paper in the short run and the delivery period. But the static literature is confined to comparisons involving static demands which here correspond to the steady state. It would be useful, in tying together the static literature to the dynamic models studied here, to find a way to make magnitude comparisons between steady-state factor price responses and those arising in dynamic demand schedules and it will be shown that there is a way to make such comparisons. It will be shown in this paper that such comparisons are indeed possible subject to an empirically plausible restriction frequently found in applied research.

Comparing factor price elasticities in a dynamic input demand schedule during the delivery period and the steady state may seem inappropriate because we would be comparing factor price responses in stock and flow relationships. But there is a practical reason for asking if we can make such a comparison. Most of the data that is available for empirical work, at least in macroeconomics, comes from sources which should not be regarded as in long-run equilibrium. For example, inventory and employment data is usually obtained for two-digit industries and data from these industries should probably be regarded as disequilibrium magnitudes since there seems to be little chance that these industries are in long-run equilibrium. The question then arises as to how one could get estimates of long-run factor demand elasticities from dynamic demand schedules that describe behavior along adjustment paths to equilibrium. It may not be possible to obtain such estimates using popular estimation methods.[4] But the analysis contained in this paper shows that, subject to a magnitude restriction on own-adjustment parameters that appears reasonable, estimates of factor price elasticities from dynamic demand schedules that have been obtained in many past applied studies, conveniently provide bounds on the factor price elasticities in the long-run demand schedules obeyed by firms.

It will be shown that the Le Chatelier Principle is indeed present in these intertemporal models. In the first model, when short-run (the time when the capital stock is fixed) and delivery period (the time when net investment in the capital stock is nonzero) factor price responses are compared, the dynamic labor demand schedule will be found to display factor price responses entirely consistent with the Le Chatelier Principle. Thus the short run displays the sort of inertia suggested in previous work because the short-run labor demand schedule is less factor price elastic than its delivery-period counterpart.

However, it is not possible to provide relative bounds on delivery-period and steady-state factor price responses. Thus no type of Le Chatelier Principle will hold essentially because relatively little is known about the relative magnitudes of parameters that arise in the model. However, there is a way to establish

---

[4] Estimated long-run factor price elasticities could be obtained by estimating a system of Euler equations arising from intertemporal models of the firm, using the delta method to construct standard errors for these elasticity estimates. Such an approach requires that all parameters that make up long-run factor demand elasticities can be identified which may not be possible even if valid instruments are available.

One could alternatively estimate cointegrating vectors to try to get estimates of these long-run elasticities. The cointegrating matrix for such a system will have rank equal to the number of quasi-fixed factors appearing in the representative firm's optimization problem [15]. Long-run factor price elasticities could be obtained with nonlinear transformations of the estimated parameters from this system. But again it is necessary that all relevant structural parameters can be identified from estimated cointegrating vectors which may not be possible.

a form of the Le Chatelier Principle in this comparison. If it is the case that own-adjustment parameters from the investment demands for capital and labor demand schedules are bounded between zero and minus unity, as is almost always found in applied work, then the Le Chatelier Principle will arise with delivery-period factor price responses that are less elastic than their steady-state analogues. Thus if these own-adjustment parameters are bounded in this way, we find that short-run factor price effects are less elastic than their delivery-period versions, and those in turn are less elastic than the factor price responses arising in the firm's steady state equilibrium. Similar results will arise for the stock and flow demands for capital.

When variable factor inputs are included in the analysis, the results hold as in the previous model and it is also found that variable factors, in the short run, will be completely price inelastic with respect to the factor prices of quasi-fixed factor inputs, although it will be argued that this result is somewhat idiosyncratic to the model in which these results are obtained. But the Le Chatelier Principle will not be found to arise when applied to the relationships between variable factor inputs and their associated factor prices when there is an arbitrary number of variable factor inputs, nor will it generalize, similarly to the static literature, to the case of more than one fixed capital good. Thus the principle survives generalization into a dynamic framework but not in every dimension in which it is considered.

This paper is organized as follows. The next section of the paper sets out the first model that will be used to study the relative magnitudes of factor price responses. For this model, Sect. 3 provides results that emerge during the delivery and steady-state periods while Sect. 4 provides an analysis of the short run. Section 5 contains the results regarding the Le Chatelier Principle as it arises during the time intervals of interest. Section 6 describe extensions to the first model involving the addition of variable factor inputs and the case of two fixed capital goods. A final section summarizes results and an appendix concludes the paper by providing all relevant derivations to support the results in the paper.

2. A dynamic model of the firm

This section examines a dynamic model of a firm producing a nonstorable output using two quasi-fixed inputs in production, capital and labor. The firm's capital stock cannot be augmented for a finite time because there is a delivery lag attached to the acquisition of new capital goods so that, during this period, the firm will be capacity-constrained. The firm operates in competitive output and input markets and factor price expectations are static. Exogenous parameters will not be assumed to be functions of time since we are comparing results from an intertemporal model with results from a literature that is concerned essentially with the results from exercises in comparative statics. All functions used in the model will be twice continuously differentiable but more will be said below about functional form restrictions that will be maintained for later purposes.

2.1. Model framework

The firm is assumed to maximize

$$\int_0^{\infty} R(t)e^{-rt}dt \tag{1}$$

where the firm's cash flow is defined to be

$$R(t) = f(k(t), m(t)) - c(h(t)) - wm(t) - g_k[d_k(t) + p_k(n_k(t)) + i_k(d_k(t))]. \tag{2}$$

Cash flow, given by $R(t)$ and discounted at the rate r ($r > 0$), is the difference between the firm's revenues and costs where the former is given partly by the technology or gross production function $f(k(t), m(t))$ where the capital stock is denoted by $k(t)$, and $m(t)$ refers to the flow of labor services. The firm's output price is normalized to unity. Net production consists of gross production less the training costs, $c(h(t))$, attached to new hires of workers, $h(t)$, measured in units of output.[5] The wage bill is the product of the real wage, w, and labor services. The firm pays for new capital at the time when new capital goods are delivered where the purchase price of new capital goods is denoted by g_k.[6] Alternatively, the firm can pay for new capital goods when new orders are placed. There is no substantive difference between either approach but it is slightly simpler to assume that payments are made at the time of delivery. There are costs, measured in units of capital, attached to the placement of new orders for capital goods, $n_k(t)$. These are given by $p_k(n_k(t))$ and there are installation costs attached to newly delivered capital, denoted by $i_k(d_k(t))$. New orders are equal to future

5 Training costs are assumed separable from the gross production function because it is convenient for nesting the static theory of the firm within an intertemporal model. Separability must ultimately be empirically justified. Relaxing these assumptions changes many of the characteristics of intertemporal models (see [23]). Absent empirical evidence to the contrary, I follow common practice and impose separability for its convenience.

6 The purchase price of capital may depend upon the delivery lag and the delivery lag can be treated as a choice variable to the firm. As an example, this would be true if suppliers offer a price-delivery lag tradeoff so that the firm could get a price discount if it waits a longer time for delivery of new capital goods. In the analysis contained here, the purchase price of capital goods will not be assumed to depend upon the delivery lag and the latter will be taken as fixed for simplicity but see [22] for an analysis of firm behavior when the switch-point is a choice variable.

deliveries of new capital, that is $n_k(t) = d_k(t+\ell)$, where the delivery lag $\ell > 0$. New order cancellations are ignored.

The firm is constrained by two accumulation equations for its inputs in production.

$$\dot{k}(t) = d_k(t), \quad k(t) = k_0 > 0 \ t \in [0, \ell] \tag{3}$$

$$\dot{m}(t) = h(t), \quad m(0) = m_0 > 0 \tag{4}$$

There are given initial stocks of capital and labor and, during the period that the delivery lag is binding upon the firm, the capital stock will remain at its initial level. Depreciation of the capital stock and any quits from the labor force are ignored for simplicity. There is thus no distinction between gross and net investment in capital and labor.

This optimization problem has an advanced time argument because of the relationship between new orders and future deliveries of new capital goods. However, the model described above can be respecified to give rise to a two-stage optimal control problem, a problem for which optimality criteria are readily available. This may be seen in the following manner. Consider

$$-g_k \int_0^\infty p_k(n_k(t))e^{-rt}dt = -g_k \int_0^\infty p_k(d_k(t+\ell))e^{-rt}dt.$$

Define $s = t + \ell$ and note that the integral with the lead time argument in this expression may be rewritten as

$$-g_k \int_\ell^\infty p_k(d_k(s))e^{-r(s-\ell)}ds.$$

As a result of these operations, the optimization problem can be specified to be maximize

$$J = J_1 + J_2 = \int_0^\ell R_1(t)e^{-rt}dt + \int_\ell^\infty R_2(t)e^{-rt}dt \tag{5a}$$

$$R_1(t) = f(k_0, m(t)) - c(h(t)) - wm(t) \tag{5b}$$

$$\begin{aligned} R_2(t) = {} & f(k(t), m(t)) - c(h(t)) - wm(t) - g_k[d_k(t) \\ & + p_k(d_k(t))e^{r\ell} + i_k(d_k(t))] \end{aligned} \tag{5c}$$

with (3) and (4) providing the relevant accounting constraints.

2.2. Optimality criteria

The optimizing model of the firm, displayed above in (5), is a two-stage optimal control problem and Tomiyama [21] provides optimality criteria for the solution of this type of optimization model.[7] These criteria may be obtained by forming the Hamiltonians

$$H_1 = f(k_0, m) - c(h) - wm + \lambda d_k + \pi h$$
$$H_2 = f(k, m) - c(h) - wm - g_k[d_k + p_k(d_k)e^{r\ell} + i_k(d_k)] + \lambda d_k + \pi h$$

where the time notation has been suppressed. In the above expressions, λ and π are adjoint variables measuring the imputed values associated with the accumulation of capital and labor. The Hamiltonian for the subinterval $t \in [0, \ell]$, H_1, has been simplified due to the fact that deliveries of new capital goods are zero over this interval ($d_k = 0$). The capital stock is thereby fixed at its initial level k_0. Payments for new capital goods and order placement costs incurred during the short run are forward-discounted into the second subinterval $t \in [\ell, \infty]$ and thus are contained in the second Hamiltonian, H_2. Aside from boundary conditions discussed below, necessary conditions for the solution of this problem, pertaining to the subinterval $t \in [0, \ell]$, are

$$\pi = c'(h) \tag{6a}$$
$$\dot{\lambda} = -f_k(k_0, m) + r\lambda \tag{6b}$$
$$\dot{\pi} = w - f_m(k_0, m) + r\pi \tag{6c}$$
$$\dot{k} = 0 \tag{6d}$$
$$\dot{m} = h \tag{6e}$$

while, for the subinterval $t \in [\ell, \infty)$, we have the necessary conditions

$$\lambda = g_k[1 + p_k'(d_k)e^{r\ell} + i_k'(d_k)] \tag{7a}$$
$$\pi = c'(h) \tag{7b}$$
$$\dot{\lambda} = -f_k(k, m) + r\lambda \tag{7c}$$
$$\dot{\pi} = w - f_m(k, m) + r\pi \tag{7d}$$
$$\dot{k} = d_k \tag{7e}$$
$$\dot{m} = h. \tag{7f}$$

To interpret these conditions, first consider (7a)–(7f). Conditions (7a) and (7c) may be interpreted by integrating (7c), the result of that integration implying that the discounted marginal product of capital equals the marginal cost of acquiring capital where the latter includes marginal planning and installation costs as well as the purchase price of capital goods. A version of Tobin's marginal q [7] may be defined within this condition as λ/g_k. Integrate (7d) and combine

---

[7] Mordukhovich [12] contains a comprehensive discussion of optimization and the techniques contained in Tomiyama [21].

the result with (7b) which will show that new hires are chosen so that the discounted marginal product of labor equals the real wage plus marginal training costs.

In the short run, the necessary conditions may be interpreted in a way similar to the interpretation of the delivery-period conditions. Since deliveries of new capital goods are zero over the short run, there is no optimality condition for deliveries d. As stated earlier, the delivery-period condition for $t \in [\ell, \infty)$ effectively incorporates an optimality criterion for both subintervals by forward-discounting the costs of new orders into the second subinterval. Also note that even though the capital stock is fixed, the shadow value of capital accumulation is not constant because the optimal choice of labor, resulting in adjustments to the employed labor force, affects the marginal product of capital (as long as $f_{km} \neq 0$), thus changing the shadow value of capital accumulation.

To complete the set of optimality criteria, boundary conditions that arise in this problem are also required.

2.3. Boundary conditions

The firm has positive initial stocks of its productive inputs that are standard boundary conditions for intertemporal problems. In addition, transversality conditions arise at the far horizon, given by

$$\lim_{t\to\infty} \lambda(t)e^{-rt}k(t) = \lim_{t\to\infty} \pi(t)e^{-rt}m(t) = 0.$$

These transversality conditions are not necessary in this framework just as in standard control problems. But this problem also has additional boundary conditions that apply at the switch-point, ℓ, given below.

$$\hat{\lambda}(\ell^-) = \hat{\lambda}(\ell^+) \tag{8a}$$

$$\widehat{\pi}(\ell^-) = \widehat{\pi}(\ell^+) \tag{8b}$$

$$e^{-r\ell}\hat{\lambda}(\ell) = -\left[\frac{\partial \hat{J}_2}{\partial k}\right]_\ell \tag{8c}$$

$$e^{-r\ell}\widehat{\pi}(\ell) = -\left[\frac{\partial \hat{J}_2}{\partial m}\right]_\ell \tag{8d}$$

The circumflex (ˆ) above a magnitude indicates the optimal value of that magnitude, conditional on the optimal choice of the instruments as described above. The conditions in (8a) and (8b) are statements showing that the adjoint variables will be continuous at the switch-point (delivery lag) ℓ. The conditions in (8c) and (8d) are the crucial optimality criteria that determine how optimal behavior in this model differs from standard control problems.

These switch-point conditions serve to tie together optimal behavior over each time interval. The conditions in (8c) and (8d) indicate that the costate variables for labor and capital must equal the maximized values of the derivatives with respect to labor and capital of the delivery-period functionals J_2, applicable to the subinterval $t \in [\ell, \infty)$, and evaluated at the switch-point ℓ, conditional on optimal choices of the instruments using the instrument conditions given above. These maximized values are functions of the initial stocks of labor and capital, $k(\ell)$ and $m(\ell)$, one of which (the labor force) can be chosen in an optimal fashion in the short run. At the switch-point ℓ, the capital stock is fixed but deliveries may arrive beyond this point. Since the initial stock of labor can be chosen optimally during the period $t \in [0, \ell]$, (8d) provides the condition which determines the optimal initial stock of labor for the second time interval $t \in [\ell, \infty)$. Thus the optimal path in the short run must achieve the optimal initial stock of labor for the second subinterval, consistent with this switch-point condition. For this consistency to be achieved, any change in the optimal path, occurring in the interval $t \in [\ell, \infty)$, will be propagated into the initial time interval when the firm is capacity-constrained. This must occur in order for the optimal short-run path to always reach the optimal level of $m(\ell)$. This requirement guarantees consistent behavior over each subinterval, thereby solving the problem posed. The boundary conditions that arise at the switch-point (delivery lag), ℓ, are the essential reasons why the Le Chatelier Principle arises during the firm's short run when it is capacity-constrained.

If the production function is strictly concave and if planning, installation, and training costs are assumed to be strictly convex, then these boundary conditions, along with the necessary conditions given earlier, are sufficient to solve this optimization problem. The existence of an optimal path is guaranteed and this path will be unique. These concavity and convexity assumptions will always be maintained in what follows below.[8]

The analysis of the subinterval $t \in [\ell, \infty)$ requires an explicit analytical solution to the transition equations describing the evolution of the state and costate variables for this time period. But because there are two state variables in this problem, optimal behavior can only be completely investigated using linear approximations to these nonlinear transition equations. To accomplish this linearization, quadratic forms will be used in deriving some of the results that follow although not all of the results in this paper require this linearization (for example, see Sect. 6.1). The functional forms that will be employed are as follows.

---

[8] A discontinuity in the optimal path may occur at ℓ for general nonlinear problems of the type analyzed here. This will not be true when quadratic forms are used (see below). If there is no such discontinuity, an additional matching condition arises for two-stage optimal control problems; the maximized Hamiltonians, defined over each subinterval, must be equal at the switch-point ℓ, i.e. $\widehat{H}_1(\ell) = \widehat{H}_2(\ell)$.

$$f(k,m) = -(1/2)\begin{bmatrix} k & m \end{bmatrix}\begin{bmatrix} \alpha_{11} & \alpha_{12} \\ \alpha_{21} & \alpha_{22} \end{bmatrix}\begin{bmatrix} k \\ m \end{bmatrix} \tag{9a}$$

$$= -(\alpha_{11}/2)k^2 - \alpha_{12}km - (\alpha_{22}/2)m^2 \tag{9b}$$

$$c(h) = (\beta/2)h^2, \quad \beta > 0 \tag{9c}$$

$$p_k(d_k) = (\gamma_k/2)d_k^2, \quad \gamma_k > 0 \tag{9d}$$

$$i_k(d_k) = (\delta_k/2)d_k^2, \quad \delta_k > 0. \tag{9e}$$

For the sake of simplicity, these functional forms are specified so as to prevent constant terms from arising in the decision rules of interest.

The production function in (9a) is a quadratic form borrowed from [6, p. 134], a functional form that is familiar since it has been so widely used in macroeconomic research. This technology is assumed to have diminishing marginal products for each productive input and to be strictly concave, implying that the Hessian of the production function is negative definite. Thus the parameter matrix $[\alpha]$ will be assumed to be positive definite and symmetric, it will have positive diagonal elements, and $\alpha_{11}\alpha_{22} - \alpha_{12}^2 > 0$. The parameter α_{12} is unrestricted in sign as is customary in the ordinary theory of the firm but the results below are unaffected by the absence of a sign restriction on this parameter.

Regarding the elements in (9c)–(9e), parameters are taken to be positive so that adjustment costs rise at the margin as in traditional neoclassical investment models.

3. Optimal behavior for $t \in [\ell, \infty)$

Beyond the switch-point ℓ, the firm can take deliveries of new capital goods and can drive its state variables to their steady-state levels. But to understand the short-run behavior of the firm first requires a discussion of the delivery period and the steady state because these solutions will be connected to the short run through the switch-point conditions given above in (8c) and (8d). Thus we begin by examining the firm's behavior for the subinterval $t \in [0, \infty)$. The details of all necessary derivations are relegated to the Appendix.

Because there is no distinction between net and gross investment in this model (recall that depreciation of the capital stock and quits are ignored), the firm will not bear costs of adjustment in the steady state and so results from the standard static theory of the firm will emerge in the firm's long-run equilibrium. Define the user cost of capital as $c_k = rg_k$ and let an asterisk (*) denote the steady-state level of a magnitude. The firm's long-run factor demands ($\dot{k} = \dot{m} = 0$) are as follows.

$$\begin{bmatrix} k^* \\ m^* \end{bmatrix} = -|\alpha|^{-1}\begin{bmatrix} \alpha_{22} & \alpha_{12} \\ \alpha_{12} & \alpha_{11} \end{bmatrix}\begin{bmatrix} c_k \\ w \end{bmatrix} \tag{10}$$

Due to the concavity assumptions that are used here, the matrix of factor-price responses has negative diagonal elements (own-factor price effects are negative) and it is symmetric [23, pp. 337–338]. Cross-factor price responses are indeterminate without any qualitative restriction placed upon the cross-derivative of the production function, measured by the parameter α_{12}. These long-run stock demand functions are homogeneous of degree zero in nominal prices and wages as is evident from the construction of (10).

When the firm can undertake net investment in both capital and labor, the investment demands for these inputs obey the multivariate flexible accelerator given by

$$\begin{bmatrix} \dot{k}(t) \\ \dot{m}(t) \end{bmatrix} = \begin{bmatrix} \omega_{11} & \omega_{12} \\ \omega_{21} & \omega_{22} \end{bmatrix} \begin{bmatrix} k(t) - k^* \\ m(t) - m^* \end{bmatrix} \tag{11}$$

where the adjustment parameters are denoted by ω_{ij}. The adjustment matrix $[\omega]$ has properties consistent with results in [9, pp. 83–84]; its eigenvalues are real and negative, its determinant is positive, and its diagonal elements obey the qualitative restrictions $\omega_{ii} < 0$. Further, the off-diagonal elements are sign-symmetric, the sign being determined by α_{12}. While we can say something qualitatively about these adjustment parameters, not much more than this can be said because determining the magnitudes of adjustment parameters requires information that is generally not at our disposal. To see this, consider the own-adjustment parameter for labor, derived in the Appendix to be

$$\omega_{22} = \frac{\alpha_{22} + \beta\kappa_1\kappa_2}{\beta(\kappa_1 + \kappa_2 - r)} < 0. \tag{12}$$

While we have made qualitative assumptions about most of the parameters in (12), this adjustment parameter involves the stable characteristic roots, denoted by $\kappa_{1,2}$, arising from the transition equations that describe the evolution of the state and costate variables during the delivery period. Qualitative information is available regarding these roots (they are each negative real numbers) and the other parameters in (12) but the magnitudes of these parameters are generally unknown and, as a result, there is no theoretical prediction that can be made about the magnitude of any of the adjustment parameters appearing in (11). However, parameters like ω_{22} are routinely estimated in applied work and it is regularly found that own-adjustment parameters are bounded between zero and minus unity. Since these parameters measure the portion of the gap between desired and actual stocks that is made up at each instant of time, these empirical findings are quite plausible. It is this empirical finding that will be used below in establishing the presence of a form of the Le Chatelier Principle in the delivery period.[9]

The dynamic demand for labor schedule can be obtained by using (10) and (11) but, for later purposes, it is more convenient to use the solution path for the adjoint variable π. This solution path is

$$\pi(t) = \sigma_{11}k(t) + \sigma_{12}m(t) + \sigma_{13}c_k + \sigma_{14}w \tag{13a}$$

$$\sigma_{11} = -\frac{\alpha_{12}}{\kappa_1 + \kappa_2 - r} \tag{13b}$$

$$\sigma_{12} = \frac{\alpha_{22} + \beta\kappa_1\kappa_2}{\kappa_1 + \kappa_2 - r} < 0 \tag{13c}$$

$$\sigma_{13} = \frac{\beta\alpha_{12}\kappa_1\kappa_2}{(\alpha_{11}\alpha_{22} - \alpha_{12}^2)(\kappa_1 + \kappa_2 - r)} \tag{13d}$$

$$\sigma_{14} = \frac{\alpha_{11}\alpha_{22} - \alpha_{12}^2 + \beta\alpha_{11}\kappa_1\kappa_2}{(\alpha_{11}\alpha_{22} - \alpha_{12}^2)(\kappa_1 + \kappa_2 - r)} < 0. \tag{13e}$$

Using this solution path and the necessary condition describing the optimal choice of new hires, the dynamic demand schedule for labor is

$$\dot{m}(t) = \beta^{-1}\pi(t) = \beta^{-1}[\sigma_{11}k(t) + \sigma_{12}m(t) + \sigma_{13}c_k + \sigma_{14}w]. \tag{14}$$

Coefficients attached to the state variables in (14) obey the relationships $\omega_{21} = \beta^{-1}\sigma_{11}$ and $\omega_{22} = \beta^{-1}\sigma_{12}$. Observe that the response of labor investment to the firm's capital costs is unrestricted because we have maintained no restriction on the cross-derivative of the production function, α_{12}. However, the own-factor price response is negative because $\beta^{-1}\sigma_{14} < 0$. It will turn out that the lack of a restriction on the cross-factor price effect in this labor demand schedule will have no impact upon the ability to bound factor price responses in order to establish the existence of the Le Chatelier Principle in this model.

4. Optimal behavior for $t \in [0, \ell]$

The firm will pursue an optimal employment decision rule while it is capacity-constrained. In order to obtain this decision rule, we require an expression for the costate variable associated with the stock of labor that corresponds to the

[9] The characteristic roots are functions of the exogenous parameters in this problem as is known from previous research. Conditional on these roots, it is easy to show that this own-adjustment parameter rises with the parameter β, a very intuitive result. This implies that the own-adjustment parameter moves towards zero as adjustment costs attached to capital become more severe. The firm thus closes a smaller fraction of the gap between desired and actual stocks of labor at each instant of time as marginal adjustment costs rise, i.e., as β rises.

expression given above for this same magnitude, but arising during the delivery period. Using the superscript s to denote magnitudes pertaining to the short run, this solution, derived in the Appendix, is

$$\pi^s(t) = \left[\frac{\Pi_1(t)}{\Pi_1(\ell)}\right]\pi(\ell) + \left[\frac{\Pi_2(t)\Pi_1(\ell) - \Pi_1(t)\Pi_2(\ell)}{\Pi_2(\ell)}\right]m(0) \tag{15}$$

where the parameters $\Pi_1(t)$ and $\Pi_2(t)$ are given by

$$\Pi_1(t) = \frac{\kappa_1^s e^{\kappa_2^s t} - \kappa_2^s e^{\kappa_1^s t} + r\left[e^{\kappa_1^s t} - e^{\kappa_2^s t}\right]}{\kappa_1^s - \kappa_2^s}, \quad \Pi_2(t) = \frac{\alpha_{22}\left[e^{\kappa_1^s t} - e^{\kappa_2^s t}\right]}{\kappa_1^s - \kappa_2^s}.$$

In the expression above, $\kappa_{1,2}^s$ are the characteristic roots arising from the transition equations that apply to the short run; these roots are real numbers of opposite sign.[10] The crucial part of this solution is the fact that $0 < \Pi_1(t)/\Pi_1(\ell) \leq 1$. Given its magnitude, the ratio $\Pi_1(t)/\Pi_1(\ell)$ will be referred to later as a damping factor. At $t = \ell$, (15) reduces to $\pi(\ell) = \pi(\ell)$. In this way, the solution over $t \in [0, \ell]$ will achieve consistency with behavior over the delivery period. To obtain the short-run solution path that is required, combine (15) with (13a)–(13e) to obtain

$$\begin{aligned}\pi^s(t) = &\left[\frac{\Pi_1(t)}{\Pi_1(\ell)}\right][\sigma_{11}k(\ell) + \sigma_{12}m(\ell) + \sigma_{13}c_k + \sigma_{14}w] \\ &+ \left[\frac{\Pi_2(t)\Pi_1(\ell) - \Pi_1(t)\Pi_2(\ell)}{\Pi_2(\ell)}\right]m(0).\end{aligned}$$

The optimality condition for new hires may be used as it was above to derive the labor demand schedule that applies to the short run, and it is given below.

$$\begin{aligned}\dot{m}^s(t) = \beta^{-1}\pi^s(t) = \beta^{-1}&\left\{\left[\frac{\Pi_1(t)}{\Pi_1(\ell)}\right][\sigma_{11}k(\ell) + \sigma_{12}m(\ell) + \sigma_{13}c_k + \sigma_{14}w]\right\} \\ +\beta^{-1}&\left\{\left[\frac{\Pi_2(t)\Pi_1(\ell) - \Pi_1(t)\Pi_2(\ell)}{\Pi_2(\ell)}\right]m(0)\right\}.\end{aligned} \tag{16}$$

Inspection of (16) reveals that all factor price effects come through the short-run costate solution that arises in $t \in [0, \ell]$.[11]

---

[10] Note that, unlike the standard infinite horizon control problem, there is no requirement here to eliminate the positive characteristic root by the choice of a constant term because there is no need to achieve a steady-state equilibrium in this interval. All that is required is that costate variables achieve their optimal values consistent with the switch-point boundary conditions in (8c) and (8d)

[11] It is also true that variation in the length of the short run, given by the parameter ℓ, will also shift the optimal path in the short run. This effect is given by $\partial\pi^s(t)/\partial\ell = \dot{\pi}(\ell)$. Since the length of the short run is assumed fixed throughout, this effect is suppressed.

5. Comparisons of factor price responses

The literature that exists about the Le Chatelier principle is essentially confined to static analyses so that there is no sense in which one can compare fixed-capacity parameters to analogous parameters arising while capacity adjustments can be made. The only comparisons that could be made involved full equilibrium and situations where one or more choice variables were fixed arbitrarily. In the present framework, however, the results derived for each subinterval can be used to make additional comparisons; namely, we can compare factor price responses during the delivery period ($\dot{k} \neq 0$) to those arising in the short run and the steady state (where, in both cases, $\dot{k} = 0$). These comparisons between input price responses in the labor demand schedule will determine if the Le Chatelier Principle holds in this model and three pairwise comparisons will be made. The first one will be a comparison of the short-run and the delivery period ($\dot{k} \neq 0$), followed by a discussion of the delivery period and the steady state. We may then infer the relationship between the fixed-capacity period and the steady state from these results.

5.1. The short run and the delivery period

The first set of results concerns the relative magnitudes of the real factor price coefficients in the dynamic labor demand schedules in the short run and delivery periods. These results are summarized in the following proposition.

Proposition 1. *In the dynamic demand for labor schedule, the responses of labor demand to variations in real wages and capital costs in the short run ($\dot{k} = 0$) and the delivery period ($\dot{k} \neq 0$) obey the following relationships:* $\left|\frac{\partial \dot{m}(t)}{\partial w}\right| > \left|\frac{\partial \dot{m}^s(t)}{\partial w}\right|, \left|\frac{\partial \dot{m}(t)}{\partial c_k}\right| > \left|\frac{\partial \dot{m}^s(t)}{\partial c_k}\right|.$

The proof of this proposition, for the real wage responses, requires the following condition, using results derived above.

$$\frac{\partial \dot{m}^s(t)}{\partial w} - \frac{\partial \dot{m}(t)}{\partial w} = \beta^{-1}\sigma_{14}\left[\frac{\Pi_1(t)}{\Pi_1(\ell)} - 1\right] > 0$$

It was stated above that the real wage responses in the labor demand schedule were negative and, therefore, as long as $0 \leq t < \ell$, the Le Chatelier Principle holds in this case because the fixed-capacity response is smaller, in absolute value, as compared to its delivery-period counterpart. Thus the Le Chatelier Principle holds when we compare short-run to delivery-period real wage responses in the labor demand schedule.

Regarding capital cost responses, the proof of this proposition uses

$$\frac{\partial \dot{m}^s(t)}{\partial c_k} - \frac{\partial \dot{m}(t)}{\partial c_k} = \beta^{-1}\sigma_{14}\left[\frac{\Pi_1(t)}{\Pi_1(\ell)} - 1\right] > 0$$

If $\alpha_{12} > 0$, it is evident from (13d) and (14) that the response of labor demand to capital costs is negative, in which case $\partial \dot{m}^s(t)/\partial c_k - \partial \dot{m}(t)/\partial c_k > 0$ and the Le Chatelier Principle arises just as in the case of real wages. If $\alpha_{12} < 0$, then labor demand is positively related to the firm's capital costs and the short-run and delivery-period responses obey $\partial \dot{m}^s(t)/\partial c_k - \partial \dot{m}(t)/\partial c_k < 0$. The Le Chatelier Principle holds once again and so the fact that the cross-derivative of the production function is unrestricted has no impact on the existence of the Le Chatelier Principle in this comparison.

Regarding investment in quasi-fixed capital, the Le Chatelier Principle holds trivially in this context simply because capital investment is zero in the short run. Because the firm is capacity-constrained in $t \in [0, \ell]$, capital investment is completely inelastic with respect to the factor prices in the model. Thus in comparing short-run and delivery-period factor price responses, short-run factor price responses will be smaller than their delivery-period counterparts (which are of course generally nonzero) and thus the Le Chatelier Principle holds.

5.2. The delivery period and the steady state

We may now consider the factor price responses in the delivery period and the steady state. In this context, a form of the Le Chatelier Principle holds but with a qualification involving the own-adjustment parameter contained in the investment demand for labor. To see this, use (10) and (14) to form

$$\frac{\partial \dot{m}(t)}{\partial w} - \frac{\partial m^*}{\partial w} = \frac{\alpha_{11}\alpha_{22} - \alpha_{12}^2 + \alpha_0\beta\kappa_1\kappa_2 + \alpha_0\beta(\kappa_1 + \kappa_2 - r)}{\beta(\alpha_{11}\alpha_{22} - \alpha_{12}^2)(\kappa_1 + \kappa_2 - r)}.$$

With only qualitative information on the elements of this expression, it is not possible to bound this relation without further restrictions of some sort. Inspection of the expression above, along with (12), suggests that a plausible restriction might involve the own-adjustment parameters from the flexible accelerator in (11). Pursuing this possibility, it can be shown that this factor price comparison above can be rewritten as

$$\frac{\partial \dot{m}(t)}{\partial w} - \frac{\partial m^*}{\partial w} = \frac{(1 + \omega_{22})\beta(\kappa_1 + \kappa_2 - r) - \alpha_{12}^2}{\beta(\alpha_{11}\alpha_{22} - \alpha_{12}^2)(\kappa_1 + \kappa_2 - r)}$$

The above expression will be positive if $1 + \omega_{22} > 0$.[12] The implication of this restriction is summarized in the following proposition.

[12] Discrete time models do restrict own-adjustment parameters in just this way. Quadratic form adjustment cost models, now familiar from Sargent [17], provide numerous examples of this fact.

Proposition 2. *Suppose that the own-adjustment parameter from the dynamic demand for labor schedule satisfies the restriction* $0 > \omega_{22} > -1$. *Then it will be true that* $\left|\frac{\partial m^*}{\partial w}\right| > \left|\frac{\partial \dot{m}(t)}{\partial w}\right|$.

A similar result may be established if capital cost responses in the dynamic labor demand schedule were to be compared. Therefore, if we maintain the bound on the own-adjustment parameter in this way, we have the result that steady-state responses, in absolute value, exceed those in the delivery period which, in turn, exceed those arising in the fixed-capacity period.[13] Thus estimation of factor price elasticities in the dynamic demand for labor readily provide a bound on the factor price elasticities contained in the long-run stock demand for labor. Thus estimates of dynamic demand schedules can be relied upon to provide some information about long-run factor input responses to variations in factor input prices.[14]

The restriction that own-adjustment parameters are bounded between zero and minus unity seems a plausible one on the basis of a wide array of empirical work.[15] For example, empirical studies in the inventory investment literature (see [1]) have repeatedly estimated own-adjustment speeds for inventory stocks and, while there has been some controversy over the plausibility of these magnitudes when they are estimated, there is little disagreement in the empirical evidence that own-adjustment parameters are bounded as they are in the above proposition. Similarly, the money demand literature contains estimates of adjustment speeds for the stock of money with similar results and one can find estimates of own-adjustment parameters in a variety of dynamic factor demand studies.[16]

To summarize, the Le Chatelier Principle holds with qualifications when delivery-period and steady-state factor price responses are compared. If costs of adjustment cause firms to make up only a fraction of the gap between desired and actual stocks at each instant of time, this same manifestation of inertia will cause the Le Chatelier Principle to hold when factor price responses are compared in delivery-period (dynamic) demand schedules and steady-state factor demands.

[13] It should be clear that we could derive the same sorts of results in the capital investment demand schedule if we restrict the own-adjustment parameter in that schedule as we have in the labor demand equation.

[14] These long-run factor price effects would be contained in the cointegrating vectors describing the long-run behavior of the firm.

[15] I am, of course, glossing over the difficult issue of aggregation as is customarily done in macroeconomics. For the most part I am proceeding here as most economists do, which is to simply derive microeconomic relationships and then act as though these decision rules hold in the aggregate.

[16] See the survey by Goldfeld and Sichel [4] for evidence of partial adjustment in estimated money demand schedules. For empirical results from factor demand studies, see, for example, [5, Chap. 7] who provides evidence on estimated adjustment speeds in dynamic labor demand schedules.

Thus the Le Chatelier Principle can be viewed as a companion result to the effects of costs of adjustment.

6. Extensions

The analysis to this point has ignored two issues that need to be addressed. One concerns the role that variable factor inputs might play in affecting any of the results that were obtained above. The second issue concerns how the results might change if we were to incorporate additional fixed state variables into the analysis. I first study a model with one variable factor input (extending the model to include an arbitrary number of variable factors will be discussed as well) and then a model with two capital goods subject to delivery lags will be examined. It will be seen that the Le Chatelier Principle generalizes into these contexts but not in every direction that is considered.

6.1. Variable factor inputs

A variable factor input is defined as one that is not subject to adjustment costs. To augment the model with such a variable factor input is straightforward. The problem to be solved is maximize

$$J = J_1 + J_2 = \int_0^{\ell} R_1(t)e^{-rt}dt + \int_{\ell}^{\infty} R_2(t)e^{-rt}dt \tag{17a}$$

$$R_1(t) = f(k_0, m(t), v(t)) - c(h(t)) - wm(t) - p_v v(t) \tag{17b}$$

$$R_2(t) = f(k(t), m(t), v(t)) - c(h(t)) - wm(t) - p_v v(t) - g_k[d_k(t) + p_k(d_k(t))e^{r\ell} + i_k(d_k(t))] \tag{17c}$$

where the accounting constraints that apply to this problem are those used before in (3) and (4). The production function has been augmented with a variable factor input, denoted by v, and the purchase price of this input is given by p_v. Factor payments for this variable factor input are subtracted from the firm's revenues. Otherwise, the problem is identical to that discussed above.

The addition of the variable factor only adds a marginal productivity condition for the variable factor to each set of optimality conditions. For $t \in [0, \ell]$, necessary conditions are given by

$$\pi = c'(h) \tag{18a}$$

$$p_v = f_v(k_0, m, v) \tag{18b}$$

$$\dot{\lambda} = -f_k(k_0, m, v) + r\lambda \tag{18c}$$

$$\dot{\pi} = w - f_m(k_0, m, v) + r\pi \tag{18d}$$

$$\dot{k} = 0 \tag{18e}$$

$$\dot{m} = h \tag{18f}$$

and, for the delivery period, necessary conditions are given by

$$\lambda = g_k[1 + p_k'(d_k)e^{r\ell} + i_k'(d_k)] \tag{19a}$$
$$\pi = c'(h) \tag{19b}$$
$$p_v = f_v(k, m, v) \tag{19c}$$
$$\dot{\lambda} = -f_k(k, m, v) + r\lambda \tag{19d}$$
$$\dot{\pi} = w - f_m(k, m, v) + r\pi \tag{19e}$$
$$\dot{k} = d_k \tag{19f}$$
$$\dot{m} = h. \tag{19g}$$

The boundary conditions for this problem are identical to those given previously.

The structure of each solution path for this problem is very similar to the problem given in (5) as long as we maintain the curvature assumptions that were used in the previous model. Specifically, the solution path for the delivery period will still display saddlepath stability. The characteristic roots will again be symmetric about $r/2$ with two stable real roots and two roots that are unstable and positive. The solution path for the costate variable π will have the same form as (13a) except that, with the addition of the variable factor input, the coefficients of this expression will differ from those given above in (13b)–(13e) and the factor price for the variable factor will also appear as an argument of this path. The flexible accelerator for capital and labor will arise just as it did in the previous problem. The short-run solution path for this costate variable will be of the form given previously by (15). Although the characteristic roots in this expression will differ from those arising in the problem without the factor input v, they will still be real with one root that is negative and one that is positive. The damping factor will arise in the short-run solution just as it did in the previous problem.

Since the solution paths for this augmented problem display these similarities, it is clear that the propositions discussed earlier for the labor demand schedules will also apply to this problem. Whatever the delivery-period factor price responses for real wages and capital costs that arise while the firm can take deliveries of new capital or in the steady state, smaller ones will apply to the short run assuming that own-adjustment parameters are bounded as discussed above. In this sense, the addition of the variable factor is of little consequence. Additional variable factors could be added with the same result. But it will also be true that the short-run dynamic demand for labor will respond to p_v (as well as other variable factor prices if there other such inputs contained in the problem) and this response in the short run will be smaller than it will be during the delivery period and the steady state as can be established with similar reasoning. Our results for the capital investment flow and stock demands will go through just as they did before.

But now we can ask if there are Le Chatelier effects that apply to variable factor inputs and here the results are somewhat idiosyncratic to the model at hand. That is, the results that arise are specific to a model where the costate variable π does not appear in the optimality condition describing the optimal choice of the variable factor, a fact which need not arise in other contexts.[17] Because this costate variable does not appear in the marginal productivity condition, there is thus no scope for variable factor inputs to be elastic with respect to the firm's real wage and capital costs. This fact is summarized in the following proposition.

Proposition 3. *Variable factor inputs will be completely inelastic with respect to the firm's real wage and capital costs in the short run. Thus the response of variable factor inputs will be smaller in magnitude in the fixed-capacity period with respect to these factor input prices than they will be in either the delivery period or the steady state.*

Finally, the variable factor inputs will be elastic with respect to all variable factor input prices with responses given directly from the necessary conditions describing the optimal choices of variable inputs. For example, inverting the optimality condition for v in the short-run necessary condition above gives the short-run response of v to its own input price; this response is $f_{vv}^{-1} < 0$ assuming that we maintain the assumption that there are diminishing returns to this variable factor input in production. Thus with diminishing returns in production, the variable factor input is inversely related to its own input price. While variable factors will be elastic with respect to all variable factor input prices, it is not be possible to show that Le Chatelier effects, associated with the responses of variable factors to variable factor input prices, arise for these inputs in models with one or more variable inputs in production. Thus this principle does not generalize in this direction.[18]

6.2. Additional fixed state variables

The final model to be studied is one where we augment the original problem statement with an additional quasi-fixed state variable that will also be subject to a delivery lag. There will now be two state variables fixed for the same length

---

[17] For example, if the firm were to produce output to stock, thus holding a stock of finished goods, it will evaluate the marginal productivity of variable factor inputs using the shadow price of inventory accumulation. Thus a costate variable would appear directly in the marginal productivity condition for the variable factor, unlike the problem at hand.

[18] In the current problem, it is not possible to show that $\left|\frac{\partial v^*(t)}{\partial p_v}\right| > \left|\frac{\partial v^s(t)}{\partial p_v}\right|$ which would be needed to establish Le Chatelier effects in this case. This proof is not provided but it is available upon request.

of time. This is of course somewhat artificial. It seems more reasonable, at least as an empirical matter, to assume that heterogeneous capital goods would be subject to delivery lags that differ in length. But the static literature on the Le Chatelier Principle has been concerned with the magnitudes of factor price effects as additional choice variables are fixed. Thus this experiment seems a natural one to undertake in order to see if the results from the static literature carry over to the dynamic case.

The problem to be solved may be stated as the maximization of the following objective functional

$$J = J_1 + J_2 = \int_0^{\ell} R_1(t)e^{-rt}dt + \int_{\ell}^{\infty} R_2(t)e^{-rt}dt \tag{20a}$$

$$R_1(t) = f(k_0, m(t), x_0) - c(h(t)) - wm(t) \tag{20b}$$

$$\begin{aligned} R_2(t) = {} & f(k(t), m(t), x(t)) - c(h(t)) - wm(t) - g_k[d_k(t) \\ & + p_k(d_k(t))e^{r\ell} + i_k(d_k(t))] \\ & - g_x[d_x(t) + p_x(d_x(t))e^{r\ell} + i_x(d_x(t))] \end{aligned} \tag{20c}$$

where g_x denotes the purchase price of the capital good x and d_x refers to deliveries of this additional capital good. Both capital goods are treated in exactly the same way: there is no depreciation of either one and payments for new capital goods of either type are made at the time that deliveries are received. Planning and installation costs are associated with each capital good. An additional accounting constraint for x will apply that is similar in form to (3).

Necessary conditions for this problem will arise by forming the Hamiltonians for each interval as before and these expressions lead to the following necessary conditions. Let φ denote the adjoint variable measuring the imputed value of accumulating the capital good x. For the initial interval we have the necessary conditions

$$\pi = c'(h) \tag{21a}$$

$$\dot{\lambda} = -f_k(k_0, m, x_0) + r\lambda \tag{21b}$$

$$\dot{\pi} = w - f_m(k_0, m, x_0) + r\pi \tag{21c}$$

$$\dot{\varphi} = -f_x(k_0, m, x_0) + r\varphi \tag{21d}$$

$$\dot{k} = 0 \tag{21e}$$

$$\dot{m} = h \tag{21f}$$

$$\dot{x} = 0 \tag{21g}$$

and, for the second interval we obtain

$$\lambda = g_k[1 + p_k'(d_k)e^{r\ell} + i_k'(d_k)] \tag{22a}$$
$$\varphi = g_x[1 + p_x'(d_x)e^{r\ell} + i_x'(d_x)] \tag{22b}$$
$$\pi = c'(h) \tag{22c}$$
$$\dot{\lambda} = -f_k(k, m, x) + r\lambda \tag{22d}$$
$$\dot{\pi} = w - f_m(k, m, x) + r\pi \tag{22e}$$
$$\dot{\varphi} = -f_x(k, m, x) + r\varphi \tag{22f}$$
$$\dot{k} = d_k \tag{22g}$$
$$\dot{m} = h \tag{22h}$$
$$\dot{x} = d_x. \tag{22i}$$

Boundary conditions are familiar at this point and need not be repeated.

The crucial part of the analysis will concern what, if any, differences there are in the short-run solution path, compared to our previous analysis, as a result of adding an additional state variable that is fixed for a finite time. If results from the static literature apply here, then we should find that factor price responses in the dynamic demand schedule for labor will be smaller than they would be with only one capital good fixed for a finite time.

It is evident from these necessary conditions that the solution path for the costate variable π is required as it was previously to establish factor price responses in the short run. The dynamic demand for labor continues to be related to the costate variable π as in the earlier models. The solution path for this adjoint variable during the delivery period will be of the form

$$\pi(t) = \begin{bmatrix} \tilde{\sigma}_{11} & \tilde{\sigma}_{12} & \tilde{\sigma}_{13} & \tilde{\sigma}_{14} & \tilde{\sigma}_{15} & \tilde{\sigma}_{16} \end{bmatrix} \begin{bmatrix} k(t) \\ m(t) \\ x(t) \\ c_k \\ w \\ c_x \end{bmatrix}$$

where $c_x = rg_x$, the user cost of capital good x. If additional state variables were added, the dimension of each vector would increase in the obvious way with additional state variables and their associated capital costs appearing in this solution path. The coefficients in the vector $[\tilde{\sigma}]$ are not the same as the parameters in (13a) for variables appearing in each problem. Thus the impact on π of variation in, say, the real wage will not be the same in this problem as it was in earlier problems described above.

Now suppose for the moment that the damping factor, arising in the short-run solution path, is identical to that in the first problem examined above.[19] Consider the impact of real wages in the relevant decision rules in the current problem and the first problem studied above. The only way that we could get smaller factor price effects in the short run, now that there is an additional fixed state variable in the initial interval, would be if $|\sigma_{14}| < |\tilde{\sigma}_{14}|$. These parameters generally cannot be bounded in this way if only because such comparisons involve the characteristic roots (see 13a–13e) from different problems which cannot generally be compared. In fact these coefficients will differ for other reasons as well and so there will not be a ready way to bound parameters in factor price comparisons between models. Therefore, the result from the static literature, namely that fixing additional choice (state) variables results in reduced price elasticities, does not generalize in this dynamic context.

7. Concluding remarks

It is commonly believed that the Le Chatelier Principle, introduced into the economics literature by Samuelson [16], arises in the demand schedules obeyed by economic agents. This principle provides an explanation of why economic agents respond sluggishly to changes in incentives because it asserts that demands for choice variables will less elastic in the short run (that is, while subsets of choice variables are fixed) than they will be in full equilibrium when all choice variables can be set in an optimal fashion. Previous literature studying this idea has been done in a static context and there is no study that examines a neoclassical dynamic model of the firm for the existence of this principle when there are costs of adjustment attached to inputs used in production by the firm.

In this paper, three models of the firm are examined to see if the demand schedules for productive inputs display the properties of the Le Chatelier Principle when the Marshallian short run is embedded within the model solved by the firm. The short run arises by assuming that there is a finite delivery lag associated with the receipt of new capital goods so that unanticipated movements in the purchase prices of inputs or other magnitudes will cause the firm

[19] In fact, the damping factor will be the same here as it was in the earlier problem above as may be found by forming the transition equations for the short run that arise in each problem. The damping factor involves the characteristic roots associated with the transition equations from each problem and it happens that the coefficient matrix, used to form these characteristic roots, is the same in each problem. It seems likely, however, that this is not a general property of this class of model and so it seems reasonable to suppose that this finding is specific to the model at hand.

to be capacity-constrained while awaiting delivery of new capital goods. During the short run, the firm can adjust its labor force in anticipation of future deliveries of new capital goods and therefore, in this paper, comparisons can be made about the magnitudes of factor price responses in the short run, the period when capital goods deliveries arrive, and the long-run equilibrium of the firm when all of its inputs are at optimal levels (full stock adjustment). The analysis also considers a form of the Le Chatelier Principle which differs from previous research because factor price response comparisons are made between delivery-period and steady-state factor price responses.

Results are obtained in this paper showing that the Le Chatelier Principle does indeed hold when we compare short-run and delivery-period factor price responses in the dynamic demand schedule for labor. The dynamic demand for labor in the short run will have smaller factor price elasticities when compared to its delivery-period counterpart. Similar results are true for the dynamic demand for capital. In addition, the principle will hold when we compare delivery-period and steady-state factor price responses but with the additional restriction that own-adjustment parameters in the model are bounded between zero and minus unity. Such a restriction on adjustment speeds is plausible and consistent with a considerable body of empirical evidence.

Two extensions are considered: one is where there are an arbitrary number of variable factor inputs (i.e., inputs that are not subject to adjustment costs) and the second is where there is more than one capital good that is fixed for a finite time. With additional variable factor inputs, the Le Chatelier Principle generalizes in a straightforward manner for the quasi-fixed inputs but not the variable inputs. When there are two capital goods fixed for a finite time, the additional fixed capital good does not reduce factor price elasticities in the short run from what they would be with one fixed capital good. Thus the Le Chatelier Principle survives many, but not all, of the generalizations considered in this paper. But it seems fair to conclude that the Le Chatelier Principle is indeed a feature of economic systems and that it is one reason, among others advanced in previous research, for the inertia evident in economies.

There are some extensions to this analysis that should be mentioned. One possible avenue for future research on this topic would be to incorporate finished goods inventories into a model of the type studied here. By holding a buffer stock of finished goods, the firm would have an additional degree of freedom in dealing with a fixed-capacity constraint and it may be true that the results in this paper regarding the existence of the Le Chatelier Principle may need to be tempered by the presence of these buffer stocks. The existence of substantial input delivery lags may also have a role to play in providing an explanation of why firms may choose to produce to stock or to order. These two possible subjects are left for future research on this topic.

8. Appendix

8.1. The delivery period

The delivery-period transition equations are

$$\begin{bmatrix} \dot{\lambda}(t) \\ \dot{\pi}(t) \\ \dot{k}(t) \\ \dot{m}(t) \end{bmatrix} = \begin{bmatrix} r & 0 & \alpha_{11} & \alpha_{12} \\ 0 & r & \alpha_{12} & \alpha_{22} \\ [g_k(\gamma_k e^{r\ell} + \delta_k)]^{-1} & 0 & 0 & 0 \\ 0 & \beta^{-1} & 0 & 0 \end{bmatrix} \begin{bmatrix} \lambda(t) \\ \pi(t) \\ k(t) \\ m(t) \end{bmatrix} + \begin{bmatrix} 0 \\ w \\ -(\gamma_k e^{r\ell} + \delta_k)^{-1} \\ 0 \end{bmatrix} \tag{23}$$

To establish the properties of the solution path that arises from these differential equations, an analysis of the characteristic roots is required. To find these roots, form the quartic equation given by

$$|\Omega - \kappa I| = 0$$

where the roots are denoted by κ and $[\Omega]$ is the matrix of constant coefficients in this linear system of equations. The roots of the system are given by

$$\kappa = \frac{r}{2} \pm \sqrt{\left(\frac{r}{2}\right)^2 + \frac{\alpha_{11}\Omega_{31} + \beta^{-1}\alpha_{22}}{2} \pm \sqrt{\left(\frac{\alpha_{11}\Omega_{31} - \beta^{-1}\alpha_{12}}{2}\right)^2 + \alpha_{12}^2\beta^{-1}\Omega_{31}}}$$

where $\Omega_{31} = [g_k(\gamma_k e^{r\ell} + \delta_k)]^{-1}$. Inspection of this expression reveals that the roots are symmetric about $r/2$ [24, p. 850] and they are real. Assuming that the roots are distinct (a slight perturbation of underlying parameters will induce distinct roots) and eliminating the unstable roots by the choice of constant terms, the solution path for this system is

$$\lambda(t) = C_1\rho_1^1 e^{\kappa_1 t} + C_1\rho_1^2 e^{\kappa_2 t} + \lambda^* \tag{24a}$$
$$\pi(t) = C_1\rho_2^1 e^{\kappa_1 t} + C_1\rho_2^2 e^{\kappa_2 t} \tag{24b}$$
$$k(t) = C_1\rho_3^1 e^{\kappa_1 t} + C_1\rho_3^2 e^{\kappa_2 t} + m^* \tag{24c}$$
$$m(t) = C_1\rho_4^1 e^{\kappa_1 t} + C_1\rho_4^2 e^{\kappa_2 t} + k^* \tag{24d}$$

where the stable roots are defined as $\kappa_{1,2}$. The elements of the characteristic vectors are found from

$$\begin{bmatrix} r - \kappa_j & 0 & \alpha_{11} & \alpha_{12} \\ 0 & r - \kappa_j & \alpha_{12} & \alpha_{22} \\ [g_k(\gamma_k e^{r\ell} + \delta_k]^{-1} & 0 & -\kappa_j & 0 \\ 0 & \beta^{-1} & 0 & -\kappa_j \end{bmatrix} \begin{bmatrix} \rho_1^j \\ \rho_2^j \\ \rho_3^j \\ \rho_4^j \end{bmatrix} = 0.$$

One element of the characteristic vectors may be set arbitrarily. Set $\rho_4^j = 1$ and the remaining elements may be found to be

$$\rho_1^j = -\frac{[\alpha_{11}(r-\kappa_j)\beta\kappa_j + \alpha_{11}\alpha_{22} - \alpha_{12}^2}{\alpha_{12}(r-\pi_j)}$$

$$\rho_2^j = \beta\kappa_j$$

$$\rho_3^j = \frac{[(r-\kappa_j)\beta\kappa_j + \alpha_{22}]}{\alpha_{12}}.$$

To obtain the solution path for π, eliminate the constants and exponentials from (24) using the elements of the characteristic vectors. Doing so gives (13a)–(13e).

The investment demand equations can be derived in a similar fashion. Differentiate the solution path (24) above for $k(t)$ and $m(t)$ with respect to time and eliminate the constants and exponentials from the resulting expressions. This gives the multivariate flexible accelerator

$$\begin{bmatrix} \dot{k}(t) \\ \dot{m}(t) \end{bmatrix} = \begin{bmatrix} \omega_{11} & \omega_{12} \\ \omega_{21} & \omega_{22} \end{bmatrix} \begin{bmatrix} k(t) - k^* \\ m(t) - m^* \end{bmatrix}$$

where the adjustment parameters ω_{ij} are

$$\omega_{11} = \frac{\kappa_2\rho_3^2 - \kappa_1\rho_3^1}{\rho_3^2 - \rho_3^1} = -\frac{[\alpha_{22} + \beta\kappa_1\kappa_2 - \beta(\kappa_1+\kappa_2)(\kappa_1+\kappa_2-r)]}{\beta(\kappa_1+\kappa_2-r)} < 0$$

$$\omega_{12} = -\frac{(\kappa_2-\kappa_1)\rho_3^1\rho_3^2}{\rho_3^2-\rho_3^1} = \frac{[(r-\kappa_2)\beta\kappa_2+\alpha_{22}][(r-\kappa_1)\beta\kappa_1+\alpha_{22}]}{\alpha_{12}\beta(\kappa_1+\kappa_2-r)}$$

$$\omega_{21} = \frac{\kappa_2-\kappa_1}{\rho_3^2-\rho_3^1} = -\frac{\alpha_{12}}{\beta(\kappa_1+\kappa_2-r)}$$

$$\omega_{22} = \frac{\kappa_1\rho_3^2 - \kappa_2\rho_3^1}{\rho_3^2-\rho_3^1} = \frac{\alpha_{22}+\beta\kappa_1\kappa_2}{\beta(\kappa_1+\kappa_2-r)} < 0.$$

The adjustment parameters are negative along the diagonal of the adjustment matrix and are sign-symmetric off the diagonal, the sign depending upon the parameter α_{12}. The long-run factor demand functions arise by setting $\dot{\lambda}(t) = \dot{\pi}(t) = \dot{m}(t) = \dot{k}(t) = 0$ in (23) and solving the resulting equations to obtain (10).

8.2. The short run

The analysis of the short run requires the solution to the transition equations

$$\begin{bmatrix} \dot{\pi}(t) \\ \dot{m}(t) \end{bmatrix} = \begin{bmatrix} r & \alpha_{22} \\ \beta^{-1} & 0 \end{bmatrix} \begin{bmatrix} \pi(t) \\ m(t) \end{bmatrix} + \begin{bmatrix} w - \alpha_{12}k_0 \\ 0 \end{bmatrix}$$

because these transition equations are partially uncoupled from the costate equation for the shadow price of capital. The solution to these equations must incorporate the switch-point conditions (8c) and (8d). To do this, the homogeneous component of the solution path will be obtained following methods in [2, pp. 316–317]. The solution can be written as

$$\begin{bmatrix} \pi(t) \\ m(t) \end{bmatrix} = \Phi(t, \tau) \begin{bmatrix} \pi(\tau) \\ m(\tau) \end{bmatrix}$$

where the transition matrix $\Phi(t, \tau) = \psi_0(t, \tau)I + \psi_1(t, \tau)[\Lambda]$ and

$$[\Lambda] = \begin{bmatrix} r & \alpha_2 \\ \beta^{-1} & 0 \end{bmatrix}.$$

The elements ψ_i are given by

$$\psi_0(t, \tau) = \frac{\kappa_1^s e^{\kappa_2^s(t-\tau)} - \kappa_2^s e^{\kappa_1^s(t-\tau)}}{\kappa_1^s - \kappa_2^s}$$

$$\psi_1(t, \tau) = \frac{e^{\kappa_1^s(t-\tau)} - e^{\kappa_2^s(t-\tau)}}{\kappa_1^s - \kappa_2^s}.$$

where $\kappa_{1,2}^s$ are the eigenvalues arising in this problem. The solution for π is therefore

$$\pi(t) = [\psi_0(t, \tau) + r\psi_1(t, \tau)]\pi(\tau) + \alpha_{22}\psi_1(t, \tau)m(\tau).$$

To derive the solution that is required, set $\tau = 0$ in the above expression, then take the resulting expression and set $t = \ell$. These operations give

$$\pi(t) = [\psi_0(t, 0) + r\psi_1(t, 0)]\pi(0) + \alpha_{22}\psi_1(t, 0)m(0)$$
$$\pi(\ell) = [\psi_0(\ell, 0) + r\psi_1(\ell, 0)]\pi(0) + \alpha_{22}\psi_1(\ell, 0)m(0).$$

Eliminate $\pi(0)$ from this pair of equations and the resulting expression is (15) with the superscript s used to denote magnitudes pertaining to the short run. The nonhomogeneous component of this costate solution is zero.

References

1. Blinder, A.S., Maccini L.J.: The resurgence of inventory research: what have we learned? J. Econ. Surv. **5**(4), 291–328 (1991)
2. Brogan, W.L.: Modern Control Theory, 3rd edn. Prentice-Hall, Englewood cliffs (1980)
3. Epstein, L.G.: The le chatelier principle in optimal control problems. J. Econ. Theory **19**(1), 103–122 (1978)
4. Goldfeld, S.M., Sichel, D.E.: The demand for money. In: Friedman, B.M., Hahn, F.H. (eds.) Handbook of Monetary Economics, vol. I, pp. 300–356. Elsevier, Amsterdam (1990)
5. Hamermesh, D.S.: Labor Demand. Princeton University Press, Princeton (1993)
6. Hansen, L.P., Sargent, T.J.: Linear rational expectations models for dynamically interrelated variables. In: Lucas, R.E., Sargent, T.J. (eds) Rational Expectations and Econometric Practice, vol. 1, pp. 127–156. The University of Minnesota Press, Minneapolis (1981)
7. Hayashi, F.: Tobin's marginal q and average q: a neoclassical interpretation. Econometrica **50**(1), 213–224 (1982)
8. Kydland, F.E., Prescott, E.C.: Time to build and aggregate fluctuations. Econometrica **50**(6), 1345–1370 (1982)
9. Lucas, R.E.: Optimal investment policy and the flexible accelerator. Int. Econ. Rev. **8**(1), 78–85 (1967)
10. Maccini, L.J.: Delivery lags and the demand for investment. Rev. Econ. Stud. **40**(2), 269–281 (1973)
11. Milgrom, P., Roberts, J.: The LeChatelier principle. Am. Econo. Rev. **86**(1), 173–179 (1996)
12. Mordukhovich, B.S.: Variational analysis and generalized differentiation. In: Basic Theory, vol. 1. Springer, Heidelberg (2006)
13. Nickell, S.: Uncertainty and lags in the investment decisions of firms. Rev. Econ. Stud. **44**(1), 249–263 (1977)
14. Rossana, R.J.: Delivery lags and buffer stocks in the theory of investment by the firm. J. Econ. Dyn. Control **9**(2), 153–193 (1985)
15. Rossana, R.J.: Technology shocks and cointegration in quadratic models of the firm. Int. Econ. Rev. **36**(1), 5–17 (1995)
16. Samuelson, P.A.: Foundations of Economic Analysis. Harvard University Press, Cambridge (1983)
17. Sargent, T.J.: Macroeconomic Theory, 2nd edn. Academic Press, New York (1987)
18. Silberberg, E.: The le chatelier principle as a corollary to a generalized envelope theorem. J. Econ. Theory **3**(2), 146–155 (1971)
19. Silberberg, E.: A revision of comparative statics methodology in economics, or, how to do comparative statics on the back of an envelope. J. Econ. Theory **7**(2), 159–172 (1974)
20. Suen, W., Silberberg, E., Tseng, P.: The LeChatelier principle: the long and the short of it. Econ. Theory **16**(2), 471–476 (2000)
21. Tomiyama, K.: Two-stage optimal control problems and optimality conditions. J. Econ. Dyn. Control **9**(3), 317–337 (1985)
22. Tomiyama, K., Rossana, R.J.: Two-stage optimal control problems with an explicit switch-point dependence: optimality criteria and an example of delivery lags and investment. J. Econ. Dyn. Control **13**, 319–337 (1989)

23. Treadway, A.B.: Adjustment costs and variable inputs in the theory of the competitive firm. J. Econ. Theor **2**(4), 329–347 (1970)
24. Treadway, A.B.: The rational multivariate flexible accelerator. Econometrica **39**(5):845–855 (1971)

Adv. Math. Econ. 11, 147–155 (2008)

Advances in MATHEMATICAL ECONOMICS

Interdependent utility functions in an intergenerational context

Tomoichi Shinotsuka*

Graduate School of Humanities and Social Sciences, University of Tsukuba, Tennodai 1-1-1, Tsukuba, Ibaraki 305-8571, Japan
(e-mail: shino@social.tsukuba.ac.jp)

Received: August 31, 2007
Revised: November 12, 2007

JEL classification: D11, D64

Mathematics Subject Classification (2000): 91B42, 91B62

Abstract. We investigate the question of representing nonpaternalistic functions (aggregators) in paternalistic form, which was posed by Ray (J. Econ. Theory 41:112–132, 1987), in an intergenerational setting. As in Hori (Jpn Econ. Rev. 52:137–155, 2001), the aggregators in this paper may differ across generations and depend possibly on the utility levels of all other generations. We discuss two approaches to deal with an infinite horizon. The first one explores monotonicity structures inherent in nonpaternalistic altruism. By means of lattice-theoretic arguments, we establish the existence of representations of nonpaternalistic functions in paternalistic form. The second approach uses the requirement of small degree of altruism.

Key words: nonpaternalistic intergenerational altruism, paternalistic representation, aggregator

1. Introduction

To analyze intertemporal economic problems, the notion of intergenerational altruism has been playing an important role.[1] Researchers in this field identified

* I thank seminar and conference participants in Hitotsubashi, Kansai, Waseda, and Caltech (Social Choice and Welfare Meeting) for helpful comments. I am also grateful to an anonymous referee for pointing out a gap in the proof of Theorem 1 and other valuable suggestions. Research grant from Zengin Foundation for Studies in Economics and Finace is gratefully acknowledged.

[1] For prominent examples, the reader is referred to the references in Ray [14] and Hori and Kanaya [10].

two models of intergenerational altruism. To borrow terminologies from Ray [14], the paternalistic model, on the one hand, incorporates intergenerational altruism into the utility function of each generation as a function of consumption allocations among all generations. On the other hand, the nonpaternalistic model captures intergenerational altruism by means of aggregators which relate the utility level of each generation to the utility levels of other generations as well as one's own consumption. The idea of nonpaternalistic altruism was formulated by Becker [3] in the context of altruism among family members. In intergenerational contexts, the same idea was employed by Barro [2], Kimball [11], Ray [14], Hori and Kanaya [10], Hori [7], and Hori [8].

Ray [14, pp. 113–114] addressed the following question concerning the two approaches:

> The representation of nonpaternalistic functions in paternalistic form has also been the object of limited attention; .... But a systematic analysis of the relationship between these two frameworks is yet to be written, and appears to be quite a challenge, especially for models with an infinite horizon.

Several interesting results on this question have been delivered recently. Bergstrom [4] identified the relevance of an infinite version of McKenzie's [13] dominant diagonal condition for a given list of linear aggregators to possess a unique representation. Hori [9] considered the representation problem for the case of a finite number of agents with possibly nonlinear aggregators. Hori [9] showed that McKenzie's [13] dominant diagonal matrix can be useful in the case of non-linear aggregators as well. The model in this paper is an extension of Hori's [9] to the case of countably many generations. As in Hori [9], the aggregators in this paper may differ across generations and depend possibly on the utility levels of all other generations.

We discuss two approaches to deal with an infinite horizon. The first one explores monotonicity structures inherent in nonpaternalistic altruism. By means of lattice-theoretic arguments alone, we establish the existence of representations of nonpaternalistic functions (aggregators) in paternalistic form. Becker [3] discussed the problem of infinite regress to require that the degree of altruism be small. The second approach uses the requirement of the same spirit expressed in terms of uniformly small Fréche derivative (with respect to the utility level of other generations). We regard this approach as a natural extension of Hori's [9]. We also discuss the case of linear aggregators. As Bergstrom [4] showed, a certain infinite matrix with a dominant diagonal expresses the idea of small degree of altruism in this case and it offers a powerful tool to represent nonpaternalistic functions in paternalistic form. Our treatment is different from Bergstrom [4] in that we view the infinite matrix as a representation of a continuous linear operator on l_∞ (the set of bounded utility allocations of all generations) into itself while Bergstrom viewed it as a certain limit of finite dimensional square matrices.

The rest of this paper is organized as follows. In Sect. 2, we present the model. In Sect. 3, we discuss the lattice-theoretic approach to the representation problem. In Sect. 4, we discuss the approach based on the contraction mapping theorem. In Sect. 5, we consider the case of linear aggregators. In the last section, we show that the contraction approach is an extension of Hori's [9] to the case of an infinite horizon.

2. The model

For simplicity, we assume that there is one consumer for each generation. The integers $t = 1, 2, \dots$ denote generations. For each t, $X_t = \mathbb{R}^l_+$ denotes the consumption set of generation t.

Let $X = \prod_{t=1}^{\infty} X_t$. For each t, let $U_{-t} = \mathbb{R}^{\infty}$. A generic element $u_{-t} = (u_1, \dots, u_{t-1}, u_{t+1}, \dots) \in U_{-t}$ signifies a profile of utilities other than generation t.

We employ the following terminologies. Let f be a real-valued function on an ordered set Y. We say that f is non-decreasing (respectively, strictly increasing) if $f(x) \geq f(y)$ [respectively $f(x) > f(y)$] for all $x, y \in Y$ with $x \geq y$ and $x \neq y$.

For each t, a real-valued function G_t on $X_t \times U_{-t}$ is given. We call it the **aggregator for generation** $\boldsymbol{t}$. Let $G = (G_1, G_2, \dots)$ be the profile of the aggregators.

Representation problem (RP): Given the profile G of aggregators, find a profile $u = (u_1, u_2, \dots)$ of real-valued functions on X such that for each $x \in X$ and t, $u_t(x) = G_t(x_t, u_{-t}(x))$, where u_{-t} denotes the profile with the t-th component u_t deleted, $u_t(x)$ is strictly increasing in x_t and non-decreasing in $x_{-t} = (x_1, \dots, x_{t-1}, x_{t+1}, \dots)$.

If RP has a solution $u = (u_1, u_2, \dots)$, we call it **a paternalistic representation of** $\boldsymbol{G = (G_1, G_2, \dots)}$. We call the t-th component u_t of the representation u the **utility function of generation** $\boldsymbol{t}$. Two questions immediately arise.

Question 1: Does G have a paternalistic representation?

Question 2: Is the representation unique?

3. The lattice-theoretic approach

In this section, we assume the following on the aggregators.

Pointwise boundedness (PB): For each t and $x_t \in X_t$, $\{G_t(x_t, u_{-t}) : u_{-t} \in U_{-t}\}$ is bounded.

Monotonicity (MON): For each t, $G_t(x_t, u_{-t})$ is strictly increasing in x_t and non-decreasing in u_{-t}.

Now, we present the first main result.

Theorem 1. *Under PB and MON, there exists a paternalistic representation of a given profile of aggregators.*

Proof. By PB, we can define the following real-valued functions. For each t and $x = (x_1, x_2, ...) \in X$, let $\alpha_t(x) = \inf\{G_t(x_t, u_{-t}) : u_{-t} \in U_{-t}\}$, $\beta_t(x) = \sup\{G_t(x_t, u_{-t}) : u_{-t} \in U_{-t}\}$. We consider the following function spaces. $\mathcal{U}_t = \{u_t : u_t$ is non-decreasing and for each $x \in X$, $\alpha_t(x) \leq u_t(x) \leq \beta_t(x)\}$. The set $\mathcal{U}_t$ is non-empty since α_t and β_t belong to it. Let $\mathcal{U} = \prod_{t=1}^{\infty} \mathcal{U}_t$. We equip $\mathcal{U}$ with the natural order $\geq$, i.e., $u \geq v$ if $u_t(x) \geq v_t(x)$ for every x and t. For $u = (u_1, u_2, \ldots), v = (v_1, v_2, \ldots) \in \mathcal{U}$, let $u \wedge v = \inf\{u, v\}$ and $u \vee v = \sup\{u, v\}$. Then, for each $x \in X$, $(u \wedge v)(x) = (\min\{u_1(x), v_1(x)\}, \min\{u_2(x), v_2(x)\}, \ldots)$ and $(u \vee v)(x) = (\max\{u_1(x), v_1(x)\}, \max\{u_2(x), v_2(x)\}, \ldots)$. These operations, $\wedge$ and $\vee$, make $\mathcal{U}$ a complete lattice, i.e., for every non-empty subset $\mathcal{T}$ of $\mathcal{U}$, $\inf \mathcal{T}$ and $\sup \mathcal{T}$ exist and belong to $\mathcal{U}$. Indeed, $\inf \mathcal{T}(x) = (\inf\{u_1(x) : u \in \mathcal{T}\}, \inf\{u_2(x) : u \in \mathcal{T}\}, \ldots)$ and $\sup \mathcal{T}(x) = (\sup\{u_1(x) : u \in \mathcal{T}\}, \sup\{u_2(x) : u \in \mathcal{T}\}, \ldots)$ are non-decreasing in x and belong to $\mathcal{U}$.

For each $u = (u_1, u_2, \ldots) \in \mathcal{U}$ and t, let $F_t(u)(x) = G_t(x_t, u_{-t}(x))$ and $F = (F_1, F_2, \ldots)$. Clearly, $F_t(u)(x)$ is strictly increasing in x_t and non-decreasing in x_{-t}. It is also trivial that $F_t(u) \in \mathcal{U}_t$. Hence, the operator F maps $\mathcal{U}$ into itself. Clearly, $F_t(u)$ is non-decreasing in u. Hence, by Tarski's fixed point theorem [15], there exists $u = (u_1, u_2, \ldots) \in \mathcal{U}$ such that for every x and t, $u_t(x) = G_t(x_t, u_{-t}(x))$. By MON, u_t satisfies the desired monotonicity properties. □

Example 1. To see how crucial PB is in Theorem 1, let us consider the following profile of aggregators $G = (G_1, G_2, G_3, \ldots) : G_1(x_1, u_{-1}) = p \cdot x_1 + \alpha u_2, G_2(x_2, u_{-2}) = p \cdot x_2 + \beta u_1, G_t(x_t, u_{-t}) = p \cdot x_t \ (t = 3, 4, \ldots)$, where p is an l-dimensional vector with strictly positive components, and α and β are positive constants satisfying $\alpha\beta > 1$. Clearly G satisfies MON but violates PB. Suppose G possesses a system of utility functions $u = (u_1, u_2, u_3, \ldots)$. Then, $u_1(x) = p \cdot x_1 + \alpha u_2(x)$ and $u_2(x) = p \cdot x_2 + \beta u_1(x)$ for all x. Hence, $u_1(x) = \frac{p \cdot x_1 + \alpha p \cdot x_2}{1 - \alpha\beta}$. Since $1 - \alpha\beta < 0$, $u_1(x)$ cannot be strictly increasing in own consumption x_1 (or non-decreasing in x_2 for that matter). A contradiction obtains. Therefore, there is no paternalistic representation. Of course, we have no contradiction if $1 - \alpha\beta > 0$. In Theorem 1, PB excludes this case which is covered by Sect. 5.

4. The contraction approach

In this section, we obtain a unique paternalistic representation of a given profile of aggregators.

To this end, we add a few more assumptions on the aggregators. For simplicity, we put a restriction on the domains of the aggregators: For each t, U_{-t} is equal to $\boldsymbol{l}_\infty$. For $u \in \boldsymbol{l}_\infty$, $\|u\|_\infty$ denotes the sup norm of u. $\mathbf{1}$ denotes the constant sequence $(1, 1, \dots)$. Note that the domain of the aggregator, $X_t \times U_{-t}$ is a subset of $\mathbb{R}^\infty$. We equip $X_t \times U_t$ with the relative product topology. From now on, we refer it as the product topology.

Continuity(CONT): For each t, the aggregator G_t is product continuous.

Uniform boundedness(UB): For every $\alpha \in \mathbb{R}$, $\sup_t \sup_{x_t \in X_t} |G_t(x_t, \alpha\mathbf{1})| < \infty$.

Lipschitz condition (LC): There exists $\delta \in (0, 1)$ such that for every t, x_t, u_{-t} and v_{-t}, $|G_t(x_t, u_{-t}) - G_t(x_t, v_{-t})| \leq \delta\|u_{-t} - v_{-t}\|_\infty$.

CONT is standard. UB may be weakened at the cost of elaborating the choice of relevant function spaces [6], which we do not pursue in this paper. LC expresses the idea that the utility level of each generation does not depend too much on those of other generations.

Theorem 2. *Under CONT, UB, and LC, there uniquely exists a paternalistic representation of a given profile of aggregators.*

Proof. We set up different function spaces from those in the previous section. Let$\mathcal{U} = \{u = (u_1, u_2, \dots) :$ For each t, u_t is a product continuous, real-valued function on X, and $\sup_{x\in X} \sup_t |u_t(x)| < \infty\}$. For $u = (u_1, u_2, \dots) \in \mathcal{U}$, let $\|u\|_\infty = \sup_{x\in X} \sup_t |u_t(x)|$. By the standard argument, $\mathcal{U}$ is a Banach space under the norm $\|u\|_\infty$.

Let $\mathcal{U}^{inc} = \{u = (u_1, u_2, \dots) \in \mathcal{U}$: For each t, u_t is non-decreasing$\}$. Clearly, $\mathcal{U}^{inc}$ is a closed subset of $\mathcal{U}$ so that it is a complete metric space.

Now, we define an operator T on $\mathcal{U}^{inc}$. For $u = (u_1, u_2, \dots) \in \mathcal{U}^{inc}$ and $x \in X$, let $T(u)(x) = (G_1(x_1, u_{-1}(x)), G_2(x_2, u_{-2}(x)), \dots)$, where $u_{-t}(x) = (u_1(x), u_2(x), \dots, u_{t-1}(x), u_{t+1}(x), \dots)$ for every t. To see that T maps $\mathcal{U}^{inc}$ into itself, for every $x \in X$, $u = (u_1, u_2, \dots) \in \mathcal{U}^{inc}$, and t, $G_t(x_t, -\|u\|\mathbf{1}) \leq G_t(x_t, u_{-t}(x)) \leq G_t(x_t, \|u\|\mathbf{1})$ by MON.

Thus, for every t, $|G_t(x_t, u_{-t}(x))| \leq \max\{\sup_{x\in X} \sup_\tau |G_\tau(x_\tau, \|u\|\mathbf{1})|, \sup_{x\in X} \sup_\tau |G_\tau(x_\tau, -\|u\|\mathbf{1})|\}$. Thus, by UB, $\sup_{x\in X} \sup_t |G_t(x_t, u_{-t}(x))| < \infty$. Clearly, for every t, $G_t(x_t, u_{-t}(x))$ is non-decreasing in x and product continuous in x. Hence, T maps $\mathcal{U}^{inc}$ into itself.

By LC, T is a contraction. Hence, by the contraction mapping theorem, there exists a unique $u^* = (u_1^*, u_2^*, \dots) \in \mathcal{U}^{inc}$ such that $u^* = T(u^*)$, i.e., for every $x \in X$ and t, $u_t(x) = G_t(x_t, u_{-t}(x))$. By MON, $u_t(x)$ is strictly increasing in x_t. □

5. Linear representation problem

We call a real-valued, increasing function ν_t on X_t a **felicity function of generation t**. $\nu = (\nu_1, \nu_2, \dots)$ denotes a profile of felicity functions. Let $\nu = (\nu_1, \nu_2, \dots)$ be a profile of felicity functions and let $\{a_{tj}\}_{t=1}^{\infty}{}_{j=1}^{\infty}$ be a double sequence such that for each t and j, $a_{tj} \geq 0$ and $a_{tt} = 0$, and $\{a_{tj}\}_{j=1}^{\infty}$ is summable. We say that the aggregator G_t is **linear** if it is of the form $G_t(x_t, U_{-t}) = \nu_t(x_t) + \sum_{j=1}^{\infty} a_{tj} U_j$.

Linear representation problem (LRP): Given a profile of linear aggregators, find a paternalistic representation.

Two immediate questions arise.

Question 3: Does LRP possess a solution?

Question 4: Is a solution to LRP unique?

To give a positive answer to each question, we propose a condition which generalizes Hori's [9]. To this end, let B be the infinite matrix defined by

$$\begin{bmatrix} 1 & -a_{12} & -a_{13} & \dots \\ -a_{21} & 1 & -a_{23} & \dots \\ -a_{31} & -a_{32} & 1 & \dots \\ \vdots & \vdots & \vdots & \ddots \end{bmatrix}.$$

Let b_{ij} be the (i, j)-element of the matrix B, i.e., $b_{ij} = 1$ if $i = j$, and $b_{ij} = -a_{ij}$ otherwise. Let n be a positive integer and let $I_1 = \{1, 2, \dots, n\}, \dots, I_k = \{n(k-1)+1, n(k-1)+2, \dots, n(k-1)+n\}$ $(k = 2, 3, \dots)$. Then, the set $\{I_k\}_{k=1}^{\infty}$ partitions the set $\mathbb{N}$ of all positive integers. For every i and $j \in \mathbb{N}$, let B_{ij} be the sub-matrix $[b_{lm}]_{l \in I_i, m \in I_j}$. Note that the sub-matrix B_{ij} depends on the choice of n.

Dominant diagonal blocks (DDB): The matrix B has a dominant diagonal blocks, i.e., there exists $n \in \mathbb{N}$ such that for all i, B_{ii} satisfies the Hawkins–Simon condition, and there exists a norm $\|\cdot\|$ on $\mathbb{R}^n$ such that $\sup_i \sup_{x \in \mathbb{R}^n : \|x\|=1} \|B_{ii}^{-1} x\| < \infty$ and $\sup_i \sup_{x \in \mathbb{R}^n : \|x\|=1} \sum_{j \neq i}^{\infty} \|B_{ii}^{-1} B_{ij} x\| < 1$.[2]

DDB means that off-diagonal blocks are small in terms of some norm. This intuition may easily be seen in a special case $n = 1$. In this case, all the diagonal blocks B_{ii} degenerate into 1×1 matrix 1.

Dominant diagonal (DD): $\sup_t \sum_{j \neq t}^{\infty} a_{tj} < 1$.

The series $\sum_{j \neq t}^{\infty} a_{tj}$ may be regarded as the degree of intergenerational altruism. Then, DD clearly expresses the idea that the degree of intergenerational altruism is small.

To see the relevance of DDB, let us look at the system of simultaneous equations:

---

[2] Araujo and Scheinkman [1] applied this version of diagonal dominance assumption to deliver comparative dynamics results in infinite horizon optimization problems.

$$U_t = G_t(x_t, U_{-t}) = v_t(x_t) + \sum_{j=1}^{\infty} a_{tj} U_j \quad (t = 1, 2, \dots).$$

We search for a bounded sequence $U = (U_1, U_2, \dots)$ that solves the simultaneous equation. This immediately raises a question of invertibility of the continuous linear operator $T : \boldsymbol{l}_\infty \to \boldsymbol{l}_\infty$ represented by the infinite matrix B.

Let $I : \boldsymbol{l}_\infty \to \boldsymbol{l}_\infty$ be the identity operator. By DDB, $\|T - I\| < 1$. Hence, T is invertible and $T^{-1} = \sum_{j=0}^{\infty}(I - T)^j$. See Lang [12, Chap. 5], for example. The last formula shows the inverse of operator T is represented by a nonnegative infinite matrix. Thus, by DDB, the system has the unique solution:

$$U(x) = T^{-1}v(x) = v(x) + \sum_{j=1}^{\infty}(I - T)^j v(x).$$

Let $U(x) = (U_1(x_1, x_{-1}), U_2(x_2, x_{-2}), \dots)$. Since each $v_t(x_t)$ is strictly increasing in x_t, each $U_t(x_t, x_{-t})$ is strictly increasing in x_t. Since $\sum_{j=1}^{\infty}(I-T)^j$ is nonnegative, $\sum_{j=1}^{\infty}(I - T)^j v(x)$ is non-decreasing in x. Hence, $U(x)$ gives the unique solution to LRP.

Now, we discuss diagonal dominance introduced by Bergstrom [4].

Bergstrom dominant diagonal (BDD): There exists a bounded sequence $d = (d_1, d_2, \dots)$ such that for all t, $d_t > 0$, and $\inf_t(d_t - \sum_{j=1}^{\infty} a_{tj} d_j) > 0$.

Suppose that the infinite matrix B satisfies BDD. Then, the continuous linear operator $T : \boldsymbol{l}_\infty \to \boldsymbol{l}_\infty$ represented by the infinite matrix B is invertible. The infinite matrix representing the inverse operator of T is of the following form: $DC^{-1}D^{-1}$, where $D = \mathrm{diag}(d_1, d_2, \dots)$, $C = (c_{tj})$, $c_{tj} = (a_t d_j)/d_t$. Note that the existence of the inverse matrix of C follows from $\|C - I\| < 1$, where I denotes the identity matrix and $\|\cdot\|$ denotes the sup-norm. Since $C^{-1} = \sum_{j=0}^{\infty}(I - C)^j$, C^{-1} is nonnegative. Hence, $DC^{-1}D^{-1}$ is nonnegative also. Hence, under BDD, LRP has a unique solution.

6. Link between the contraction approach and DDB

In this section, we consider the logical implications of differentiable aggregators. To be more specific, we extend Hori's result [9] by means of the contraction approach.

Smoothness (S): For each t and x_t, $G_t(x_t, u_{-t})$ is continuously Fréchet differentiable with respect to u_{-t}.

Let $D_{u_{-t}}G_t(x_t, u_{-t})$ be the derivative of $G_t(x_t, u_{-t})$ with respect to u_{-t}. Note that $D_{u_{-t}}G_t(x_t, u_{-t})$ is a sup norm continuous, linear functional on $\boldsymbol{l}_\infty$. By MON, it is nonnegative. By definition of the dual norm, $\|D_{u_{-t}}G_t(x_t, u_{-t})\| = \sup_{h \in \boldsymbol{l}_\infty : \|h\|_\infty = 1} |D_{u_{-t}}G_t(x_t, u_{-t})(h)|$. Since $D_{u_{-t}}G_t(x_t, u_{-t})$ is nonnegative,

$\|D_{u_{-t}}G_t(x_t, u_{-t})\|$ can be written as $D_{u_{-t}}G_t(x_t, u_{-t})(\mathbf{1})$. To see the link between the contraction approach in the previous section and the condition developed by Hori [9], it is useful to consider the following condition.

Limited utility dependence (LUD): $\sup_{u \in \mathcal{U}^{inc}} \sup_t \sup_{x_t \in X_t} \|D_{u_{-t}} G_t(x_t, u_{-t}(x))\| < 1$.

By the mean value theorem (see [12, Corollary 1, Chap. 5] for example), for every t, x, u_{-t} and v_{-t},

$$|G_t(x_t, u_{-t}) - G_t(x_t, v_{-t})| \le \sup_{w_{-t}} \|D_{u_{-t}}G_t(x_t, w_{-t})\| \|u_{-t} - v_{-t}\|_\infty,$$

where the $\sup_{w_{-t}}$ is taken over any w_{-t} on the line segment between u_{-t} and v_{-t}. Let $\delta = \sup_{u \in \mathcal{U}^{inc}} \sup_t \sup_{x_t \in X_t} \|D_{u_{-t}}G_t(x_t, u_{-t}(x))\|$. Then, by LUD, $\delta < 1$. Since $\sup_{w_{-t}} \|D_{u_{-t}}G_t(x_t, w_{-t})\| \le \delta$, we have $|G_t(x_t, u_{-t}) - G_t(x_t, v_{-t})| \le \delta \|u_{-t} - v_{-t}\|_\infty$. Thus, LUD implies LC.

In order to see the link between our results and Hori's [9], we need to invoke the Yosida–Hewitt decomposition theorem (see [16]): $D_{u_{-t}}G_t(x_t, u_{-t})$ can be expressed as

$$D_{u_{-t}}G_t(x_t, u_{-t})(h) = \sum_{j \ne t}^{\infty} p_{tj}(x_t, u_{-t})h_j + \lambda_t(x_t, u_{-t})(h) \quad \text{for every } h \in \boldsymbol{l}_\infty,$$

where $\{p_{tj}(x_t, u_{-t})\}_{j \ne t}^{\infty}$ is an absolutely summable, nonnegative sequence and $\lambda_t(x_t, u_{-t})$ is a purely finitely additive, nonnegative linear functional on $\boldsymbol{l}_\infty$.

Let $j_0 \ne t$, and let $e^{j_0} = \{e_j^{j_0}\}_{j \ne t}^{\infty}$ be the sequence defined by $e_{j_0}^{j_0} = 1$ and $e_j^{j_0} = 0$ for $j \ne t, j_0$. Then, $D_{u_{-t}}G_t(x_t, u_{-t})(e^{j_0}) = p_{tj_0}(x_t, u_{-t})$. Since $D_{u_{-t}}G_t(x_t, u_{-t})(e^{j_0})$ is the partial derivative of $G_t(x_t, u_{-t})$ with respect to u_{j_0}, denoted by $G_{tj_0}(x_t, u_{-t})$, $\{G_{tj}(x_t, u_{-t})\}_{j \ne t}^{\infty}$ is absolutely summable and nonnegative.

Let $a_{tj} = \sup_{u \in \mathcal{U}^{inc}} \sup_{x \in X} G_{tj}(x_t, u_{-t}) (t \ne j)$. Clearly, $\sup_{u \in \mathcal{U}^{inc}} \sup_t \sup_{x \in X} \{\sum_{j \ne t}^{\infty} G_{tj}(x_t, u_{-t})\} \le \sup_t \sum_{j \ne t}^{\infty} a_{tj}$. Now, let us consider the following two conditions. The first one is from Bewley [5].

Exclusion (EX): For each t, $x \in X$, and u_{-t}, the purely finitely additive part $\lambda_t(x_t, u_{-t})$ of the Fréchet derivative $D_{u_{-t}}G_t(x_t, u_{-t})$ vanishes.

Uniformly dominant diagonal blocks (UDDB): There exists a nonnegative infinite matrix $A = [a_{tj}]_{t=1}^{\infty}{}_{j=1}^{\infty}$ such that for each t, j, and (x_t, u_{-t}), $a_{tt} = 0$, $a_{tj} \ge \partial G_t(x_t, u_{-t})/\partial u_j$ and that the infinite matrix $I - A$ satisfies DDB.

It follows from the above discussions that UDDB, along with EX, imply LUD. This explains why UDDB, the analogue of Hori's condition (4.1) in Hori [9], is useful in obtaining the unique solution to RP.

References

1. Araujo, A., Scheinkman, J.A.: Notes on Comparative Dynamics. In: General Equilibrium, Growth, and Trade: Essays in Honor of Lionel Mckenzie Green, J., Scheinkman, J.A. (eds.) 1979
2. Barro, R.: Are government bond net wealth? J. Polit. Econ. **82**, 1095–1117 (1974)
3. Becker, G.S.: A theory of social interactions. J. Polit. Econ. **82**, 1063–1093 (1974)
4. Bergstrom, T.C.: Systems of Benevolent utility functions. J. Public Econ. Theory **1**, 71–100 (1999)
5. Bewley, T.F.: Existence of equilibria in economies with infinitely many commodities. J. Econ. Theory **43**, 514–540 (1972)
6. Boyd, J.: Recursive utility and the Ramsey problem. J. Econ. Theory **50**, 326–346 (1990)
7. Hori, H.: Utility functionals with nonpaternalistic intergenerational altruism: the case where altruism extends to many generations. J. Econ. Theory **56**, 451–467 (1992)
8. Hori, H.: Non-stationary Intergenerational Altruism, mimeo. Tohoku University 2000
9. Hori, H.: Non-paternalistic altruism and utility interdependence. Jpn Econ. Rev. **52**(2), 137–155 (2001)
10. Hori, H., Kanaya S.: Utility functionals with nonpaternalistic intergenerational altruism. J. Econ. Theory **49**, 241–265 (1989)
11. Kimball, M.S.: Making sense of two-sided altruism. J. Monetary Econ. **20**, 301–326 (1987)
12. Lang, S.: Real Analysis. Addison-Wesley, Reading 1969
13. McKenzie, L.W.: Matrices with dominant diagonals and economic theory. In: Arrow, K.J., Karlin, S., Suppes, P. (eds.) Mathematical Methods in the Social Sciences. Stanford University Press, Stanford, pp. 47–62, 1959
14. Ray, D.: Nonpaternalistic intergenerational altruism. J. Econ. Theory **41**, 112–132 (1987)
15. Tarski, A.: A Lattice-theoretical fixed point theorem and its applications. Pacific J. Math. **5**, 285–309 (1955)
16. Yosida, K., Hewitt, E.: Finitely additive measures. Trans. Am. Math. Soc. **72**, 46–66 (1952)

Subject Index

Instructions for Authors

A. General

1. Papers submitted for publication will be considered only if they have not been and will not be published elsewhere without permission from the publisher and the Research Center for Mathematical Economics.

2. Every submitted paper will be subject to review. The names of reviewers will not be disclosed to the authors or to anybody not involved in the editorial process.

3. The authors are asked to transfer the copyright to their articles to Springer-Verlag if and when these are accepted for publication.

The copyright covers the exclusive and unlimited rights to reproduce and distribute the article in any form of reproduction. It also covers translation rights for all languages and countries.

4. Manuscript must be written in English. Its pdf file should be submitted to:
Office of Advances in
Mathematical Economics
c/o Professor Toru Maruyama
Department of Economics
Keio University
maruyama@econ.keio.ac.jp

5. **Offprints**: Twenty-five (25) **offprints** of each paper will be supplied free of charge. Additional offprints can be ordered at cost price.

B. Preparation of Manuscript

1. Manuscripts must be double-spaced (not 1.5), with wide margins (at least 25 mm), and large type (at least 12 point) on one side of A4 paper. Any manuscript that does not meet these requirements will be returned to the author immediately for retyping.

2. All manuscripts would finally be composed using our Springer LaTeX macro package. The Springer macros use standard LaTeX packages - if you do not have these packages refer to `http://www.ctan.org` or `http://www.dante.de/tex`. If authors make manuscripts by word-processing software other than TeX, please follow our styles as possible. For authors who prepare their manuscripts by TeX, we strongly recommend to visit our homepage, `http://www.springeronline.com/economics/`. You can download all the necessary macro packages with instructions for LaTeX2e from `ftp://ftp.springer.de/pub/tex/latex/svjour/global/`. For support, please contact `texhelp@springer.de`.

3. **The title page** must include: title; short (running) title of up to 60/85 characters; first names and surnames of all coauthors with superscript numerals indicating their affiliations; full street addresses of all affiliations; address to which proofs should be sent; fax number; and any footnotes referring to the title (indicated by asterisks*).

4. **Summary/abstract**: Each paper must be preceded by a summary/an abstract, which should not exceed 100 words.

5. **The Journal of Economic Literature index number (JEL classification)** should be indicated and the statement of the **2000 Mathematics Subject Classification (MSC) numbers** is desirable. You can check JEL classification with Internet at `http://ideas.repec.org/JEL/` as well as 2000 MSC numbers at `http://www.ams.org/msc`.

6. **Main text**: All tables and figures must be cited in the text and numbered consecutively with Arabic numerals according to the sequence in which they are cited. Please mark the desired position of tables and figures in the left margin of the manuscript.

Do not italicize, underscore, or use boldface for headings and subheadings. Words that are to be italicized should be underscored in pencil.

Abbreviations must be spelled out at first mention in summary/abstract and main text. Abbreviations should also be spelled out at first mention in figure legends and table footnotes.

Short equations can be run in with the text. Equations that are displayed on a separate line should be numbered.

7. **References**: The list of references should be in alphabetical order and include the names and initials of all authors (see examples below). Whenever possible, please update all references to papers accepted for publication, preprints or technical reports, giving the exact name of the journal, as well as the volume, first and last page numbers and year, if the article has already been published or accepted for publication.

When styling the references, the following examples should be observed:

Journal article:
1. or [F-M] Freed, D.S., Melrose, R.B.: A mod *k* index theorem. Invent. Math. **107**, 283-299 (1992)

Complete book:
2. or [C-S] Conway, J.H., Sloane, N.J.: Sphere packings, lattices, and groups (Grundlehren Math. Wiss. Bd. 290) Berlin Heidelberg New York: Springer 1988

Single contribution in a book:
3. or [B] Border, K.C.: Functional analytic tools for expected utility theory. In: Aliprantis, C.D. et al. (eds.): Positive operators, Riesz spaces and economics. Berlin Heidelberg New York: Springer 1991, pp. 69-88

8. **Citations in the text** should be either by numbers in square brackets, e.g. [1], referring to an alphabetically ordered and numbered list, or by the author's initials in square brackets, e.g. [F-M], or by author and year in parentheses, e.g. Freed and Melrose (1992). Any of these styles is acceptable if used consistently throughout the paper. In the third system, if a work with more than two authors is cited, only the first author's name plus "et al." need be given and if there is more than one reference by the same author or team of authors in the same year, then a, b, c should be added after the year both in the text and in the list of references.

9. **Tables** are to be numbered separately from the illustrations. Each table should have a brief and informative title. All abbreviations used in a table must be defined in a table footnote on first use, even if already defined in the text. In subsequent tables abbreviations need not be redefined. Individual footnotes should be indicated by superscript lowercase a, b, c, etc. Permission forms must be provided for any tables from previously published sources (same procedure as with figures; see below).

10. **Figures**: If you have access to suitable software, you can design your figures directly on a computer, but creation by other means is of course also possible. In any case the originals should be pasted into the camera- ready copy at the appropriate places and with the correct orientation. If necessary, the figures may be drawn overscale, but in this case suitably reduced copies should be pasted into the script.

If a figure has been published previously, acknowledge its source and submit written permission signed by author and publisher. The source must be included in the reference list. If a permission fee is required, it must be paid by the author. Responsibility for meeting this requirement lies entirely with the author.

MIX
Papier aus verantwortungsvollen Quellen
Paper from responsible sources
FSC® C105338

If you have any concerns about our products,
you can contact us on
ProductSafety@springernature.com

In case Publisher is established outside the EU,
the EU authorized representative is:
Springer Nature Customer Service Center GmbH
Europaplatz 3, 69115 Heidelberg, Germany

Printed by Libri Plureos GmbH
in Hamburg, Germany